HD
8081
.A65
H37

Harris, William
   Hamilton, 1944-

The harder we run

DATE		

© THE BAKER & TAYLOR CO.

The Harder We Run

We tell you to go to work; and to work you must go or die. Men are not valued in this country, or in any country, for what they are; they are valued for what they can do. It is vain if we talk about being men, if we do not do the work of men.

FREDERICK DOUGLASS

The Harder We Run:

BLACK WORKERS
SINCE THE CIVIL WAR

WILLIAM H. HARRIS
Indiana University

New York • Oxford
OXFORD UNIVERSITY PRESS
1982

Library of Congress Cataloging in Publication Data
Harris, William Hamilton, 1944–
The harder we run.
Bibliography: p.
Includes index.
1. Afro-Americans—Employment—History. I. Title.
HD8081.A65H37   331.6′3′96073009   80-27897
ISBN 0-19-502940-2   ISBN 0-19-502941-0 (pbk.)

Printing (last digit): 987654321
Printed in the United States of America

For Cindy and Bill, and their generation, with hope that the stories in these pages will remind them of their heritage and inspire them in the future.

Preface

Writing *The Harder We Run* was more than an intellectual enterprise for me, for not only did I learn more about the efforts black men and women have made to earn decent wages and to support their families in the United States, but I came to appreciate far more fully the sacrifices others made so that I could have the opportunity to tell their stories. Indeed, the struggles and failures, as well as the few successes, took on a different meaning as I looked at them anew. The experience of writing the book rekindled in me feelings I had known as a child. I remembered that my father, who knew as much about fixing locomotives as anyone in town, always remained a machinist's helper while younger whites, who learned their work from him, became machinists. Little did I know back then in Georgia that my feeling of frustration over that situation was one that young black boys— and even more, their fathers—shared all over the country, and that it was a condition that had existed for most black people for the whole period of their existence as free men and women in the United States. My father's comment to me years ago that black people were already so poor in the 1920s that in the 1930s they did not even know that the Great Depression had come, took on a new meaning as well as I tried to organize and retell the story of black workers since the Civil War.

I have written this book with as little passion as possible, but with a clear appreciation of the pathos that has been so much a part of the history of black people in America. I have taken pains to place the history of black people into a discussion of the major developments in American history in the period since the Civil War, but always with a clear understanding that the history of blacks has a dateline of its own.

I obviously owe an enormous debt after having written a book such as this. In addition to my own work in archives and libraries, *The Harder We Run* is built upon the work of numerous scholars who have written on this subject during the whole period that it covers. I acknowledge many of these scholars in the notes. Many others influenced my thinking, but their work was not particularly related to the story I wanted to tell in this book.

In addition to their published work, several historians were personally helpful to me in this endeavor. Herbert Gutman, whose work stands as a benchmark for all who write in labor history, has been aware of this project from the time I began to think about it, and he graciously gave of his time through long conversations with me as I developed the ideas for this book. A no less distinguished labor historian, David Brody, read the entire manuscript and made several suggestions that contributed to improving the book. Several colleagues at Indiana University, especially William B. Cohen, George Juergens, and Walter Nugent, read various drafts and offered helpful and encouraging comments.

The accurate and enthusiastic efforts of my graduate research assistants, Peter Murray and Ronald Hartzer, relieved me of the tiring tasks of running down details and locating obscure sources, thereby enabling me to spend more of my time writing. That task of writing was eased even more by the sincere hospitality I received from Günter Moltmann and his colleagues at the Historisches Seminar at the University of Hamburg, where I spent a delightful and productive year as a Fulbright Fellow and Guest Professor in 1978–79. Near the end of the project, another of my research assistants and graduate students, Linda Reed, provided essential help to me in the tedious work of reading proof and preparing the index, as did Wynetta Lee of my office staff. I am, of course, grateful to Nancy Lane, my editor at Oxford University Press, who believed in this project from the beginning and offered encouragement all along the way. And I can never overlook the contribution of Debra Chase who typed the manuscript from my sometimes confusing drafts.

Finally, I want to thank my wife, Wanda, and our children Cynthia and Bill, whose love and warmth endured through the long nights that I spent staring at blank pages in the typewriter, and who were always there to remind me of the importance of family. I dedicated this book to our children. Though Wanda's and my generation may never see it, perhaps theirs will develop a just society.

Bloomington   W.H.H.
July 1981

Contents

Contents

The Harder We Run

Introduction

The history of black workers in the United States spans more than three and a half centuries and touches the lives of all black people who have lived in America. At the same time, black workers have been deeply involved in the development of all major black institutions, from churches to protest and advancement organizations. Black working-class people were closely involved in such activities because all black people were either workers themselves or had close relatives who were. Despite advances of some blacks into the professions and skilled crafts, as late as the 1980s far too many were still the "first" to hold certain jobs, like the first black person to teach history at Indiana University. Accordingly, then, the history of black workers is the history of discrimination, not to say downright oppression.

As I prepared to write this book, it became increasingly clear that the crucial issue was not so much how blacks got along on their jobs but whether they got jobs at all. Thus, this book is not only about black workers who had jobs; it is also about the right to earn a living and about the millions of blacks who looked for work and were unable to find it. And it is about the various efforts of white unions, white management, and the white government throughout much of the post-Civil War period to deny employment to blacks in any but the meanest positions. And even when the government changed its stance under pressure from increasingly well-organized blacks, it did so only halfheartedly, and never effectively by 1980. In short, this book is about the

3

racism that has made it impossible for blacks to participate fully in American society.

This book emphasizes one of the fundamental differences between black and white workers in the United States: the fact that large numbers of black women participated in the labor force for decades while white women entered the work force in large numbers only recently. Indeed, the discussion of black female workers emphasizes how "phenomena" become important only when they affect whites. In recent years, we have heard a great deal about the tremendous number of women entering the labor force. Even now awaiting ratification is a much-needed Equal Rights Amendment to the Constitution which will help to protect the rights of working women. But the discussion of the rising number of women at work, and the recent development of that trend, should legitimately focus on white women; black women have, of necessity, been involved in the labor force throughout their history on this continent.

Chapters 1 to 3 cover the period from the end of the Civil War through 1925. Much of the discussion in these chapters focuses on black agricultural workers in the South and their dispersal into southern industry during the rise of the New South. Likewise, these chapters trace relationships between black and white workers—particularly those in unions—and follow the increasing migration of southern blacks into northern urban areas and the development of an urban black population during and after World War I.

The year 1925 is a reasonable and natural break in a book on black workers. On the one hand, it is a time when some evaluation can be made of the advancement of blacks in the labor market since the Civil War and before the start of real problems for black and white workers with the onslaught of the Great Depression. On the other hand, 1925 is an important year for black workers because it marks a distinct change in the attitude of blacks toward trade unionism. For example, the National Urban League created a bureau of industrial relations to find ways to improve relations between blacks and organized white labor and to use the influence of the growing number of black unionists to improve the status of black workers. American Communists also took a major step forward in their efforts to radicalize black workers and to force improvement of relations between blacks and organized white labor in 1925 when they founded the American Negro Labor Congress (ANLC). Though short-lived, the ANLC, forerunner of the International Labor Defense, laid the groundwork for an important Communist movement among blacks in the United States. Most important, 1925 marks a change in relationships between blacks and organized labor—and an improvement in the status of black workers in general—because it is the year in which the Brotherhood of Sleeping Car Porters was founded.

Chapters 4 and 5 cover the Brotherhood of Sleeping Car Porters, the Great Depression, during which black workers suffered disproportionately, and World War II. Even during the great upsurge in employment during World War II, discrimination against blacks and limitation of their rights as workers continued. Chapter 6 deals with the postwar years down to 1956. That year serves as a cutoff not because it marks the completion of the merger of the American Federation of Labor and the Congress of Industrial Organizations, though I do discuss that event. Chapter 6 ends in 1956 because that year saw the first successful effort of black workers to demonstrate their combined might when they united under the leadership of Martin Luther King and forced an end to discrimination in Montgomery, Alabama, during the Montgomery Bus Boycott.

Chapters 7 and 8 concentrate on black workers in the period of the Civil Rights Movement and affirmative action, particularly the 1960s and 1970s. It was a time of growing militance among black workers, especially those in the industrial unions, but it was also a period of increased black unemployment under pressure from accelerated automation and a generally unstable economy. Moreover, during the latter part of the period, whites generally abandoned their efforts to improve the conditions of black workers. Affirmative action, which critics called "reverse discrimination," was particularly under fire by the 1980s.

I used a wide range of sources for this book, including archival collections, scholarly books and articles, and primary data from governmental agencies. I have finished this project more convinced than ever of the official collusion, or at best lack of concern, of the United States government in efforts to deprive black Americans of the chance to gain jobs and earn a decent living in this rich country. Report after report of federal agencies, especially those of the Census Bureau and the *Monthly Labor Review*, tells the grim tale of economic depression in which blacks have generally lived. And administration after administration did practically nothing to alleviate the situation.

Thus, contrary to my fondest hopes at the outset of this project, this is not an optimistic book. Despite the various victories of blacks, and the times at which it seemed that black workers would be permitted to function as equals in the American work force, far too much opposition remains to be overcome. Indeed, *The Harder We Run* underscores the fact that there is no such thing as a melting pot operating in American society. And perhaps that is good, for a melting pot would at best produce a mush, and there is little excitement in that. In sharp contrast, the presence of blacks in the United States makes our society more like a huge kettle in which simmers a rich gumbo soup. The pity is that whites have tried to keep the black portion of that dynamic concoction at the bottom of the kettle, and in so doing have diluted the impact of both blacks and whites on efforts to create a just society. By the 1980s the lid was about to blow off the kettle, and indeed off the whole country, as blacks imprisoned in ghettos and low-paying jobs determined to end the oppression under which they lived.

1

The Legacy of Slavery

> The South, after the war, presented the greatest opportunity
> for a real national labor movement which the nation ever
> saw or is likely to see for many decades. Yet the labor move-
> ment, with but few exceptions, never realized the situation.
> It never had the intelligence or knowledge, as a whole, to
> see in black slavery and Reconstruction the kernel and
> meaning of the labor movement in the United States.
>
> W. E. B. DU BOIS, *Black Reconstruction* (1935)

Black workers entered the American free labor force at a time
of massive disruption. They had lived for practically two and a
half centuries on the American continent as slaves, a status that
ended only after 200,000 blacks joined the North in all-out war
against the slave forces of the South.[1] The victorious North abol-
ished slavery by constitutional amendment and added 4 million
new workers to the free population. The major battles of the
Civil War had taken place in the South, where 95 percent of the
blacks lived; the region lay in shambles. Its white residents, especially the once proud and haughty landowners, suffered the psychological damage of military defeat and now had to live under
the occupation of a conquering army that included blacks, some
of them former slaves. Most of those whites continued to hold to
the myth of racial superiority, refusing to see black people as
social and political equals despite the reality of war-mandated
freedom. Indeed, some even refused to see blacks as human at all.

Despite the overwhelming conditions of disaster in the South,
Afro-Americans entered the new era of freedom with hope and

determination. Convinced that the federal government would protect them, they were ready to make their way to self-sufficiency.
They faced fearful obstacles in doing so. Slave codes that outlawed the education of blacks had left 95 percent of them illiter-
ate, unable to write so much as their names, let alone understand
legal contracts. More important, though they had performed most
of the work in southern agriculture for centuries, they came to
freedom with absolutely no capital, possessing neither cash nor
land. They had only the ability to work. But without land they
could find work only by offering their services in southern cities
or by returning to the same plantations on which they had labored before the war. In either case, they were expected to work
under circumstances not much different from those of slavery.

Blacks saw such labor as unacceptable and held out hope that
the federal government would confiscate the property of southern
rebels and redistribute it among the loyal people of the South.
Above all else, blacks wanted land in the postwar South. Though
the legal bases for redistribution may have been shaky,[2] blacks
had an absolutely defensible moral right to expect land as com-
pensation for the tremendous contribution they had made to the
wealth of the nation, to say nothing of the mental and social
degradation they had suffered under the inhuman conditions of
slavery. Activities of certain Union generals who had in fact confiscated land and distributed it among blacks during the war had
given grounds for hope, a hope intensified by the demands of
farsighted federal legislators like Thaddeus Stevens. He demanded that blacks have land to protect their recently acquired
political and social rights.

White southerners sensed the great desire for landownership
among blacks and knew well the importance of land in their society. Thus they were determined that blacks should remain landless laborers. Not only did whites oppose federal schemes of confiscation and redistribution, they would not even consider selling
land to those few blacks able to pay for it. Whitelaw Reid re-
corded their sentiment during his tour of the South soon after
the war:

The feeling against any ownership of the soil by Negroes is so strong [among whites] that the man who should sell small tracts to them would be in actual personal danger. Every effort will be made to prevent Negroes from acquiring land; even the renting of small tracts to them is held to be unpatriotic and unworthy of a good citizen.[3]

Unwillingness of whites to sell land to blacks or otherwise allow them to become independent workers resounds in the comment of an Alabama resident, who maintained:

the nigger is going to be made a serf, sure as you live. It won't need any law for that. Planters will have an understanding among themselves: "you won't hire my niggers and I won't hire yours." Then what's left to them? Whites are as much the masters of blacks as ever.[4]

In the end the government acceded to white southern demands and refused to redistribute land in the South. This action sealed the failure of Reconstruction and locked blacks into a system of perpetual poverty, the inevitable status of people unable to acquire land in an agriculture-dominated society.[5] Indeed, the government's action placed blacks whose past employment had been largely in agriculture at the mercy of their former owners. They could return to the plantations and make the best deals possible. Refusal to redistribute land relegated all but the most talented and very lucky blacks to a lifetime of drudgery and left them little chance of improving their economic standing or of protecting the flimsy freedom that had come with the Civil War.

When it became clear that the northern victory would mean abolition of slavery, southern whites began to fashion a system that would ensure only partial freedom at best for blacks. In state after state in the old Confederacy, legislatures passed laws that were "an astounding affront to emancipation."[6] Through a series of vagrancy, apprenticeship, enticement, and other restrictive measures, southern whites practically bound blacks to their previous slave status. Most heinous were the laws of vagrancy, a concept southern whites defined broadly when applied to blacks. Afro-Americans found that moving about, even when looking for work, could cause them to be arrested and hired out to the highest bidder, provided the previous owner had first preference.

Moreover, minor children of black parents deemed unable to provide for them could be "apprenticed" to their former owners until they reached adulthood. Such apprenticeship amounted to peonage. In desperate efforts to find work, blacks signed agreements that committed not only the head of the family, but other members as well, to labor from sunup to sundown in the fields and to accept numerous other tasks that made them responsible for the crops and the surrounding real property. In addition, they had to suffer the indignity of calling their employers "master."[7]

In an illuminating bit of insight, the historian Harold D. Woodman suggests that more than racism might have been involved in the new harsh labor conditions southern whites imposed on blacks. The new laws demonstrated the realization and admission by whites that they lacked the experience and knowledge to deal with a free labor force. Woodman is undoubtedly right in part, but racism is clearly the reason landowners did not impose such laws on nonlandowning white southerners.[8]

Blacks were fortunate in not having to face these developments alone. Though unprepared to take the essential step of confiscating and redistributing land, the federal government had no intention of seeing emancipation wholly undone. Congress refused to accept the civil governments established by former white rebels and stationed the army in the South to maintain martial law. The presence of the military forces provided time for blacks to fashion a brief alliance with various white groups, enabling them to forestall the harshest elements of the system envisioned by the majority of southern whites. More important, Congress extended the life of the Freedmen's Bureau which, under the protection of Reconstruction governments and the U.S. Army, guaranteed the contract rights of black workers. These developments provided relative peace in which characteristic relations between black workers and white landowners were established. Labor conditions that developed soon after the Civil War remained in effect well into the twentieth century throughout much of the South.

The dominant type of southern agricultural labor was a form of tenantry or sharecropping in which all members of the black family worked in the fields and on other farm tasks to provide the highest possible yield. Payment for their labor, usually at the end of the harvest season, came in the form of a share of the crop. The crop-sharing system developed because the war had left the South largely devoid of liquid capital. Hence the South existed as a noncash economy. Circumstances required the creation of a labor system through which essential tasks could be performed while payment of wages was deferred until the crops were marketed. Though land use arrangements varied widely, they usually took one of two main forms. In one system, landowners and laborers agreed that each would own specific shares of the crops at harvest time. The second type of agreement gave the croppers use of the land for a fixed sum, payable in goods at the end of the year. To distinguish between the two systems, we here define the former as sharecropping and the latter as tenantry.

Landowners preferred sharecropping to tenantry for several reasons, including their belief that black farmers were incapable of working without supervision. Moreover, sharecropping left the major decisions on which crops to plant, how much fertilizer to use, and when the cropper and his family would work largely to the landowner. Under normal circumstances, the two parties agreed that for shares of the harvest—usually one-third for the cropper and two-thirds for the landowner—the landowner would provide seeds, fertilizer, draft animals, and food and clothing for the cropper's family for the year of the contract. The cost for such items would be charged to the cropper's account. In return, the cropper agreed to provide all the labor required to produce the most bountiful crop, usually cotton. In addition, the cropper and his family were to maintain the farm and its properties in proper condition. Clearly, such a system provided little incentive for the workers. If they worked hard and produced an above-average crop, in the end they simply paid more for use of the land. The more they produced the more they got, but the landowner got more as well.

If the sharecropping system provided little incentive for the workers, tenantry, the system by which they rented land for a fixed sum, usually an established number of bales of cotton, was far more desirable. Though the basic arrangement was much like that for sharecroppers, tenant farmers could look forward to increasing their incomes without paying more for use of the land. Workers obviously favored that system. Tenantry also provided a means by which black farmers could accumulate a little capital and thus eventually escape the system. Accordingly, it found little favor among landowners. As late as 1880, renting to blacks accounted for only 9.6 percent of all southern farms and only 3.4 percent of land planted in cotton.[9] In order to control the land and workers, southern landowners stifled black incentive and delayed for decades the economic development of the South.

Given the lack of capital in the South after the Civil War, the cooperation of bankers and state governments was needed for the tenantry system to work. Despite a large work force, landowners still faced the problem of how to provide for workers between crops. A loan and furnishing system through which landowners borrowed goods from central stores and made them available to their workers provided the remedy. Southern law protected landowners and storekeepers through crop lien laws that gave landowners title to the workers' share of the crop until payment had been made for the goods advanced them throughout the year. The crop lien system eventually came to serve a second major purpose as well: it became a mode of social control, a system based largely on racism.[10] Fixed in a cashless system and without land of their own, blacks had little choice but to depend on the landowners for subsistence during the year. At year's end the workers often found that their share of the crops barely paid for the goods they had received, hardly providing the margin of capital required to finance themselves. Thus they had little choice but to renew their contracts, locking themselves into a cycle of perpetual poverty from which there was little hope of escape.

One immediate outcome of the changed land-use patterns in the postbellum South was a decrease in the average size of farms, though little change in land ownership occurred. In 1870 farms in the cotton South averaged about 60 percent of their size in

1860, by 1880 only 39 percent. Continued decrease in the size of farms occurred as more and more blacks began to work for fixed wages, demonstrating to once skeptical whites that if treated fairly, blacks could and would perform well on their own. By 1880 about one-third of black agricultural workers labored for wages,[11] but the vast majority were still sharecroppers.

A more unfortunate outcome of the furnishing system was the large-scale development of peonage, a labor system through which large numbers of workers were bound to their employers for long periods, ostensibly because of indebtedness. Through the years, many states came to legalize this involuntary servitude—in direct contradiction of the U.S. Constitution. In many more cases, plantation owners simply colluded with local judges and sheriffs to keep black workers—and some whites as well—entangled in a labor condition little removed from slavery. It must be kept in mind, though, that peonage was not restricted to agriculture. Many industrial concerns, particularly sawmills and mines, used peonage as well as the equally obnoxious convict-lease system. Indeed, one of the most notorious examples of peonage, convict leasing, and enticement laws working hand in hand under protection of the local government is that of Henry Flagler, who built the Florida East Coast Railroad from Miami to Key West. In 1908, when U.S. attorneys finally brought charges against three of Flagler's agents and produced extensive evidence in federal court that the company held several thousand men against their will, a U.S. circuit judge directed a not-guilty verdict because the government had failed to prove that the agents had entered "an agreement of minds with evil intent to conspire."[12] In 1917 the U.S. Supreme Court finally declared peonage laws unconstitutional, but neither federal nor local authorities spent much energy in enforcement. Thus, well into the twentieth century, southern landowners continued to hold workers against their will, extracting from them enormous physical and psychological toil.[13]

Black workers who made agriculture profitable in the postwar South existed at barely a subsistence level. Their homes were small, drab, and poorly furnished. As late as 1900, for example, one-third of all black farm families in the South still lived in one-room cabins.[14] Though they undoubtedly received sufficient food, it was of the most ordinary and unvaried sort. But even with this food they often showed creativity, turning greens, okra, hog's feet, and chitlings into highly palatable dishes. Some modern-day gourmets have thought it fashionable to sample small portions of these "soul foods," but poor rural families hardly considered their steady diet to consist of delicacies. They possessed a bare minimum of the most simple clothing, and they went barefoot most of the year. Labor in the fields from dawn to dusk left little time to clean either clothes, homes, or bodies.

Given the meanness of their daily lives, it is somewhat remarkable that poor rural blacks were able to maintain their families. Yet, maintain them they did. Herbert G. Gutman, in his classic study of black family life, points out that "the typical black family everywhere [in the South in 1880] contained only the members of the core nuclear family." Moreover, most black families were male-headed—or at least a man lived in the typical home, though we cannot say whether he or his spouse actually ran it. What is crucial is that black rural families would have found it hard to survive without males to do most of the backbreaking work of making a crop before the advent of air-conditioned farm implements. This is not to deny, of course, that there were some black female-headed families in the rural South after the Civil War, or that some black families were not nuclear. In fact, children often lived in extended families with their grandparents. They all divided up the tasks so that the family could make a living.[15]

Another matter of long-term importance to the black working class is that their burdensome labor and the prime importance of the crops to the landowners made it impossible for black children to utilize fully the public schools, institutions Du Bois described as the most important development of Reconstruction governments. Despite the well-documented thirst among blacks for learning, the crops came first.[16] School years were notoriously short. We hear a great deal about the tremendous decline in illiteracy which took place in the South during the late nineteenth century, but in fact a large proportion of the black population remained unlettered. Their ignorance affected their immediate lives, making them easy prey for quick-counting clerks who kept account books in local furnishing stores. Of equal importance, labor demands that prevented many blacks from going to school greatly retarded the development of a large group of educated blacks able to fashion well-thought-out responses to American racism or to prepare for jobs whose requirements were constantly changing. Nor did the discrimination in education end with the twentieth century. The crop remained supreme, and as late as the 1960s black children in rural Georgia and other southern states attended school for short days in the fall so as to spend at least part of their time in cotton patches.

A complicated set of factors prevented blacks from finding much employment in southern industry. Of prime importance were the attitudes and actions of leading industrialists, advocates of a New South based on manufacturing, railroads, and other industrial development. But the South could not industrialize without capital, which was in short supply in the first decades after the Civil War. Indeed, investment capital was hard to find anywhere. The nation languished in the depression of 1873, which reached its trough in 1876. But those who envisioned a New South suffered from more than merely a temporary cash flow shortage. As the historian C. Vann Woodward observes, "no ruling class of our history ever found itself so profoundly stripped of its economic foundations as did that of the South in this period. Involved in the downfall of the old planter class were the leading financial, commercial and industrial families of the region." These people were willing to try desperate methods to recoup their losses. Accordingly, they turned to the hated North and the federal government for the funding they needed and made extravagant promises of exceptional returns on investments. As it turned out, the disputed presidential election of 1876 provided the leverage southerners needed to extract commitments from Washington. In return for a deal that threw the election to the Republicans, the so-called Compromise of 1877, the Republicans agreed to support internal improvement bills that would benefit southern industry. Northern financing for investments in the South settled the dispute. But the rising industrial class of the South got more than money. The new president, Rutherford B. Hayes, also agreed not to protect the political and civil rights of southern blacks. The failure of Reconstruction was complete. The South could reconstruct itself in its own image, grafting industrial development onto the agricultural base so firmly that by 1880 the same people who had lost the Civil War on the battlefields were securely in power, to the detriment of both black and white workers.[17]

Spokesmen for the New South assured their lenders "a large body of strong, hearty, active, docile and easily contented negro laborers," a cadre reinforced by large numbers of "hearty native Anglo-Saxon stock."[18] Nor should lenders fear loss of their capital in labor strikes. Even though they shared the same miserable wages and working conditions, white and black workers would hardly join together in common cause. The reason was simple: race. Though poor whites and blacks often labored side by side for miserable pay, whites suffered the exploitation because of their simple consciousness that they were racially superior to the equally suffering blacks. Furthermore, class consciousness was unlikely to overcome soon the racism that seemed inherent in the American character. Though aware that they would remain poor, white laborers tried to prove their superiority by keeping certain skilled jobs for themselves while relegating blacks to unskilled and menial tasks. And in one segment of southern industry, the cotton mills, whites did succeed in keeping blacks out completely. Indeed, cotton mill villages became miserable enclaves of poor whites no less owned by the mill companies than black sharecroppers were owned by their plantation masters.[19]

Most black workers in the postbellum South remained in agriculture. But not all of them did so, and not all remained in the South after the war. Afro-Americans, particularly those in the South, had had broad experience in nonfarm labor under slavery, and as the postwar decades wore on, many of them moved from the South to the urban North and the West. When the war ended, blacks in the South were equally represented with whites in skilled labor categories. Yet, despite these skills and job experience, industrial developments made it more and more difficult for black men to hold on to the positions they had acquired. In the building trades, for example, the organization of large construction companies caused a rapid decline in the percentage of black workers. In Savannah, Georgia, the proportion of black carpenters declined from 40 percent in 1870 to 32 percent by 1880. During the same period, the proportion of black plasterers declined from 73 percent to 44 percent, while that of black painters fell from 32 percent to 23 percent.[20] Large companies preferred white workers, and the newly developing white labor unions discriminated against blacks as both apprentices and members. These forces combined to relegate black men to the status of common laborers and domestic employees, both examples of casual employment. Consequently, black male workers suffered greatly. Also, black men experienced much more unemployment than did white men, a development whose full impact would be felt only in the twentieth century.

Nonetheless, blacks provided crucial labor for the growth of industry in the developing New South. They worked in the turpentine, lumber, mining, and shipping industries, and though their numbers were seriously curtailed they did not disappear from the building trades. Many black men also became deeply committed to the improvement of working conditions and participated in the development of unions.

It is well to keep in mind that hundreds of southern black industrial workers had not fully abandoned agriculture. In fact, farm work remained the primary occupation of many; they worked on other jobs during the off season after the crops had been laid by or during the winter when there was little to do on the farms. In this fashion they earned cash to supplement their farm earnings. Perhaps more important, they gained experience and an introduction to industrial rigor. This would help to ease their transition to urban life when many of them joined the massive northern migrations in the early twentieth century.[21]

Black forestry workers in Florida were representative of their work in that industry, generally. Work in the forests was tiring and unpleasant. There was the daily danger of being killed by falling trees. And since forestry usually took place in semi-swamplands, workers often had to brave icy water in winter and deadly snakes in summer, not to mention an occasional alligator. At the same time, black forest workers received good pay compared to what sharecroppers earned. Nonfarm workers also received their money on a regular weekly or monthly basis; no longer did they have to work all year without wages. While farmers paid black field hands in Florida about $10 a month plus food and housing, axemen in the cedar forests received $20 to $30 plus board. Some Florida sawmills even employed unskilled laborers for wages ranging from $20 to $30 per month.[22] These wage differentials for farm and forest work added to the stigma of farming. When we also consider that despite the tight control of forest companies their laborers enjoyed more freedom of movement and decision making than field workers, it is not surprising that many men sought work in the woods.

By the early 1870s as many as 5,000 black men worked as axemen in the forests of Florida alone; by 1900 approximately half of the 262,000 forest workers in southern woods were black.[23] Many other workers gathered turpentine, the least desirable work in the forests. The relatively good wages they received, rising as high as $35 per month, mitigated the difficulties somewhat. But even in the woods, where survival often depended upon mutual support, black workers suffered racial discrimination. They frequently received less pay than immigrant Swedes; for the lower pay, they performed as much as 25 percent more work under the task system.[24]

Closely associated with forestry, though in some ways different, were the sawmills that developed throughout the South. There, too, blacks made up a large share of the work force, though whites occupied the most prized skilled positions. In fact, in 1890 blacks comprised 41.6 percent of all sawmill workers in the South, a percentage that increased to 46.1 in 1900. That year, the total number of blacks in the sawmills stood at 33,366.[25] To protect their interests and in response to the refusal of whites to unionize with them, black sawmill workers in Jacksonville, Florida, founded the Labor League of Jacksonville in the early 1870s. During the summer of 1873, they went on strike when the mill owners refused to grant a minimum wage of $1.50 per day. Their strike failed. It failed because the incipient union had no strike fund and because white workers in the mills refused to support its actions, while other whites came in as strikebreakers.[26]

Black employees on the docks of Pensacola fared somewhat better in protecting their jobs. A majority of the dock workers in Florida, they faced increasing competition from imported Canadian stevedores who came to work in Florida during the winter when the Canadian ports were too cold. As early as 1868, blacks in the Pensacola area formed the Workingmen's Association to organize their efforts to keep Canadian whites from taking over their jobs. Peaceful entreaties to shipping companies brought little remedy, and in 1872 the Workingmen's Association violently protested this foreign intrusion. During late 1872 and early 1873, competition between black and white workers on the Pensacola docks led to violence and almost caused an international confrontation between the U.S. and British governments over whether the United States would protect British subjects who wished to work in America. The incident ended in victory for the Workingmen's Association. In 1874 the Florida legislature required licensing for any person who wished to work on the docks of that state. This act worked to the advantage of blacks and effectively got rid of the Canadians because the legislature set a minimum of six months' residence in Florida as a qualification for a license.[27]

Those who foresaw rapid improvement of southern industry generally placed their hopes largely in mining, where more blacks were employed than in any other southern industry. Large numbers of blacks mined coal and iron ore in the fields of northern Alabama, and in other mining regions as well. Conditions in min-

ing camps differed little from those on the plantations in the postwar South. Companies not only required long working days at
miserable wages but also often demanded that miners accept payment in script redeemable only at company-owned stores. One
miner complained of receiving only 75 cents for a long ton of coal
and of paying exorbitant prices for goods in the company stores.[28]

Miners suffered from depressed wages caused by the wide use
of convict laborers, mainly black prisoners whom southern states
hired out to private businesses for fixed fees. Convict leasing was
one of the most humiliating acts ever perpetrated against workers, both those leased and those whose wages and working conditions deteriorated because of state-controlled slavery. But blacks,
particularly in mining, suffered most. Many even had to pay kick-
backs to white supervisors to hold on to their jobs. In an extreme
case of this practice, a major corporation of the New South, the
Tennessee Coal, Iron, and Railroad Company, gained access in
1883 to all the prisoners in the Tennessee penitentiary. These
1,300 men, whom the company put to work in its mines, provided
a convenient hedge against unionism by free workers.[29]

As the postwar decades wore on, blacks found jobs in the
North. The Pullman Palace Car Company of Chicago employed
many blacks as porters and maids on sleeping cars to perform
personal services for the increasing number of passengers who
traveled across the country. Other blacks trickled north to become domestics in the homes of white families, while still others
went to work in the private service sector.

But blacks were not totally absent in northern industry. Particularly in mining, their presence had a heavy impact. Most observers hold that blacks first found employment in northern mines
in the 1870s, when mine owners brought them into Illinois and
Ohio to help break strikes by white miners. Any discussion of
black workers and strikes raises crucial questions about the rights
of workers. Apparently many black miners worked with mine
owners to break a series of strikes in the Hocking Valley of Ohio
during the depression of 1873. Miner T. Ames, a Chicago capitalist and a mine owner of the region who had used blacks as

strikebreakers in Brazil, Indiana, encouraged their use in the Ohio strikes. In June, Ames recruited 400 to 500 black miners mainly from Memphis, Louisville, and Richmond and brought them together in Columbus, Ohio, prepared to "go dig coal in the beautiful country" near the Ohio capital. According to Herbert Gutman, the historian of this strike, they were promised good wages and inexpensive accommodations and were told nothing about the labor strife in the mines.[30]

When the new black miners arrived, they received sympathy from neither the white miners nor the mine operators. White miners called to the blacks to leave the mines with the promise that they would "be good to them and send them back home to their families."[31] As was traditional among white workers, the white miners never considered these blacks as simply workers who, like themselves, were exploited by the employers to maintain low wages and poor working conditions for the entire working class. Accordingly, they made no effort to make common cause with black miners and to enlist them as permanent workers in a region where plenty of work was available.

The use of black miners in the Hocking Valley strikes takes on wider significance when we realize that blacks were employed to break other strikes in Indiana, Illinois, and Ohio in 1874, and in Ohio, Indiana, and Kansas in 1875. These activities added to the relish with which whites tagged blacks as scabs, men incapable of developing class consciousness and unworthy of unionizing with white workers. But two points must be made here. First, blacks were by no means the only group of workers who broke strikes. During the 1870s and 1880s, for example, labor agents regularly brought in large numbers of foreign workers not only to break strikes but also to swell the labor supply in various localities so as to keep workers docile. And native-born whites showed up regularly as strikebreakers, too. But the second point is more important to our discussion. Black workers who wished to work were justified in going into the mines during strikes. In fact, when they did so under the protection of company guards, it was because that was the only way they could obtain work in the

industry. Under normal circumstances, white workers themselves
would have gone on strike to oppose the employment of blacks.
Between 1880 and 1900, federal sources reported at least thirty
strikes by whites in protest over employment of blacks—eight from
1880 to 1890 and twenty-two from 1890 to 1900.[32] Moreover, since
white miners did not see a connection between their interests and
those of black workers, it is unthinkable that black workers would
do so. Blacks saw little reason to honor a strike by whites when
the sure result of victory would be continued denial of employment for blacks. Though it did little to develop class consciousness among black and white workers, blacks sided with the employers—who at least gave them jobs, even if at pitiably low
wages.

Not all diversity of black employment took place in the basic
industries of the urban North, nor did blacks always enter new
fields only in competition with whites. A generation of Americans
who have grown up with television western shows in which all
cowboys are white find it difficult to believe that 25 percent of
the more than 35,000 cowboys during the heroic age of the cattle
industry, 1866 to 1895, were black. Black cowhands were particularly numerous in the Texas Gulf Coast and in parts of the Indian
Territory. Records show that blacks performed a variety of tasks,
from top hand to chief cook, though few actually became fore-
men. Unlike the romanticized versions we see on television, work
on the cow trails was rough. But the pay was good, and cowboys
had freedom unavailable almost anywhere else. Black range workers certainly faced discrimination and isolation, particularly in the
generally all-white towns of the West. But there was apparently
little discrimination on the job. Strange as it may seem, there is
no evidence that black cowboys received less pay than whites of
equal experience, though it is clear that Mexicans who rode the
western range sometimes received as little as one-third the wages
of whites for the same work.[33]

A major factor in black employment after the Civil War is the
large number of black women in the labor force. Of course, the
fact that black women and children worked was nothing new,

particularly in agriculture. Since under slavery all blacks had worked, after the war both men and women had work experience. Much has been made in recent years of the phenomenal increase in the number of women workers. But it is much more accurate to speak of white female workers, for black women have always worked. As early as the 1640s, Maryland and Virginia law declared black women eligible for employment in agriculture, work not allowed for white women, even servants.[34] In 1870, 49.5 percent of black women of all ages and marital statuses were in the labor force. In contrast, only 16.5 percent of white women worked. The situation changed little over the next decade—in 1880 the percentages for black and white women were 55.1 and 18.1, respectively.[35] This differential began to narrow only in the mid-twentieth century. While labor force participation for white women more than doubled between 1890 and 1960, increasing from 16.3 to 33.7 percent, for black women it remained almost constant (39 percent in 1890 and 41.7 percent in 1960).[36]

There is no simple explanation for the much higher participation rate of black women than white women, though discrimination against black men that resulted in lower family income is clearly a factor. Yet, numerous black artisans, particularly in southern cities, refused to allow their wives to work and, as Carter G. Woodson observed, many white women from poor families held no jobs because they were "too proud to work." Claudia Goldin, in her study of the female labor force, confirms this view. She points out that only 14 percent of white women with low family labor incomes ($0–$299) worked in 1880, while 44 percent of low-income black women had jobs.[37] The truth is that the harsh requirements of slavery which had forced black women—and children—to work had removed the stigma of labor. When faced with the economic realities of making a living, black women found little difficulty in going to work.

Black women worked largely in low-paying, dead-end jobs. In 1870, for example, when black women comprised 31.6 percent of the total black labor force and 26.0 percent of black professionals, 32.6 percent of those in the cities were employed as servants,

Table 1-1. Female labor force participation by race and marital
status, 1870–1890

	1870	1880	1890
Black			
Married	31.0%	35.4%	22.5%
Single		73.3	59.5
White			
Married	4.0	7.3	2.5
Single	26.4	23.8	38.4

laundresses, and cooks. Another 3.4 percent listed their job classifications as "unskilled." Occupational data on rural black women
are even more difficult to obtain or to explain because enumerators often listed women as "at home." But the fact is that white
landowners expected the whole family to participate in crop production and farm maintenance. Black women and children worked
in the fields alongside black men.[38]

Despite severe restrictions on their movements and freedom of
action, black workers did not live in a vacuum. Many of them,
unfortunately few of those in agriculture, knew of efforts by white
workers to organize in order to improve their conditions. Blacks
attempted to join these movements. When whites set up discriminatory organizations, overlooking the necessity of class solidarity,
black workers formed their own unions to protect themselves
against both white workers and white employers.

During Reconstruction black and white workers in New Orleans made notable progress in creating strong class consciousness
across racial lines. Longshoremen in that city showed remarkable
unity, even surviving efforts of capitalists to divide them during
the depression of 1873. In 1881 black and white workers in New
Orleans joined together to form the Central Trades and Labor
Assembly (CTLA). By 1882 the CTLA represented 15,000 workers, and its vice president was a black worker.[39]

The grave misfortune for U.S. workers in the Reconstruction
years and after is that that situation was rare, and black and
white workers never came to recognize their common interests.

In fact, deep antagonism marked the relations between black and white workers, and white workers became a bulwark of American racism. This was particularly true of organized labor, where blacks and whites never created firm working-class consciousness.

In the years immediately following the Civil War, organized labor got a new start in the United States. The first nationwide group, the National Labor Union, convened for its first session in Baltimore in 1866. Composed mainly of national unions of skilled craftsmen which refused membership to blacks through constitutional prohibitions or subterfuge, the union mouthed platitudes about the need to organize black workers; for a short time, black delegates actually attended its meetings. But the union failed to recognize the particular interests of black workers, and disagreements between blacks and whites over the relative merit of U.S. political parties made it impossible for them to settle their differences.

At the same time that white labor organized on a national level, a similar movement occurred among blacks. As early as 1866, black caulkers in Baltimore worked collectively to protect their jobs when whites drove them from shipyards. Under the leadership of Isaac Myers they organized their own company, secured government contracts, and eventually rehired all the blacks who had been dismissed. In 1869 Myers called a meeting in Washington, D.C., of blacks interested in the problems of workers. That meeting, attended by delegates from eighteen states and representatives of the white National Labor Union, endorsed efforts of workers to organize and became the first session of the black National Labor Union.[40] It was also the session at which a black spokesman made it clear to white workers that black laborers must be able to protect their right to work. Myers told the gathering:

American citizenship is a complete failure if [blacks are] proscribed from the workshops of this country—if any man cannot employ him who chooses, and if he cannot work for any man whom he will. If citizenship means anything at all, it means the freedom of labor, as broad and as universal as freedom of the ballot.[41]

The black group worked energetically to organize black workers throughout the country, a difficult and deadly task in the South. The National Labor Union's Alabama affiliate, the Labor Union of Alabama, founded by James Rapier in 1871, even tried to organize farm workers in that state.[42] At the same time, the national leaders also tried to convince the white group that success for all laborers rested on the ability of black and white workers to make common cause. Blacks were particularly unable to agree with denunciations of the Republican party that often circulated in the white labor press and punctuated the speeches of leaders of the white National Labor Union. As far as blacks were concerned, the Republican party had freed the slaves. What better gesture could be made to show that the party had the interests of working people at heart? Differences remained when the two groups ceased to exist by 1872.

Even before the demise of the two National Labor Unions, a new national movement had developed that promised better relations between black and white workers. In 1869 the Knights of Labor began. This order, composed of both craft and industrial unions, offered more than the lip service of leaders of the white National Labor Union and actively sought to recruit black members, even to the extent of hiring black organizers. Employing the slogan "An injury to one is the concern of all," the Knights tried to recruit all laborers, regardless of race or sex. Nor did the class of work matter to them. Unskilled workers had as much right to organized protection as the most skilled. This basic rejection of the craft orientation of the white National Labor Union, as well as the advanced racial views of the two principal leaders, Uriah Stephens and Terence Powderly, made the Knights of Labor palatable to black workers. At the height of its power in 1886, an estimated 60,000 to 90,000 blacks belonged to the Knights out of a total membership of 700,000.[43] Indeed, in the South during the 1870s and 1880s fewer and fewer whites joined the order, and the Knights became a haven for blacks.[44]

The Knights of Labor was one of the most militant and egalitarian organizations in the history of the American working-class movement. Though keenly aware of racial hostility in the South and of the basically antiunion sentiment of that region, the Knights attempted to organize black and white workers in all industries and all sections of the South. Most revolutionary of all, the national leaders insisted that race was of no consequence in economic questions facing workers. They repeatedly pointed out to workers—both black and white—that talk about workers' solidarity was inconsistent with segregated meetings and separate locals. But when the realities of social conditions of their day prevailed and their attempts at integration failed, the national leaders organized segregated locals.

Despite the intentions of its leaders, then, the Knights failed largely because of racism, particularly in the South, where by the late 1880s most of its members were rural blacks. In Oxford, North Carolina, for example, where the mayor was a Knight, the master workman reported the scorn with which residents had called Knights "Nigger! Nigger! until the two words 'nigger' and Knight became almost synonymous terms." To be sure, race was always a strong emotional peg on which opponents could hang their arguments. They could, and did, argue that the racial policies of the Knights of Labor threatened the economic and social order of the South. Those policies sometimes flagrantly violated the rules of racial separation—as in Richmond, Virginia, during the Knights General Assembly in 1886, when black delegate Frank Ferrell of District Assembly 49 of New York spoke from the same podium that Governor Fitzhugh Lee had just vacated. Ferrell later occupied an orchestra seat in the city's most famous theatre to see a production of *Hamlet*. When such events occurred, southern whites were willing to listen to anti-Knight arguments. The incidents surrounding Ferrell's visit to Richmond even caused animosity between black and white Knights and contributed much to the breakup of the fragile reform political alliance that existed in that city. When verbal arguments failed to break up the Knights, southern capitalists turned to violence. They ended a strike by blacks in Arkansas with guns in 1886; they killed a black organizer of the Knights at Warrenton, Georgia, in

1887; they browbeat and intimidated workers throughout the section where attempts to organize occurred.[45]

The eventual decline of the Knights of Labor in the South ended in an explosion of violence in Louisiana in 1887. The order had started organizing in the state in 1883 and by 1887 had about 5,000 members and enough regular funds to publish a weekly newspaper. The sugar crop was poor in 1886, so the owners cut wages in 1887 to make up the shortfall. In October, members of District Assembly 194 of the Knights of Labor threatened a strike unless their wages were raised by November. The sugar growers, organized in the Louisiana Sugar Planters' Association, did not deign to reply. Consequently, 6,000 to 10,000 laborers, mostly blacks, refused to work after November 1. The planters and the powers of the state reacted with vigor to put down this group of blacks who were "plotting insurrection." By November 10, the governor had dispatched ten companies of state militia to Lafourche Parish, the scene of most of the strike activity, at least one company of which reportedly brought along a Gatling gun. The militia evicted strike leaders and intimidated other workers. But the strike had not been broken after three weeks of strife, and the planters faced a critical situation: the first ice came on the night of November 21 and the cane was damaged. The next night the planters' gunners moved in and when the shooting ended, at least thirty blacks had died and many others fled the region. The strike had been crushed, and the Knights had been destroyed in the sugar country.[46]

Yet, despite this failure and the almost simultaneous decline of the order as a whole, the Knights of Labor came closest to understanding Du Bois's assertion that in the South lay the hopes for a unified movement of workers. The opportunity lost in the 1880s would not occur again until the 1960s.

2

The Nadir

Now I started at the bottom and I stays right there, don't seem like I'm gonna get nowhere.

Line from the Blues

If Reconstruction ever set the bottom rail on top, it was not for long and never securely. Redemption seemed to leave little doubt that the bottom rail was again on the bottom—whatever its temporary dislocation. It remained for the New South to find what Reconstruction had failed to find: the measure of the emancipated slave's freedom and a definition of free labor. . . .

C. VANN WOODWARD, *Origins of the New South* (1951)

As the nineteenth century gave way to the century of hope, the lot of most blacks remained wretched. In many areas of the South as late as 1910, it was difficult to see what improvement General Lee's surrender had made possible for blacks. Indeed, one historian has concluded that the position of black people reached its nadir during these years.[1] Evidence is abundant to support this view; black working people had by now lost much of their political, social, and economic status throughout the South.

Conditions worsened in both agriculture and industry as white landowners, industrial managers, and white workers, particularly unionists, combined to relegate blacks to unemployment or casual labor. This worsening of status of blacks was an index of their utter powerlessness in the South. And the federal government was in no mood to help. Its various branches actually helped to weaken them. You will recall President Hayes's pullback in 1877.

Congress, for its part, refused to pass a major piece of legislation to protect the rights of blacks in the last two decades of the nineteenth century. And even if Congress had acted, the Supreme Court stood ready to dismantle its work. The Court invalidated the Civil Rights Act of 1875 in a series of decisions in 1883, and in 1896 it handed down a decision in *Plessy* v. *Ferguson* that gave official recognition to "separate but equal" facilities for black and white citizens. This decision removed all doubt that a caste system relegating blacks to second-class status was the law of the land.[2]

Nonetheless, the vast majority of blacks remained in the rural South as oppressed and ignorant farm workers, while some moved to southern cities to seek employment in the developing industries. Still others had tired of conditions in the South and looked on the North as a land of social and economic opportunity. Blacks quit the South in a steadily increasing trickle that would become a flood of migration by World War I. They soon found that life in the northern cities was "no crystal stair," but they provided the base from which new generations of blacks would enter the urban industrial class.

In 1910 the U.S. black population stood at 9,827,763, more than double the 4,441,830 in 1860; 83.3 percent of the black population in 1910 resided in the twelve southern states, compared to the 86.6 percent who had lived there in 1860. The vast majority of southern blacks remained on the farms, reaching an all-time high of 6,592,505 in 1910. But the urban black population had increased sharply as well, growing from 190,518 in 1860 to 1,597,260 by 1910.[3]

Agriculture remained the dominant occupation of southern blacks into the twentieth century. Indeed, the number of black farmers increased during the first decade of the twentieth century. The 1900 census reported 746,715 black farmers; by 1910 893,370 black farmers operated 14 percent of all the farms in the United States, a disproportionate number, given that blacks made up 10.7 percent of the national population that year. The number of black farmers was increasing more rapidly than that of white farmers. Between 1900 and 1910 the number of black farmers increased by 19.6 percent, while whites registered a 9.5 percent gain.[4]

It is not enough to look at the increased number of black farmers to gauge their improvement; to do so would produce misleading conclusions. In fact, though in real numbers more black farmers owned the land they worked in 1910 than in 1900, more and more blacks were falling into tenantry. In 1910 only 25 percent of black farmers owned their land; the rest were tenants of some sort. Most of them were, as Du Bois stated, "those half-million black men who hire[d] farms on various terms . . . a large part of whom stand about midway between slavery and ownership."[5] In contrast, in the same year more than two-thirds of white farmers owned the land they worked.[6] Moreover, while

Fig. 2-1. Percentage of farms operated by black farmers, 1910. (U.S. Census Bureau: Bulletin 129, *Negroes in the U.S.* (Washington, D.C.: GPO, 1915).

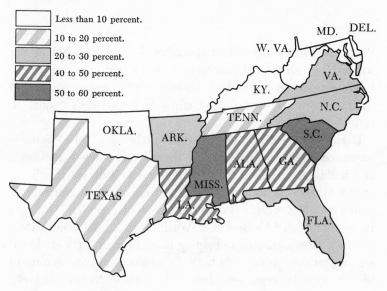

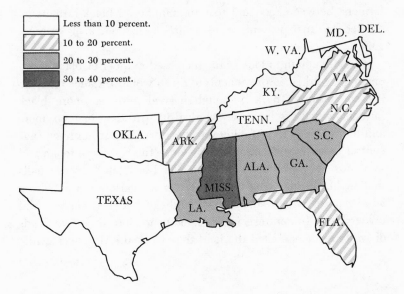

Fig. 2-2. Percentage of land in farms operated by black farmers, 1910.
(U.S. Census Bureau: Bulletin 129, *Negroes in the U.S.* (Washington,
D.C.: GPO, 1915).

the average black farmer had 47.3 acres, the average white farmer
worked 153 acres. Differences in farm sizes in part reflect the
larger proportion of blacks than whites who were tenants, but
sizes of farms also had a direct effect on the farmer's annual income.[7]

Despite their unfavorable conditions, the lot of black farmers
improved. Between 1900 and 1920 the value of black-owned lands
and buildings increased from $69,636,420 to $522,178,137. Some
of the increase undoubtedly resulted from inflation and regular
increments. But organized activities contributed as well. Tuskegee
Institute, founded by Booker T. Washington in Alabama in 1881,
played a prominent part in helping black farmers, both landowners and tenants, to improve both their lands and their quality of
life. In 1892 Tuskegee established the Annual Negro Congress,

which provided information and education so that farmers could improve their lands. By 1895 the Annual Negro Congress attracted 2,000 delegates to discuss a wide range of common problems. Tuskegee's activities did not stop there. Dr. George Washington Carver made available results of his plant research, and Thomas M. Campbell used the Jesup Wagon, a vehicle laden with equipment and new seeds—and even a nurse—to carry directly to the farmers, for demonstration on their own farms, the latest information and procedures for developing bountiful crops. The Tuskegee representatives also gave instruction in good housekeeping, personal hygiene, and food preservation.[8]

Not all efforts to improve conditions for southern black workers consisted of self-help. In 1890, Walter R. Vaughn, a white southerner then resident in Omaha, Nebraska, began agitating for reparations payments and bounties for the ex-slaves. He even wrote a bill that would have provided reparations and had his Republican representative introduce it in Congress. The bill died in committee, but by the mid-1890s blacks had joined the effort, even establishing the National Ex-Slave Mutual Relief Bounty and Pension Association in 1894. Despite official harassment and allegations of fraud, the organization worked until 1915, with at least five reparations bills introduced in Congress.[9]

Black farmers themselves made a more practical attempt to improve their lives. In March 1888 black farmers met in Lovejoy, Texas, to found the Colored Farmers' National Alliance and Cooperative Union. Its general superintendent and best-known leader was Richard Manning Humphrey, a southern white preacher. This fact has caused some scholars to wonder whether the Alliance was a black organization at all. Indeed, some black Alliance members objected to Humphrey's leadership, one murmuring that though he had nothing against Humphrey personally, why did he not belong to the white alliance instead? The reasonable explanation is that though blacks undoubtedly exercised strong influence over the Alliance's activities, they recognized the grave difficulties a black person would encounter in serving as spokesman for a militant farmers' organization in the nineteenth-century

South. Accordingly, they used Humphrey as their spokesman. Despite underlying dissensions the organization experienced remarkable growth. At its peak in 1891 the Alliance claimed a membership of 1,200,000 in twelve states, sponsored cooperative stores in several southern cities, obtained loans to pay off mortgages of members who fell on hard times, published newspapers, and in some regions helped to raise money to provide longer school terms for black children.[10]

The Colored Farmers' Alliance undertook its most militant action, and the one that proved its undoing, when it attempted a cotton pickers' strike in 1891. When Humphrey called for the strike under the auspices of the Cotton Pickers' League, a new name used to circumvent opposition of some Alliance leaders to the scheme, he attempted to solve a serious problem for an oppressed group of workers. Cotton pickers received a wage of 50 to 60 cents per 100 pounds. Picking cotton by hand is a grueling task. Pickers spend the day either with their backs bent or crawling on their knees to reach the cotton that grows generally within two feet of the ground. All the while they drag a bag that they fill with cotton that comes to weigh as much as twenty or thirty pounds. Moreover, cotton ripens in August, when temperatures in the South reach 100 degrees in the shade. In order to pick as much as 200 pounds of cotton, and thus earn $1.20, a good picker would have to go into the field at daybreak and remain at work until dusk, with little time off to escape the life-draining heat.

Humphrey set the cotton pickers' strike for September 12, 1891, but in general it did not come off. Those who did attempt to strike failed miserably. Strike leaders suffered from inadequate communication facilities and from opposition of some Alliance members who themselves were cotton farmers. Moreover, this was a period of general union weakness, and the Cotton Pickers' League had no strike fund to tide its members over. But most important was the opposition of the white cotton farmers, some of whom were members of the white farmers' alliances. Leonidas L. Polk, president of the influential Southern Farmers' Alliance, even advised white farmers to leave their cotton in the fields rather than pay more than 50 cents per 100 pounds to have it picked. In Lee County, Arkansas, the one area in which the black cotton pickers made a determined effort to strike, white farmers crushed the effort with brutal violence. More than twenty-five blacks died, including nine "taken" from a deputy sheriff and lynched.[11] After the strike of 1891, the Alliance was only a paper organization.

Though the failure of the cotton pickers' strike marked the end of the Colored Farmers' Alliance, it was hardly the end of attempts by blacks and white Populists to form a political alliance to improve conditions for working-class people. When the Peoples' Party of Texas organized in 1892, the convention elected two black men to the state committee. The historian Lawrence Goodwyn has written a revealing account of the cooperation between black and white Populists in Grimes County, Texas, in the 1890s. In other parts of the region, some Populist leaders, particularly Thomas "Tom" Watson of Georgia, argued vociferously for a while that blacks should be included in all aspects of the party's activities. Watson even claimed that "the accident of color can make no difference in the interest of farmers, croppers, and laborers" and counseled both blacks and whites that landowners and other big businessmen were keeping the two groups apart to deprive them of the benefits of their labor. But, given the centrality of race in American economic and political thought, particularly in the post-Reconstruction South, the Populists' efforts were doomed to failure. The majority of southern whites, particularly the leaders of the Democratic party, saw the activities of the Populists as a threat to the economic and social status quo. Accordingly, they joined forces to crush the incipient interracial movement, eliminating blacks from southern politics for more than a half century. Nonetheless, as Goodwyn points out, in the post-Reconstruction South,

during which the social order has been organized hierarchically along racial lines, Populism intruded as a brief, flickering light in parts of the South. For a time, some white Southerners threw off the romanticism that has historically been a cover for the region's pessimism and ventured a larger, more hopeful view about the possibilities of

man in a free society. Under duress and intimidation this public hope
failed of persuasion at the ballot box; under terrorism it vanished
completely.[12]

Given this context, then, it is clear that the white farmers reacted so violently to the cotton pickers' strike because it threatened the whole labor situation in the South. Cotton, like peanuts,
tobacco, and sugar cane, is a labor-intensive crop, requiring large
numbers of unskilled workers for a short time to harvest the product. Thus, although many blacks lived a marginal existence in
which there was little work for much of the year, they had to be
available to pick the cotton.

The concept of black workers as a reserve or surplus labor supply is central in understanding their continued relative poverty.
In some ways, it is more central than unemployment. It was only
in the 1950s that the unemployment ratio of blacks to whites became 2 : 1. But since the end of the Civil War, southern agriculture has demanded a large supply of hands at harvest time, thus
reducing black workers, particularly males, to a condition of casual labor. As long as their lives remained centered on the farms,
they could not become permanent industrial workers. And the
casual nature of this farm labor, particularly for those who lived
in towns and villages, left them with no money with which to
improve their living conditions or—in the case of many—to leave
the rural South for the prospect of better jobs in the cities. Casual work provided no hope that they would someday improve
their social standing, and the idea of a career was almost non-
existent.

If southern black farmers had problems earning a living around
the turn of the century, their efforts to move into southern industry were equally unavailing. Black women found it particularly
difficult to find any but menial or domestic work when they left
the farms. Yet, it would be inaccurate to conclude that the majority of black women were servants in the homes of southern
whites. Indeed, one myth of the Old South that exists to this day
is that of the faithful and loyal black "mammy" who served pa-
tiently and seemingly forever in the home of her master. Recent

evidence shows that the average black house servant was a young girl rather than an experienced older woman. Black women declined such work after marriage and the start of families, under pressure from their fathers and husbands to remain at home. Most women preferred work as washerwomen which, though heavy and onerous, left them time to care for their families and their own homes.[13]

The historian Carter G. Woodson has written an extremely tender history of one group of these black women, the washerwomen, whom he claims were responsible for all the progress made by black people since the Civil War. To be sure, these women, who labored long, hard hours carrying heavy pails of water, rubbing their hands to the bones on scrub boards as they cleaned the clothes of whites, undoubtedly contributed greatly to black family incomes. Generally, their work went unappreciated.

Woodson's claim about the impact of these women is undoubtedly excessive, but washerwomen were anything but passive in the developing New South, as an episode in Atlanta, Georgia, in 1881 demonstrates. The women formed the Washerwomen's Association of Atlanta and went on strike, demanding a wage of $1 for twelve pounds of wash. As many as 3,000 women eventually joined the strike, showing the militance of black women at the end of Reconstruction. But the strike, particularly the manner in which it was put down, also demonstrated the powerlessness of the black community. Whites threatened to refuse to help destitute blacks during the oncoming winter, some landlords evicted black washerwomen, and the city council introduced a bill that would require washerwomen to buy a $25 license. The Washerwomen's Association at first scoffed at the proposed license resolution and informed the mayor that they would gladly pay the fee if it would assure them a decent wage. But the strike had been broken by the full might of whites. After two weeks of disruption, the washerwomen returned to work at their earlier rates.[14]

If the abortive washerwomen's strike shows the powerlessness of the black people in the South, their wages are representative of the depressed black economic condition. Already in the South blacks were experiencing high rates of unemployment and low family income. Few black families earned as much as $30 a month during the 1870s and 1880s. Accordingly, poor incomes relegated urban blacks to poor housing and a diet of the worst quality. Moreover, lack of cash also placed them at the mercy of grocery store owners, who sold on credit at inflated prices, and to nonfood merchants, who sold cheap goods at high prices on the installment plan.[15] Most blacks grew up in the South fearing that their meager belongings would be repossessed because they missed a payment at the store. They were trapped in perpetual poverty.

In spite of these difficult circumstances, black male workers made some headway in expanding into industry, which took off at the turn of the century. The nation's gross national product (GNP), which stood at $13 billion in 1890, increased to $40 billion by 1910. Total employment rose as well, from an annual average of 27 million between 1889 and 1898 to 39 million from 1909 to 1918. During these heady times, employment of black males in mining, manufacturing, and mechanical industries increased from 275,000 in 1900 to 693,000 in 1910. These three fields employed almost 1,000,000 black workers nationally by 1920.[16]

In the South, blacks still held on to many of the industrial jobs they had attained during slavery. In Savannah, Georgia, blacks held important jobs during the 1870s and 1880s, their numbers and percentages actually increasing in some trades during those decades. And in 1890 most artisans in Charleston, South Carolina, were black. Indeed, as R. R. Wright stated in 1913, in the South "its railroads and streets, its sewers and water works have been largely constructed by Negroes. The writer was in his twenty-first year before he had ever seen as many as a dozen white men at one time working on the streets, digging sewers or laying railroads. Reared in the black belt of the South, he had seen only Negroes do this work and had come to believe it was their work until a visit to Chicago introduced him to the first large group of white sewer diggers."[17] Black firemen and brakemen, employed in positions previously described as "Negro jobs," were particularly numerous on southern lines at a time when they had been wholly excluded from such jobs in the North. In Birmingham, Alabama, in 1900, for example, blacks accounted for more than 70 percent of the brakemen and 56.5 percent of the firemen. Moreover, there were still many blacks in the building trades and municipal services of various cities.[18]

Yet change was clearly in the air as blacks lost more ground than they gained. Black male employment dropped even in "Negro jobs." In fact, census figures for both 1890 and 1900 dispute the widely held view that in certain occupations black workers held a monopoly. By 1900 very few job classifications employed more blacks than whites. Blacks lost ground rapidly in jobs like barbering, bricklaying, blacksmithing, carpentry, and even housekeeping. Even more ominous for the long-term future of blacks as skilled workers was the fact that black craftsmen were considerably older than whites in the same trades.[19]

One of the clearest signs of decline was the decreasing number of black draymen, teamsters, and hackmen in the South. The number of blacks in these jobs increased 50.5 percent between 1890 and 1900, but the number of whites increased 74.9 percent. More telling, whereas there had been 1,079 more black than white draymen in 1890, by 1900 there were 6,044 fewer. In 1900, 83.6 percent of all black workers were employed as agricultural laborers, farmers, planters, overseers, unspecified laborers, servants and waiters, and launderers and laundresses. Hardly had they attained wide industrial employment.[20] And by the end of the decade, white workers were attempting to remove blacks from even those few positions they had attained. Blacks faced intimidation, subterfuge, violence, and threats of death as they attempted to find work as free citizens in the burgeoning American economy.

Though figures are mixed for various occupations, black employment decreased greatly in the building trades during the late nineteenth and early twentieth centuries, largely because of the actions of white unions. The most impressive losses occurred among carpenters and joiners. The number of blacks employed in these fields nationwide declined from 22,581 in 1890 to 21,591 in 1900, while in the South the number of black carpenters and joiners fell from 20,591 to 19,451. During the same decade, the number of whites in these fields increased from 94,861 to 100,459. Black brickmasons suffered as well. A classic example of a white union using its influence to keep black craftsmen out of work occurred in Indianapolis, Indiana, in 1903. Robert Rhodes, a black brickmason, went to work on a federal project in that city, and all the whites employed there walked off the job rather than work with him. The contractor, under pressure to finish the job on time, fired Rhodes, and the whites returned to work. Rhodes, a card-carrying member of his union, appealed to the local for relief. The union found no merit in Rhodes's claim that he had been fired because of discrimination; indeed, it fined him $25 for scabbing because he had taken a job on a nonunion project while his case was under review at the local.[21] Under such circumstances, blacks could hardly expect to find work in the building trades.

Eliminated from key construction occupations at this crucial time of technological innovation and refused by whites as apprentices, a generation of black construction workers were left with only the most basic skills. They were wholly unprepared to work on the skyscrapers that rose to blot out the sun in city after city. Also, white unionists could deny employment to blacks because they were "unqualified" to do the work they had been denied the right to learn.

Despite the success of the Indianapolis brickmasons in keeping blacks from finding work, U.S. labor unions generally have been weak and in a poor position to control access to jobs. But railroad unions have been an exception. In fact, from the end of the Civil War, these skilled workers in the nation's leading industry of the time formed strong unions and bargained with railroads to protect their members' wages and working conditions. The railroad unions, known as the Big Four Brotherhoods—the Brotherhood of Locomotive Engineers, the Order of Railway Conductors, the Brotherhood of Locomotive Firemen and Enginemen, and the

Brotherhood of Railway Trainmen—were both social and economic organizations, and restrictionist in the worst way. They
made no effort to include unskilled white workers, and blacks, regardless of skill or occupation, were denied membership by their
constitutions. The railroad brotherhoods even refused to frater-
nize officially with the American Federation of Labor (AFL), the
leading federation of trade unions after 1881, and bitterly opposed efforts to establish industrywide unions that would work
to improve the status of unskilled workers.

When Eugene V. Debs, secretary of the Brotherhood of Locomotive Firemen, resigned in 1893 and founded the industrywide
American Railway Union (ARU), he met total opposition from
his former brothers. When the ARU called a strike against the
Pullman Company and the General Managers' Association—the
organization of railroads with terminals in Chicago—the next
year, causing one of the greatest upheavals in American labor
history, the Big Four stood aloof. In fact, they actually collabo-
rated with management. And though the Pullman Strike of 1894
resulted in federal intervention and established the government's
use of injunctions to ward off future strikes on railroads, the Big
Four emerged stronger than before.[22]

The Pullman Strike of 1894 did more than demonstrate the
gulf between labor leaders like Debs, who advocated industrial
unionism, and those of the Big Four, who insisted on maintaining
craft unions. It also brought on employment problems between
black and white workers, particularly in unskilled and semiskilled
occupations. Apart from failing to enlist the Big Four in his strike
against the General Managers' Association, Debs could not convince members of his own ARU to accept black railroaders. Accordingly, blacks refused to go along with the strike. In fact,
some blacks even became strikebreakers, formalizing their action
in the Anti-Strikers Railroad Union. In a speech in 1923, Debs
said that the strike of 1894 failed because the union refused to
cooperate with black railroaders. White workers placed race
above workers' solidarity, and consequently sabotaged their own
interests.[23]

Railroad unions were not alone in denying membership to black workers and eliminating them from various occupations. In one sense it might be said that the railroad unions were simply the most honest, for though most other unions did not bar black membership officially, they accomplished the same result through various subterfuges. Methods ranged from a simple pledge that white members would recommend only other whites for membership to allowing one negative vote to decide a candidate's rejection.[24] Nor should southern whites alone carry the responsibility for holding racist views. Northern whites, in cities as small as Cleveland and as large as New York, also worked openly to keep blacks out of unions. The pretext was that they were strikebreakers and thus unworthy of membership.[25]

Indeed, by 1900 opposition to blacks typified the white American labor movement. Since the early 1880s, skilled craft unions had formed the American Federation of Labor to press their interests. Founded in Pittsburgh in 1881 as the Federation of Organized Trade and Labor Unions of the United States and Canada, the AFL soon eclipsed the Knights of Labor to become the dominant voice on union matters in the country. Early meetings of the AFL mouthed egalitarian slogans about organizing all workers, but the skilled craft unions made the AFL exclusive and discriminatory. It had little interest in organizing either blacks or white women. Indeed, though the original constitution of 1881 did not mention blacks, delegates of those sessions—including at least one black worker—debated problems organized workers would face if they refused to organize the unskilled workers. Jeremiah Grandison, the black delegate and a member of Local Assembly No. 1665 of the Knights of Labor in Pittsburgh, lectured the convention on this issue. If overlooked, unskilled workers would be pushed into the hands of antilabor employers, providing them a ready supply of strikebreakers who could harm the negotiating efforts of legitimate unions. As Grandison put it:

Our object is, as I understand it, to federate the whole laboring element of America. I speak more particularly with a knowledge of my people, and declare to you that it would be dangerous to skilled mechanics to exclude from this organization the common laborers, who might, in an emergency, be employed in positions they could readily qualify themselves to fill.[26]

Though never with enthusiasm, during its early years the AFL made noises about organizing all workers without racial discrimination. Indeed, Samuel Gompers, who was president of the Cigar Makers Union when he led in founding the AFL in 1881 and who served as its president every year but one until his death in 1924, even insisted to northern and southern national union leaders that the whole future of organized labor rested on efforts to organize all workers. In fact, Gompers even held up the application of the Machinists' Union when it refused to remove a racial discrimination clause from its constitution. But Gompers clearly operated out of a feeling of necessity and had no real interest in organizing black workers. Labor leaders were acutely aware of the power of blacks as strikebreakers.[27] Gompers wanted white unions to organize black workers so that they could be controlled.

But some international unions made real efforts to organize all workers. The United Mine Workers of America (UMW), one of the largest AFL affiliates, made notable progress in lining up all employees, regardless of race, helping to expel the myth that black and white workers could not work in the same union. From its founding in 1890, leaders of the UMW clearly recognized the impracticality of organizing only white miners. Moreover, they saw the need to include all workers employed in or about the mines without regard to craft lines. The reason for the first premise is clear. The mining industry already included numerous black miners, particularly in the bituminous fields, and white miners had bitter experience of the damage blacks or other disaffected workers could cause the union in time of strikes. The second premise is equally clear. There are many different tasks in the mining industry. Thus, it would be pure folly to attempt to organize workers along craft lines; by necessity, the union must be industrywide. Both actions, major efforts to organize blacks and elimination of craft lines, set the UMW apart from the main-

stream of AFL leadership. The tension would result in a definite
split in later years.

The miners' union had a major success in enlisting black members, partly because of the work of black organizers. Richard L.
Davis, Jr., a founder of the union and a man who dedicated his
life to organizing miners, was the most notable black contributor
to the UMW during its early years. Davis and other UMW organizers convinced large numbers of blacks to join the union. In
fact, proportionately more black miners joined than whites. In
1900 the miners' union claimed more than 20,000 black members,
approximately a quarter of the total membership.[28] But even in
the UMW, black miners faced job discrimination and limited access to responsible positions in the union. Davis had to call on
his union colleagues to grant blacks jobs in the UMW hierarchy
"in deed as well as in name" and chided white leaders for union-
tolerated discrimination against blacks.[29] Mine operators eventually blacklisted Davis for his union work, and despite appeals of
support to the UMW from white friends, he failed to find work
and the union gave him no job. In 1900 Davis died a bitter and
broken man at age thirty-five.

Despite Davis's relationship with the UMW, by 1900 it was
light years ahead of the other AFL unions. By that very year in
which Davis died, Gompers and other AFL leaders had moved
away from their position of encouraging black unionism, if for
no reason but to cut down strikebreaking. The AFL had become
a white men's movement. What caused the change in Gompers's
position is uncertain. He argued that he could not press for organizing blacks because of the opposition of southern whites to
the presence of black members. Gompers could argue that position because the AFL left the matter of membership qualification
to the affiliates. But Gompers's own racism undoubtedly influenced his decision. As the nineteenth century wore on, he increasingly retreated from his previous position that blacks had not been
admitted to labor unions because of white opposition and took
the position that blacks did not belong to unions because they
were "unorganizable." Still fearful of the damage blacks could do

to unions as strikebreakers, however, Gompers attempted to keep them in protective custody. At the AFL convention of 1900, he proposed the establishment of a "federal locals" system whereby workers—namely blacks—who could not attain membership in the normal trade unions could be organized directly by the AFL.[30]

If federal locals assuaged the fears of white unionists opposed to membership for blacks, they did little to improve conditions for black workers. When the AFL offered federal status to unorganized black workers, the international union with jurisdiction over that class of workers often objected. The AFL always backed down in the face of such opposition. And even when the international did not oppose the federal charter, the black group gained no control over negotiating contracts through its AFL affiliation. Such powers remained with the international, as did the increasingly important control over apprenticeship. Such unions could and did use these two levers practically to eliminate blacks from certain occupations. Conditions for blacks overall hardly improved. Few of them joined the federal locals, and more and more unions denied membership to black workers. When W. E. B. Du Bois studied American trade unions in 1902, he found fifty internationals that had no black members at all. And as late as 1910 a dozen unions—the Big Four railroad brotherhoods and eight AFL affiliates—had constitutional bars against black workers.[31] Animosity between blacks and the AFL that resulted from the AFL's actions persisted well into the twentieth century.

But black workers had far more reason to oppose white railroad unions. By the end of the first decade of the twentieth century, white workers in those crafts were no longer content simply to keep blacks out of certain occupations. They undertook to remove those blacks who already had attained employment and, in some cases, long tenure and seniority. A major effort to remove black firemen from southern railroads is representative. Since the Civil War, firemen's jobs had been difficult and thus considered "colored jobs." But with technological changes at the turn of the century, these jobs became more attractive to whites. In fact, they became apprentice positions from which whites moved on to become engineers. While many blacks worked as firemen in Georgia, South Carolina, Alabama, Florida, Mississippi, and the other southern states, one man in Ohio was the only black fireman in a northern state.[32]

In 1909 white firemen in Georgia went on strike to force the Georgia Railroad to dismiss black firemen who served on its lines between Augusta and Atlanta. Blacks had first gone to work as firemen for the Georgia in 1902, when the company began hiring large numbers of them in an alleged cost-saving effort. Black firemen accepted less pay than whites demanded. By 1909, 42 percent of the company's firemen were black. When the Atlanta Terminal Company dismissed ten white hostlers, those workers in the stations who prepared the locomotives for their runs, and replaced them with blacks, white firemen went on strike. They claimed that the whole economic future of whites was at stake and that this was only the first of many acts designed to remove all whites from railroad service in the South.[33] The Georgia Railroad paid little attention to the demands of white firemen that it fire its black workers. Company spokesmen maintained that black firemen did their jobs well. Moreover, from the company's point of view, black firemen were profitable because they worked for less pay than whites.

The Georgia Railroad Strike became a race strike when the white firemen, unable to get their way, called on the white public of Georgia to support them against the company's alleged efforts to eliminate white firemen. White firemen stirred up the white population, and in town after town between Augusta and Atlanta, large crowds of whites turned out to jeer black firemen and white engineers who continued to work. Jeering turned into violence as protesters stoned trains, blocked tracks, and physically abused the company's employees. Local authorities refused to enforce the law, informing Georgia Railroad officials that they could not protect the company's employees and property in view of the total public support of white firemen. The company's trains would be unsafe running through Georgia. Appeals to state authorities also failed. Indeed, Governor Hoke Smith allegedly informed the leader of the white firemen that if his term were not nearing an end, he would ensure that no more blacks got jobs on railroads in that state.[34] The violence prevailed for two weeks. Finally, absence of police protection and mob violence caused the Georgia Railroad to shut down.

Although they had stopped the trains from running, the white firemen's union failed to force the Georgia Railroad to fire black firemen. Nor would the company agree that in the future it would hire only white firemen. Unable to eliminate the impasse, the parties agreed to submit their dispute to an arbitration panel and to abide by its decision. During hearings before the all-white panel, white firemen slightly veiled the purely racist nature of their strike. Instead of arguing that blacks should be fired simply because of race, white firemen accused blacks of incompetence and claimed that they depressed the wages of whites on railroads because they worked for lower pay. They also claimed that black firemen endangered the lives of passengers and other employees, as well as valuable railroad property. They even caused some engineers to testify to the alleged incompetence of blacks. Black firemen, the story went, often fell asleep on the job and had become adept at firing their boilers to produce a lot of smoke but little steam.

The company's witnesses rebutted such testimony. Its agents admitted that black firemen received lower wages than whites, but they assured the arbitrators that blacks performed as effectively as whites, if not better. The company, they insisted, had no intention of firing its black firemen simply to make room for whites.

The three-man arbitration panel worked under considerable political and public pressure. Both the southern white press and local mobs demanded a decision in favor of the white railroad men. But in a rare bit of southern statesmanship when race was an issue, the committee voted 2 to 1 in favor of the company's position that it had a right to hire black firemen. The panel found allegations of incompetence of blacks wholly uncreditable. Yet in an apparent attempt to salve the wounds of the white firemen, the arbitration panel ordered the company to equalize the pay of blacks and whites. Equal pay for equal work, the whites believed, would eliminate the financial advantage of hiring blacks. In the absence of that incentive, the Georgia Railroad would refrain from hiring black firemen in the future.[35] But on this occasion the white firemen miscalculated, and the Georgia—as well as other southern lines—continued to hire black operating personnel until 1928.

By that year, the Big Four railway unions had taken up the effort of southern whites to remove blacks from the railroads, as had already occurred in the North. From 1928 to 1949, not a single black person found employment on a class 1 railroad as fireman, brakeman, trainman, or yardman. The ban on black operating railroad personnel held even during the emergency labor shortages of World War II.[36]

Though the Georgia Strike failed to oust blacks from the railroad industry, it did set in motion a series of efforts in the South to push blacks out of such work. Indeed, though the Georgia Strike developed wholly from local grievances, it was in keeping with the unanimous position of the white firemen's national union, the Brotherhood of Locomotive Firemen and Enginemen, that only white men would be allowed to perform such jobs on the railroads. The president of the firemen's union announced at the annual meeting in 1908, shortly before the Georgia troubles, that the "time has arrived when the railroads of the South must be made to discontinue the employment of Negroes as firemen."[37]

Unlike the AFL and the railroad brotherhoods, a smaller, more doctrinaire union movement made energetic though often misguided efforts to organize black workers. At its national convention in 1901, the Socialist party resolved to assure black workers an equal right to participate in party matters and affirmed that racism was simply an artificial invention of the capitalists. Accordingly, when prominent white Socialists and labor leaders like Eugene V. Debs, Daniel DeLeon, and William D. "Big Bill" Haywood founded the Industrial Workers of the World (IWW) in 1905, their organization became the only American union never to organize segregated locals. Known as the Wobblies, this one big union wanted to organize all workers regardless of skill, sex, or race. But like most Socialists of their day, the Wobblies had a major blind spot when it came to black workers. The union's leaders insisted that the only problem in the United States was class; blacks suffered no special disability. Their confusion on race is clearly seen in an early-twentieth-century statement which advised blacks that the only way to solve their major problems, particularly lynching, was to withhold their labor. In effect, blacks should institute a general strike. But such advice was foolish. Black workers needed employment, not leisure.[38]

It would be unfair to the IWW and to much of labor history to dismiss the Wobblies. The union gave strong support to black workers, particularly in the southern lumber mills and on the docks of Philadelphia. The Wobblies' zeal even involved some strange individuals in the cause of organizing blacks. Covington Hall, Adjutant General of the Sons of the Confederacy, was a staunch organizer for the IWW in New Orleans and even edited the union's southern journal, *The Voice of the People*. In Philadelphia, under the leadership of a black worker, Ben Fletcher, the IWW organized the mostly black Marine Transport Workers Local No. 3 in 1913. By 1916 the union had raised wages from $1.25 to $4 per day. More important, it had won time-and-a-half pay for overtime work and double time on Sundays. Partly because of his organizing work, the U.S. government tried Fletcher for espionage in 1919, found him guilty, and sentenced him to prison. President Warren G. Harding commuted the sentence in 1923, and in 1933 President Franklin D. Roosevelt granted Fletcher a full pardon.[39]

In the Piney Woods of Texas the IWW incorporated the Brotherhood of Timber Workers and helped that union in its strike against the Southern Lumber Operators' Association. Black workers were particularly important in both the union and the southern lumber industry. In the South in 1910, for example, approximately half of the 262,000 workers were unskilled blacks. Of 7,958 black workers in the planing and sawmills of Texas, for ex-

ample, 7,216 were laborers; not a single one was a sawyer.[40] After
a decade of strife, 1906–1916, which witnessed strikes, lockouts,
and violence, the union eventually lost to the Lumber Operators'
Association. But its work demonstrated wide-scale cooperation
between black and white workers in the deep South.[41]

Despite examples of racial cooperation, as exemplified by activities in the Piney Woods, the Georgia Race Strike and the
AFL's creation of federal locals typified relations between black
and white workers. And shifts in residential patterns then under
way among blacks would affect that relationship even more.
When the AFL began its segregationist policies, the vast majority
of blacks still resided in the Southeast. But beginning as early as
1910, a regular trickle of blacks began to migrate to the North.
By the time of American entry into World War I, the trickle
would become a flood as thousands of black workers anxious to
improve their life chances left the South. They moved into the
stockyards of Chicago and East St. Louis. They took jobs as laborers and semiskilled workers in the steel mills of Pittsburgh and
Gary, Indiana. They entered the mines of West Virginia and
Pennsylvania to help produce coal. In short, migration of black
workers from the South and their movement into various occupations transformed a regional problem for organized white unionists into a national issue as black workers increasingly entered the
northern urban work force.

3

Northward Migration and the Origins of an Urban Industrial Class

We affirm that it is the right and duty of every man to seek more promising opportunities and a fairer measure of justice wherever he believes they can be found.

National Urban League Resolution, 1919

Is it not time, then, that black and white labor got together? Is it not time for white unions to stop bluffing and for black laborers to stop cutting off their noses to spite their faces?

NAACP Statement, 1924

The large-scale movement of black men and women from the rural South to the urban North during the late nineteenth and early twentieth centuries seriously affected the relationships between blacks and whites, and among black people themselves. By 1925, after a decade of large-scale migration, blacks were no longer rural farmers. Although a majority of blacks remained in the South, large numbers of black workers now resided in cities and worked in industry. They worked daily in direct contact and, on occasion, in competition with whites in jobs previously reserved for whites. Accordingly, white employers and unionists who previously had paid no attention to blacks had to revise their activities in light of these rapid changes. Moreover, the presence of these black workers in northern communities, and their need for jobs and housing, sustained the growth of fledgling black protest and advancement organizations like the National Association for the Advancement of Colored People (NAACP) and the National

Urban League. Within the first decade after the outbreak of World War I, these and other black organizations began to work closely with working-class blacks in their efforts to attain industrial jobs and to join unions as equals. The war years and the early 1920s were rich in establishing institutional and community support of black workers.

It is, of course, inaccurate to assume that blacks began to move to northern cities only during the years of World War I. Indeed, the novelty lies in the number of migrants and the short time involved, and the types of jobs they found. There had been an ongoing movement of blacks out of the South since the Civil War. Census studies show that an average of 67,000 blacks had moved to the North in every decade since 1860.

The widespread migration of blacks to the North greatly affected the southern economy. The loss of essential black labor alarmed the plantation owners, who knew that without a large labor supply the cotton crops could not be harvested. Accordingly, local authorities used a variety of methods, from intimidation to legal restrictions, to keep blacks in the South. Many states dusted off decades-old emigrant agent laws. First passed in Geor-

Table 3-1. Percentage of regional black population by decade

	North	South	West
1860	7.7	92.2	0.1
1870	8.4	91.5	.1
1880	9.3	90.5	.2
1890	9.4	90.3	.4
1900	10.0	89.7	.3
1910	10.5	89.0	.5
1920	14.1	85.2	.8
1930	20.3	78.7	1.0
1940	21.7	77.0	1.3
1950	28.2	68.0	3.8
1960	34.3	60.0	5.7

Source: Marion Hayes, "A Century of Change: Negroes in the U.S. Economy, 1860–1960," *Monthly Labor Review*, vol. 85, no. 12 (December 1962), 1361.

gia in 1876, such laws required "emigrant agents" to acquire licenses and pay state taxes for the right to entice workers to leave. When the Carolinas passed such laws in 1891, an annual tax of $1,000 per agent was required for each county in which he wished to work. After the massive movement of black workers began about 1916, such laws became even more regressive. Alabama, for example, construed the term "emigrant agent" so broadly as to include messengers, assistants, and' even printers who ran off announcements. Each had to pay $5,000 per county per year.[1] But all such efforts failed to stem the tide. They failed largely because southern officials did not recognize an essential fact: blacks left the South not because white agents told them to do so but because they themselves had decided to move.

Given conditions in the South, it is understandable that black workers would wish to escape to a better life. But it would be inaccurate to assume that they found a promised land in the North. Despite the assurances of Robert S. Abbott, publisher of the Chicago *Defender*, and other urban black spokesmen that blacks would be welcomed and could find good jobs in the North, the newcomers found themselves relegated to the poorer jobs and shunted into overcrowded, depressed neighborhoods. Indeed, a major part of the problems between black and white workers is the fact that associations go beyond the workbench to the home. Whites—workers as well as managers—did not want blacks living among them. The official policy of the Pullman Company, which built a town for its workers near Chicago, was that only whites would live there. And in Gary, Indiana, the United States Steel Company would not allow blacks to live in company housing during that city's first decade. When the steel giant finally provided housing for blacks after 1917, the units were segregated for blacks only.[2]

These new black urban workers also came into conflict with blacks who had preceded them to the cities. In the beginning, the older black residents in large cities welcomed the newcomers. Abbott wrote that the migrants represented "merely one group of American citizens moving in their home country to better their conditions." But this feeling of welcome and optimism did not persist. As more and more migrants came, spokesmen for the settled blacks became increasingly aware of the problems they presented. The crude rustic ways of many of the migrants, their seeming inability to maintain accepted standards of cleanliness, and their traditionally sycophantic manner toward whites antagonized the longtime residents. These established residents found the habits of the migrants personally offensive and believed that their actions demeaned all blacks in the eyes of whites.

During the 1920s, the older urban black residents began telling themselves that discrimination in the cities had been minimal and was now caused by the arrival of the migrants. This was untrue. Residential segregation patterns, spread and solidified by the migrants, had been present from the beginning. Northern white employers had always paid black workers less than whites for the same work. Labor unions had long since learned to keep out black workers and thus deny them access to jobs.[3] The list could go on. The point is that the older residents wanted a scapegoat to blame for worsening conditions and found it in the newcomers.

Even the *Defender* joined in denouncing the new industrial workers. The paper declared on one occasion, "It is evident that some people coming to the city seriously erred in their conduct in public places, much to the humiliation of all respectable classes of our citizens, and by so doing on account of their ignorance of laws and customs necessary for the maintenance of health, sobriety and morality among people in general, have given our enemies grounds for complaint." The newspaper undertook to direct the activities of black people and published a twenty-six-point "guide to conduct." Moreover, it issued the admonition to them in bold letters: "KEEP YOUR MOUTH SHUT, PLEASE! THERE IS ENTIRELY TOO MUCH TALKING ON THE STREETCARS AMONG OUR NEWCOMERS." Given this cold reception and the virulent attitude of northern whites, black migrants fared as bady in the North as they had in the South.

White opposition to black residents in northern cities went beyond segregated housing and on several occasions even erupted into major race riots. In most cases of urban racial conflict, the two issues of jobs and residence predominated. Chicago, which because of its location and vast stockyards attracted large numbers of southern blacks between 1900 and 1920, witnessed some of the most continuous and violent conflict. When major technological changes in the stockyards in the late nineteenth and early twentieth centuries diminished the importance of butchers, large numbers of blacks and other unskilled workers found meat-cutting and packing house jobs. From approximately 500 at the turn of the century, the number of black stockyard employees jumped to 12,000 in 1916, 25 percent of the total employment.

In 1904 and again in 1905, strikes in Chicago led to widespread violence as white workers accused blacks of strikebreaking. Between May 20 and May 22, 1905, Chicago experienced the worst violence in its history prior to the major uprising in the summer of 1919. At least two persons died and dozens were wounded in this confrontation that stemmed mainly from competition in the workplace.[4]

Violence in Chicago was not an isolated event, as rioting broke out in cities throughout the country. Two major riots, one in East St. Louis, Illinois, in 1917 and the other in Chicago in 1919, showed the extremes such conflicts could reach. In both riots, particularly in East St. Louis, large numbers of blacks were killed in conflicts in which white unionists played a prominent role.[5] In Chicago black residents defended themselves effectively against the white mobs, and except for blacks killed by policemen, the number of casualties was about equal on both sides.[6] Indeed, they inflicted sufficient damage on their attackers to make such sallies too costly in the future.

During the decade of World War I, the steady trickle of northward migration of blacks had become a flood, with an estimated 500,000 southern blacks moving into northern cities, the vast majority of them coming between 1916 and 1918. The migration of the 1910s also showed a shift in the regions of origin. Whereas the earlier movement had been from the Upper South, migrants during the 1910s came from all over the region. In 1910, 48 percent of southern-born blacks who lived in the North had moved from Kentucky and Virginia; by 1920 the proportion from those states had been reduced to 31.6 percent, while migration from the cotton states had increased from 18.2 percent in 1910 to 40.5 percent in 1920. In all, by 1920 more than 1,000,000 blacks had moved from the South, the northern urban black population increasing from 452,818 in 1860 to 1,472,309.[7]

Nor did the migration cease with the end of the war. In fact, this new black industrial working class rapidly expanded during the next decade, when more blacks left the South than had migrated North during the war years. In the winter of 1922–1923, for example, thousands of blacks left the South, largely from states that had been ravaged by boll weevils. By the spring of 1923 it was clear that a new wave of movement was under way. North Carolina officials claimed that outmigration of blacks had

Fig. 3-1. Black population in the North, 1870 to 1920

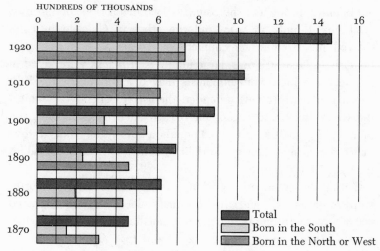

Source: Joseph A. Hill, "Recent Northward Migration of the Negro," *Monthly Labor Review*, vol. 18, no. 3 (March 1924).

Fig. 3-2. Southern-born blacks in the North: 1910 and 1920

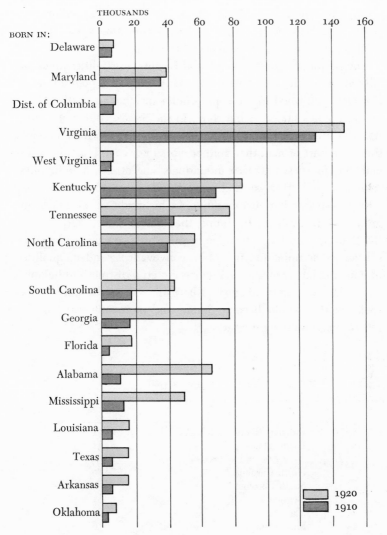

Source: Joseph A. Hill, "Recent Northward Migration of the Negro," *Monthly Labor Review*, vol. 18, no. 3 (March 1924), 5.

forced that state to close fifty road projects because of lack of labor, while in the same year the *New York Journal of Commerce* pointed out that "owing to the migration [of blacks] whites now outnumber negroes in South Carolina, a condition which has not existed before within the memory of the living."[8]

The promise of improved job and income possibilities undoubtedly attracted numerous migrants. As A. L. Harris pointed out in a survey published in 1924, per capita incomes in northern and western states far exceeded those in the South.[9] But money was not the only consideration. As W. E. B. Du Bois maintained, there is a part of man that neither works nor eats, but thinks. Social consciousness too made individuals, and often whole families, willing to pull up stakes and move hundreds of miles away from friends and familiar surroundings. In his study of the black migrants, T. J. Woofter, Jr., found that blacks were likely to quit the South because of "injustice in the courts, lynching, denial of suffrage, discrimination in public conveyances, and inequalities in educational advantages." Woofter noted a distinct public opinion on these matters among southern blacks and concluded that social factors would become "more and more influential in the future" in stimulating migration.[10]

Table 3-2. Per capita income, by region, 1920

	Income
Indiana, Illinois, Michigan, Ohio	$331
Pacific states	231
New England states	436
North Carolina	160
South Carolina	91
Georgia	81
Alabama	81
Mississippi	56
Louisiana	136
Texas	64

Source: A. L. Harris, "Negro Migration to the North," *Current History Magazine,* 20 (Sept. 1924), 923.

Mississippi economic interests, alarmed by the impact of the migration, appointed a biracial committee in 1923 to study the problem. Blacks told the committee that economic considerations in part prompted them to leave, but emphasized that they had lost faith in the fairness of Mississippi whites and could no longer tolerate violation of their civil rights. "The masses of the Negroes want to stay here," they said, "but they are not going to do it under present conditions."[11] The migration was a strike against economic and social exploitation in the South.

Massive migration of blacks to the North during the 1910s had affected not only community and union relations but the occupational distribution of black workers as well. Though blacks generally had not been a factor in industry before the war, by the 1920s most blacks, particularly men, worked in manufacturing plants. Heavy industrialization of the black migrant work force separated the newcomers from earlier black urbanites. As a government report put it in 1924, newer black arrivals became industrial laborers, finding jobs in mills, stockyards, and factories rather than in hotels, restaurants, and domestic kitchens. The report went on to point out that "if we could distinguish in the census occupational statistics between those who have migrated recently and the earlier migrants, this fact would be brought out quite strikingly. It is another distinctive feature of the new migration."[12]

Between 1910 and 1920, the black male unskilled and semi-skilled work force increased tremendously. In Chicago, 60 percent of black male workers were so employed in the latter year, compared with 20 percent of whites. The proportion of unskilled and semi-skilled black workers in Chicago mills increased from 3.5 percent in 1910 to 20.7 percent in 1920. Of the laborers in the Detroit automobile shops, 13.5 percent were black in 1920 compared with less than .05 percent in 1910. And even in general and building labor in Detroit, occupations in which only 149 blacks worked in 1910, in 1920 they numbered 1,261, 19.4 percent of all such workers.[13]

The first northern employer that hired large numbers of blacks and helped to stimulate migration to the North was the Pullman

Company, which as early as 1867 hired only blacks as Pullman porters. By World War I Pullman employed approximately 12,000 blacks, making it the largest single employer of black workers in the country. Pullman employed so many blacks as porters that the word "porter" soon became synonymous with "black." It is important to keep in mind, however, that these black workers were all service employees with no opportunity to advance to more skilled and highly paid positions within the company. The same paternalistic views that enabled southern blacks to work on the plantations of their previous owners after the Civil War contributed to George Mortimer Pullman's decision to hire blacks on his sleeping cars. His example would be followed by many other employers in later years.[14] The status of blacks as a group previously in service positions and the assumed social distance between blacks and whites made black men, in the view of Pullman officials, ideal for service as porters. White passengers could demand efficient service of black porters while at the same time ignoring their presence. Since passengers would encounter black porters in no other social context, they were content in their travels, and Pullman desired nothing more than contented passengers. In later years, A. Philip Randolph commented on the exploitative and paternalistic nature of Pullman employment of blacks. He wrote:

Burdened with the heritage of slave psychology, fearing lest they be plunged back into the sinister system of chattel slavery, [blacks] were easily induced to accept any wage system, however small and miserable, expecting to solicit gratitude from a sympathetic traveling public. In the year of the beginning of Pullman, 1867— Negroes were not only incapable of thinking in terms of collective bargaining . . . but they were uncertain of their freedom. In such a state of civil, political, and economic uncertainty, why wouldn't Pullman seek to get them to work on a semi-feudalistic basis?[15]

Efforts to improve the lot of Pullman porters are a major theme of black labor history in the twentieth century, a theme to which we will return later.

The Pullman porters were the first wave of black urban workers. Later groups worked in many basic industries. But like the porters, few blacks were able to rise above the hard, often unpleasant, unskilled jobs to find employment in skilled crafts. Lack of industrial experience itself contributed to the difficulties of blacks; lack of concern by white corporations and outright opposition by white workers—particularly unionists—were formidable obstacles as well.

During World War I, enlistment and eventual drafting of large numbers of white workers, coupled with the sharp cutback in European immigration, created a tight labor market, particularly in lower-paying unskilled jobs. In all, more than 4,000,000 men were drafted, only 400,000 of whom were black. Given the distribution of the black population at the outset of the war, most black recruits came from southern states. And whereas 1,218,480 European immigrants arrived in the United States in 1914, the first year of the war, only 326,700 came in 1915 and only 110,618 in 1918. In addition, approximately 500,000 immigrants, including some long resident in the United States and well entrenched in the American labor market, returned to Europe to join their countrymen in war.[16] This decline in manpower came at a time of unprecedented need for workers to feed, clothe, and provide weapons and munitions for the soldiers of the United States and its allies. Lower-skilled northern white workers who escaped the draft, and thousands of rural whites who migrated from the South, moved into skilled jobs created by the war and those left by soldiers off "to make the world safe for democracy." Increasingly large numbers of blacks took the unskilled positions immigrants previously held.[17] In short, no fundamental change took place between black and white workers and between black workers and white employers during the war. Employers simply experimented with the use of black labor during the emergency.

Nonetheless, in raw numbers, blacks made significant improvements and increases in industrial employment, particularly in steel, meatpacking, and automobiles. Overall, between 1910 and 1920, the number of blacks employed in industry almost doubled from just over 500,000 to 901,181.[18] Whereas there had been 37,406 blacks in the steel mills in 1910, more than 100,000 held such jobs in 1920. And the great meatpacking houses of Chicago and East St. Louis, Illinois, Omaha, Nebraska, Kansas City, Missouri, and Indianapolis, Indiana, employed more than 28,000 blacks, largely in the unskilled jobs created as the packing house industry changed. Under the new system, which began during the late nineteenth and early twentieth centuries, many workers performed specialized tasks on carcasses as they passed on conveyors, anticipating the assembly line that soon became standard in most American industries. Specialization replaced highly skilled butchers with several workers who could easily learn the tasks of one procedure.[19]

Though the Packard Motor Company, which had 1,100 black employees on its payroll in 1917, first opened the automobile industry to black workers, the Ford Motor Company eventually set the pace in Detroit and, strangely, only there. Through a mixture of paternalism and a sense of community pride, Henry Ford, founder of the company, hired a large number of black workers in his foundries and for other unskilled occupations. Ford, like George Pullman, cemented close ties with the black community in Detroit, particularly black ministers and other civic leaders, and enjoyed the reputation of being a great friend of black workers. By January 1920 Ford employed 2,500 blacks; only 50 had been there in 1916. The number increased to 10,000 by 1926. And only at Ford could black workers become apprentices. Yet Ford himself lived in a segregated neighborhood and assiduously refused to hire blacks in his shops in Dearborn and other locations outside Detroit. Indeed, some branches of the automotive industry, even in Detroit, such as the Fisher Body Shop, remained lily white, except for the normal black custodial crew.[20]

Black workers also found employment in the steel mills of western Pennsylvania, particularly in the Pittsburgh area. But here, as in most other industries, they were relegated largely to tending the blast furnaces and other unskilled tasks. By 1918, 7,000 blacks worked in the steel mills of Pittsburgh, largely in the employ of Carnegie Steel and Jones and Laughlin. In 1918, 98 percent of all black workers in the steel mills held unskilled jobs.[21] But im-

proved earnings, reportedly as high as 35 cents an hour, helped
to mitigate some of the more unpleasant aspects of the work for
laborers who had come from the South, where wages averaged
80 cents a day.[22] Even when black workers paid more for food
and housing than they had in the South, they still considered
themselves better off in the North, particularly when for the first
time, in many cases, they alone could determine when and how to
spend their money. The right to spend their own money was an
important liberating factor for many and led some to proclaim
that a black person "could be a man up North."

Government necessity during World War I led to increased
employment of blacks in shipbuilding, an important industry of
that era. Though not so stridently as during World War II, the
government demanded ships, ships, and more ships, and shipyards
worked at full capacity and for extended shifts to produce them.
There are several interesting factors about the employment of
blacks in shipbuilding. First, it underscores the fact that the black
industrial class did not develop only in the North. Like coal and
iron miners, numerous black ship workers found employment in
southern shipyards on the Atlantic and Gulf coasts. In fact, of
38,723 black shipyard workers during the war years—10.1 percent
of the 381,500 employees in the industry—11,991 worked in the
Atlantic southern district of the Emergency Fleet Corporation,
the procurement agency of the United States Shipping Board
during World War I. Another 1,830 blacks were employed at
Gulf Coast yards. By contrast, only 5,536 blacks worked in shipyards in Middle and North Atlantic ports; and on the northern
Pacific Coast and the Great Lakes, only 176 and 27 blacks, respectively, were so employed.[23] Black employment in the southern shipbuilding industry is even more striking when we consider
that more than 20 percent of blacks held skilled jobs.[24]

One could make too much of this fact. Though blacks attained
skilled shipyard work in the South, where they had acquired
skills even before the Civil War, they were singularly unsuccessful in getting such work in the North. The files of the Emergency
Fleet Corporation are full of complaints from blacks about lack

of employment opportunities in shipbuilding. Such complaints deal much more with the refusal of corporations and unions to upgrade blacks than with the inability of blacks to find work. One black riveter in California, linking his desire to advance in his job to a concern for the war effort, was quaintly eloquent in his request to have the government step in and protect employment rights of blacks. He wrote:

Can you understand what must be the feelings of our people when everyday men are called from these yards to take up for our country, to give up their life on the firing line with hundreds of thousands of colored troops in France doing their bit to make democracy safe for the world? I and any of us may be called tomorrow, and how gladly would I give this life of mine if I knew, in giving that life to make democracy safe for the Worlds I was making democracy to give for my people. . . .

We don't ask Social Equality, we only ask an equal opportunity to take our part in the industrial world, to be given the right and opportunity to perform the work, which Almighty God saw fit to give us brains and strength to do and for which hundreds of years in the most cruel school of slavery qualified and made us to do. . . .

I beg of you to take up this matter at once, don't let the word be taken from the shipyards of America that nothing is being made in the matter of even Negro labor. What will our boys feel that they have to fight for, what hopes have they to look forward to when after the war they return and the work is done. We can no longer remain silent to this condition among our people.[25]

The difficulties blacks faced in the shipyards during World War I would plague them over the decades. A new generation of workers would take far more militant action to gain their rights when ships were again needed during World War II.

Though the focus so far has been on black males, large numbers of black females also migrated to northern cities during the war years. And, as was traditional, many of them remained in the labor force. Yet in the 1910s, the percentage of black women workers declined. In 1920, 38.9 percent of black women held jobs, down from the 54.7 percent listed as employed in 1910. Unlike men, black women had not found widespread employment in industry. Census studies for 1920 reveal that from one-third to one-half of all black women were still restricted to personal and domestic service jobs.[26] They were so heavily entrenched in domestic work that a survey by the *Monthly Labor Review* omitted from its study thousands of black women because they were "known to be engaged in occupations considered *customary* for negro women, such as sweeping or cleaning, or were in laundries, hotels or restaurants."[27]

Black women apparently experienced more discrimination than black men in breaking into nonservice jobs. They entered industry at the lowest levels and had to accept the dirtiest, roughest, and most unpleasant work. In tobacco plants they worked as stemmers and strippers; in meatpacking they made up the staffs in the casing and chitterling areas. And there was more opposition among white women to working directly with black women than was found among white men at the prospect of working with black men. As the *Monthly Labor Review* pointed out, there was "strong prejudice against admitting [black women] to more skilled and better paid kinds of work, which was reserved for white women." Nonetheless, during the decade of the great migration, the proportion of black women in manufacturing and mechanical industries increased from 3.4 percent in 1910 to 6.7 percent in 1920. In the view of one observer, this increase represented "a striking change in the status of Negro women during the decade."[28]

Despite relegation to low-status, poor-paying jobs, black women were a larger proportion of the work force than any other group of women. The major reason black women were more likely than white women to work was economic: a black man alone did not earn enough money to support a family. And though it would be inaccurate to suggest that white women did not work,[29] the attitude of blacks toward working women was different in general from that of most whites. While most white women worked to attain middle-class status and "retired" once they achieved it, black women, who were not likely to achieve that status, tended to remain in the labor force even after marriage or the start of a family.[30]

The decade of World War I was a time of change, and even in domestic service a new trend developed that by 1924 led black women to show a marked lack of interest in domestic jobs that required them to "live in." Far fewer black women were willing to accept live-in positions than were white women, for several reasons. First, black women domestics were much more likely to be married and thus have family responsibilities than were whites. In Baltimore in 1924, for example, 54.2 percent of all black domestic workers were married; another 10.7 percent were separated, divorced, or widowed. Corresponding figures for white domestics in these two categories were 29.8 percent and 16.7 percent, respectively. But there were other factors as well. Black women felt ill at ease in the presence of white employers all the time. Moreover, they wanted the added independence that went with living in their own homes. Indeed, as one put it, they wanted some time in the day "to be off."[31]

This new sense of independence alarmed employers. In 1924 the president of the Domestic Efficiency Association of Baltimore, an employers' group, issued a strident denunciation of black women's desire to live in their own homes:

The desire to live out so prevalent today among the negro workers should be discouraged for many reasons, principally on the serious question of health.

Negroes are notoriously easy prey to disease, particularly to tuberculosis, a veritable scourge among them. Most negro women who demand to go home at night do so for two reasons. Either they really do go to their homes to do the work they must neglect during the day, or, particularly the younger ones, want to amuse themselves and spend much too large a portion of the nights at dances, movies, or festivals, etc. In either case, they are trying to burn their candles at both ends, and their health suffers, while the employer suffers from a tired servant utterly unequal to the requirements of her day's work.[32]

The concern expressed here clearly is not with the health of domestic workers but rather with whether the employer gets a full day's work. Domestic workers had become convinced that at some point the work day ends. More important, they had come to realize that what they did with their time off was their own concern.

Changes in the nature of the urban work force and the types of jobs now open to blacks caused severe dislocations in many large cities. The tremendous increase in the black population placed a great strain on the housing market, and the inevitable competition for jobs between blacks and whites resulted in tensions that boiled over into racial violence in East St. Louis in 1917 and in Chicago and other cities in the Red Summer of 1919.[33] The federal government often made matters worse for black workers. In May 1918 the Provost Marshall of the Army, General Enoch E. Crowder, issued a "Work or Fight" order requiring all draft-age men either to work at a war-related job or to register for the draft. The order led to a variety of similar local and state ordinances with predictable abuses. Throughout the country, particularly in the South, blacks became bound to jobs in conditions of virtual peonage. The pretext was that without stern supervision, blacks would leave essential war work.[34]

Fortunately, several institutions were now sufficiently mature to provide leadership for efforts to improve working and living conditions for blacks. Two groups in particular, the National Association for the Advancement of Colored People (NAACP), established in 1910, and the National Urban League, founded the next year, pressured employers, organized labor, and the government on behalf of blacks. Efforts on behalf of workers, particularly flirtations with organized labor, represented a major change for these groups, especially the National Urban League. Whereas some founders of the NAACP had maintained as early as its first meeting that the Association must show an interest in the right of blacks to organize, the National Urban League had generally cooperated closely with employers; on occasion its branches even served as recruitment agencies in several cities. The NAACP, generally interested in securing legal rights for blacks, had left the employment field to the National Urban League.[35]

During World War I the two organizations cooperated on several projects to improve conditions for black workers. They achieved their greatest success in 1918 when, after repeated conversations and extensive negotiations, Secretary of Labor William

B. Wilson created a special Division of Negro Economics. The secretary appointed Dr. George Edmund Haynes, a sociology professor at Fisk University and a founder of the National Urban League, to head this new division as director of Negro economics and to advise the secretary and unit heads "on matters relating to Negro wage earners, and to outline and promote plans for greater cooperation between Negro wage earners, white employers, and white workers in agriculture and industry."[36] Though apparently highly capable and likeable, Haynes was not a forceful person. He failed to work aggressively to improve the plight of blacks looking for work or to protect the jobs of those already employed. In fact, Haynes was simply an ombudsman for the Department of Labor to blacks and spent most of his time as director of Negro economics traveling throughout the country trying to establish committees to talk about the problems of workers. He busied himself making speeches and organizing surveys about black workers in various industries. In fact, he actually refused to seek to remedy some clear-cut problems brought to his attention.[37] When the war ended, black workers had gained little from the Division of Negro Economics, except that for the first time government officials admitted that blacks faced special problems in trying to make a living. Despite several requests from Secretary Wilson, Congress refused to appropriate funds to make the agency permanent, and Haynes's operation went out of business in early 1921 when the new Republican administration took office.

If black workers gained little from the Division of Negro Economics, efforts by the NAACP–Urban League group to improve relations between blacks and organized labor brought them little more. The problem was that officials of the two organizations talked with national leaders of the AFL, whereas membership decisions were made at the local level of affiliated unions. Nonetheless, some effort had to be made to increase black participation in the labor movement. During the war, unions had considerable influence as the government tried to minimize conflict between workers and employers so as to get the maximum production of war materials.

The first indication that blacks intended to make an all-out effort to improve their conditions came at an Urban League-sponsored conference on discrimination in early 1918. The conferees bitterly condemned the AFL for discriminating against black workers. Some delegates suggested that the conference go on record as encouraging blacks to become strikebreakers if that was the only way they could gain access to employment. The conference generally rejected that view but threatened that blacks would be encouraged to break strikes unless the AFL worked seriously to organize them.[38] In April, representatives of the NAACP and the National Urban League met with Samuel Gompers, president of the AFL, in an attempt to secure his help in breaking down obstacles to black membership in unions. Gompers promised his support and called on the black spokesmen to use their influence "to show Negro workingmen the advantages of collective bargaining and the value of affiliation with the AFL."[39] The black representatives had heard such sentiments from Gompers before, and this time they were unwilling to accept his comments at face value. They put forth several specific proposals. Rather than mere idle talk, they wanted Gompers to use his influence to push a resolution through the upcoming meeting of the AFL that would back up his interest in recruiting black members. Also, more concretely, the AFL should hire black organizers to do the actual work of signing up blacks.[40] When AFL delegates convened in the fall of 1918, they resolved to take steps to bring more blacks into the unions, but they stated that in so doing "no fault is or can be found with work done in the past" in organizing blacks. The matter of hiring Afro-American organizers was passed on to Gompers and the executive council to be implemented as funds became available.

The leaders of the NAACP–Urban League group knew that in practical terms the AFL resolution of 1918 was meaningless, but they thought they could exploit it eventually to bring black workers into the labor movement. Thus they continued their conversations with AFL spokesmen. But at the same time, they began to issue veiled threats against the labor movement. At its meeting in

1918, the Urban League insisted that black workers should make every effort to cooperate with the white unions "whenever conditions are favorable. But when this is not possible," the message continued, blacks "should band together to bargain with employers and organized labor alike."[41]

Blacks were far from unanimous on the matter of trade unionism, and even those who favored unions did not agree on which type. While the Urban League-NAACP group endeavored to integrate black workers into the white labor movement by affiliating with AFL unions, others argued that blacks should create their own independent unions. Some even called for opposition to unions altogether.

The clearest proponent of the latter view was Marcus Garvey of the Universal Negro Improvement Association (UNIA), the first American branch of which he established in New York in 1917. Garvey was a dashing and flamboyant leader, prone to wearing lavish uniforms and plumed hats, who bitterly opposed what he perceived as the amalgamationist views of the NAACP and the Urban League. Rather than wishing to be white, Garvey insisted, black people should recognize their own dignity and the beauty of things black. Moreover, they should look to Africa as a noble ancestral home and should make every effort to redeem that land from the Europeans. He even established a steamship company, the Black Star Line, to carry on trade with Africa. Stressing such themes, Garvey put together a huge all-black following among the urban working-class. And though his claim that the UNIA had from 4,000,000 to 6,000,000 members is undoubtedly exaggerated, he did generate a strong sense of racial pride among his followers and exercised considerable influence in northern industrial centers.

Garvey's opposition to white unions derived only in part from an antiunion philosophy; he was governed in part by deep distrust of whites as well. Accordingly, he and his associates in the UNIA argued that blacks could expect none of the spoils if they joined whites in unions; they could look forward to being led into strikes only to be fired when the strike ended and the whites returned to work. Under such circumstances, blacks would be foolish to join white unions. Instead, they should make every effort to create good relations with important employers. In one of his clearest statements on this point, Garvey even advised black workers to conspire to work for lower wages than whites, thus ingratiating themselves with white capitalists.[42]

Though Garvey undoubtedly put together an enormous following, blacks generally did not agree that they should work for less pay than whites, and they were willing to join unions to improve their lot. The most important independent efforts of black workers to organize unions during the war years were made in the railroad industry. Robert L. Mays founded the Railway Men's International Industrial Benevolent Association in 1915, and Rienzi B. Lemus organized the Brotherhood of Dining Car Employees when he merged two groups of dining car workers in 1920. Given federal supervision of the railroads under provisions of the Interstate Commerce Act, the organization of railroad workers generally preceded that of employees in other fields. Organizing was easier still during the war, when the government ran the roads under supervision of the U.S. Railroad Administration. Mays's union, which attempted to affiliate all black railroad workers, operated mainly as a paper organization until the government took over the rail lines. The Benevolent Association then grew considerably and achieved significant improvements for its members. In 1920, at its peak strength, it claimed 15,000 members. Moreover, the union took full credit for Director General William G. McAdoo's order of 1918 which required railroads to grant equal pay to black and white firemen, trainmen, and switchmen.[43] But the union was unable to undo the famous Atlanta Agreement, a complicated series of seniority rules designed to drive blacks out of railroad jobs, particularly in the South. That failure in 1921 led to the rapid decline of Mays's union, and though the Chicago *Defender* as late as 1926 called Mays "the most active and successful organizer and representative of railroad labor of our group," for all practical purposes his movement was dead.[44]

Unlike Mays, who experimented with industrial unionism,

Lemus's organization was a craft union of dining car cooks and waiters. His union never had as many members as Mays's, but President Lemus claimed that during its first decade the union, through negotiations with the railroads, won contracts that added more than $2 million to the incomes of the workers it represented.[45]

Yet another group of black labor spokesmen developed during the war years that, as it turned out, held the key for pushing the organization of black workers and making the white union movement recognize blacks during the Great Depression and the New Deal. In 1917, two young Socialists, Chandler Owen and A. Philip Randolph, founded *Messenger* magazine, "THE ONLY RADICAL NEGRO JOURNAL IN AMERICA." The magazine soon became the rallying point for the young radicals who called themselves "New Negroes," and its editorials, particularly those urging blacks to arm in self-defense against lynchers, brought charges of conspiracy to overthrow the government from both state and federal agencies and earned Randolph the Attorney General's denunciation as "the most dangerous Negro in America."[46]

For all their radicalism, the *Messenger* crowd showed considerable ambivalence on the question of blacks and unions. Their uncertainty stemmed from their strong belief in organized labor, on the one hand, and the poor treatment blacks had received from the white unions, on the other. In fact, Randolph and his associates had several complaints against the AFL. The organization, they claimed, could never improve conditions for American workers as long as it was led by reactionaries like Samuel Gompers, the "Chief Strike Breaker" in the United States, and as long as it insisted on organizing workers along craft lines. Yet their confusion was clear. When Randolph and Owen organized a small group of elevator operators in New York in 1918, they proudly announced in the *Messenger* that the group had received a charter from the AFL and proclaimed that their success ought to silence "Negro Solon-leaders" who complained that blacks could not enter the white union movement.[47] As the years went on, *Messenger* editors participated in several efforts to form independent black unions, the most important of which was their association with the National Brotherhood Workers of America. This group, founded in 1919 and composed mainly of black shipyard workers, intended to do for nonrailroad workers what Mays's group had done for black railroaders. The *Messenger* became the official organ of the union, but the relationship ended abruptly when other officials of the Brotherhood Workers of America accused its editors of being more interested in increasing *Messenger* sales than in improving the wages and working conditions of laborers. The magazine retreated increasingly from its radicalism as the postwar years wore on. The *Messenger* even carried a favorable editorial on Gompers when he died in 1924. The editors called the labor leader "one of the dynamic and interesting personalities" of his time, who deserved much credit "for the remarkable task of building up a powerful trade union movement." Gompers had been "diplomatically silent" toward blacks "not because he hated the Negro but because he feared to challenge the Southern section of the Trade Union Movement. Albeit," the piece concluded, "the number of Negro trade unionists increased under his regime."[48]

Interestingly, the NAACP seemed more militant at that point than the once-radical *Messenger* crowd. In the same year in which Gompers died, the NAACP proposed that white unions and black advancement organizations establish a joint Interracial Labor Commission to carry on the work of integrating the labor movement. The NAACP statement reminded white labor leaders that blacks had broken strikes in the past. It also pointed out that the increasing number of blacks in the cities would soon make it possible for blacks to break any strike white unionists would call. Indeed, unorganized black workers were now a menace to the whole union movement. The NAACP wondered if it was not time for organized labor to "stop bluffing [on organizing blacks] and for black laborers to stop cutting off their noses to spite their faces."[49]

These efforts came at a potentially opportune time for blacks to penetrate organized labor. William Green, who succeeded

Gompers as president of the AFL, had worked his way up through the ranks of the United Mine Workers, one of the least discriminatory unions in the country. There was at least reason to hope that he would be interested in leading the whole AFL to take a position similar to that of his own union. Green gave immediate public endorsement of the NAACP's proposal, using the *Messenger* to assure blacks that the doors of his organization were now open for them to come into the House of Labor. Yet in condescending terms showing clearly that little had changed, the AFL's new president repeated the old refrain that blacks had only themselves to blame for being outside the organized labor movement. Afro-Americans could expect to receive equal treatment from white unionists only when they developed a working-class mentality and stopped undercutting union rates by working for lower wages.[50]

More important than Green's views was the debate on trade unionism that took place among blacks themselves and the organizational developments that made 1925 a pivotal year in black labor history. The debate showed clearly that the uncertainty that blacks had felt about unions—particularly white unions—remained. But it was clear that the philosophical descendants of Booker T. Washington were losing sway. Kelly Miller, dean of the college of arts and sciences at Howard University and a leading spokesman for the Washingtonian crowd, made one last effort to keep black workers aligned with the great employers of labor. Miller wrote that black workers were like leaves in the wind, wholly unable to affect their future. Indeed, the entire U.S. labor situation was like a giant triangle "of which the Negro forms the base, with capital and white labor forming the sides. White labor presses upon the black base perpendicularly, while capital slants obliquely, with a less perceptible pressure."[51]

Miller's views met immediate opposition from other blacks. Randolph accused him of fawning before the altar of big business, while T. Arnold Hill, who became head of the National Urban League's new Department of Industrial Relations when it was established in 1925, joined in the rebuke. Hill admitted the widespread personal competition between black and white workers, but he emphasized that in the final analysis institutionalized racism was a far greater handicap to black workers. He pointed out that white workers had little control over such institutions. In effect, when Miller called on blacks to place their trust in the good will of the great employers and to seek their "protection," he was appealing to the very crowd that dominated American society and relegated blacks to the lowest levels of education, employment, and citizenship.[52]

In addition to the Urban League's creation of the Department of Industrial Relations, three other events mark 1925 as a watershed in the development of blacks as a union-conscious working class. Black Communists founded the American Negro Labor Congress, Frank R. Crosswaith established the Trade Union Committee for Organizing Negro Workers, and in August, the Pullman porters organized the Brotherhood of Sleeping Car Porters. Taken together, these actions demonstrated that blacks would no longer accept discrimination from either organized labor or organized capital, and that they would create institutions to combat it.

The Trade Union Committee for Organizing Negro Workers (TUC) was, in effect, the joint committee of trade unionists and members of black advancement organizations that the NAACP had called for in its statement of 1924. Under direction of the black Socialist Frank R. Crosswaith, the TUC also included white unionists, as well as representatives of the NAACP and the Urban League. Moreover, most of its funds came from the AFL and the Garland Fund, a New York-based foundation interested in labor causes. The TUC called on the AFL to hire black organizers and pledged to use its own standing among blacks to "remove a large portion of the opposition raised by Negro workers to the AFL."[53]

The AFL undoubtedly supported the TUC as much out of necessity as because of new views Green brought to the AFL's leadership. Soon after the TUC began, black Communists convened in Chicago and announced creation of the American Negro Labor Congress (ANLC). The ANLC condemned AFL "officialism" for its failure to integrate the working-class and vowed to create all-black unions strong enough to challenge existing white unions. AFL leadership therefore feared the ANLC not only because of its Communist ties but because of the threat of hated dual unionism.

Most black spokesmen on union affairs joined AFL officials in efforts to kill the ANLC before it became established. Leaders of the National Urban League argued that the AFL had overreacted to the new movement, pointing out that blacks "never paid attention to communist arguments" anyway. Randolph and his associates at the *Messenger* went further. They warned black workers against "being lured up blind alleys by irresponsible labor talkers," especially when their views came from abroad. Blacks should work to seek an American solution to their problems as workers. Almost alone among established black spokesmen, W. E. B. Du Bois saw much hope in the sessions in Chicago, terming the meeting "one of the most significant" gatherings in black history.[54]

Both the TUC and the ANLC served only to stimulate interest in black workers and unionism. The third significant event of 1925, the founding in August of the Brotherhood of Sleeping Car Porters (BSCP) and the subsequent rise to national attention of A. Philip Randolph, its dashing, charismatic leader, made that year pivotal in the development of a black unionized industrial group that would function as part of the mainstream of the American working-class.

4

The Brotherhood
of Sleeping Car Porters

If the porters can organize their industry, hold their ranks, prove their fighting ability in the interest of the working class, it will have a profound effect on the attitude of white organized labor. And it will have a profound effect upon the organizable capacity of Negro workers in other industries. These men who punch our pillows and shine our shoes and stow our bags under the seats bear in their hands no little of the responsibility for the industrial future of their race.

The Nation, June 9, 1926

Most observers would have thought it quite unlikely during the early 1920s that the sleeping car porters, those seemingly obsequious men, always bowing and scraping in the presence of whites with their hands held out for a tip, would ever have been able to start a union. Even more preposterous was the thought that they not only would start a union, but that their organization would become a nationally recognized symbol of the New Negro, a leader in the struggle of black people to attain their rightful place as part of the American working-class. Not only were porters servile and easily frightened men, people would say, but the vast majority of them worked for the Pullman Company, a giant among American capitalist enterprises. The company was the largest single employer of blacks in the country, and most black spokesmen believed that black people owed the Chicago-based corporation a debt of gratitude. Moreover, the Pullman Company

was notoriously anti-union. Should porters attempt anything so
foolish as forming a union, the company would crush the incipient movement before it ever began.[1]

People who held such views did not understand either the nature of the Pullman work force or the porters' working conditions.
The company had benefited so greatly from the racist labor practices of that benighted time that by the outbreak of World War
I many of the best educated and most capable black men in the
country worked as porters. The story of porter Theodore Seldon,
who died one night when his train jumped the tracks, makes the
point. Authorities identified his mangled body by his Phi Beta
Kappa key, Dartmouth, class of 1922. Many of the black men (including J. Finley Wilson, president of the Improved and Benevolent Order of Elks of the World; Perry Howard, perennial Republican national committeeman from Mississippi; and Benjamin
E. Mays, who became president of Morehouse College and of the
Atlanta school board) who went on to make names for themselves
worked for Pullman at one time. The harsh irony is that such men
accepted jobs at Pullman largely because the company offered
the best opportunities available for black men. Indeed, a porter's
annual pay of $810 plus tips in 1925 far exceeded that of a black
school teacher.[2] In addition, porters were considered cosmopo-
lites, men of the world who flitted back and forth across the country, visiting regularly places most blacks could never dream of
seeing.

Few people realized that the job, for all its appearances, was
far from glamorous. For their salary of $67.50 per month, Pullman
porters were expected to perform 400 hours of service. These
hours did not include the time porters spent in preparing their
cars for receipt of passengers or in making cars ready for storage
at the end of a run. Such dead time represented millions of dollars that porters donated to the company annually. Nor did observers realize that porters remained constantly on call for a
whole run, regardless of its duration, with no guarantee of time
off to sleep. Moreover, the company required porters to buy their
own uniforms during their first ten years in the service. These

servants on wheels even had to buy out of their own money the polish with which to shine their clients' shoes, a task Pullman required them to perform. Sleeping car porters had many long-standing grievances.[3]

Porters had tried to start a union on several occasions before 1925, only to fail each time. They had made some progress during World War I while the government operated the Pullman line, along with other railroads, and Robert L. Mays represented the porters through the Railway Men's International Benevolent Industrial Association. When the company returned to private hands after the war, Pullman management refused to deal with Mays's organization. Instead, the company established the Pullman Porters' Employee Representation Plan (ERP), a euphemism for what was in fact a company union of the type common at the time. The ERP, whose leaders were paid by the Pullman Company, steadfastly refused to take up porters' grievances on working conditions, though at times the company did grudgingly grant pay increases after "negotiating" with the employees' organization. In 1924, for example, when Mays's Railway Men's Association made new efforts to organize porters, the company called a wage conference under auspices of the ERP. This session resulted in Pullman's granting porters an 8 percent pay increase, an unheard-of percentage in those noninflationary times, until we consider that porters actually received only an additional $5 per month from the deal.[4]

Although a number of newspapers, black and white, emblazoned their front pages with headlines from Pullman press releases that read "PORTERS GRANTED MILLION DOLLAR RAISE," some porters clearly understood that ERP did not represent their interests; they laid plans to form a union of their own. A small cell in New York, which included Ashley L. Totten, William H. Des Verney, and Roy Lancaster, all of whom had worked several years for Pullman and had served as officials of the ERP, formed the nucleus of this union movement. They recognized that previous efforts to organize porters had failed largely because porters had taken leadership roles and the company had fired them, thus killing the would-be unions aborning. Accordingly, they looked for someone who could take a public lead in organizing the porters without fear of being fired.

Totten thought he knew just the man to lead the struggle. He had recently been enthralled by a young streetcorner orator, A. Philip Randolph, editor of *Messenger* magazine, and was convinced that Randolph possessed the skills for organizing porters. Totten asked Randolph to speak at a regular porters' social gathering. Randolph accepted and regaled the assembled "pillow punchers" with statements about the importance of organized labor, emphasizing that porters would never improve their wages and working conditions until they formed a union of their own. The ERP, he said, would never press the needs of employees because the company owned it and "whoever pays the fiddler calls the tune." Randolph later attended two other meetings with porters, a secret affair in June 1925 and a public meeting at St. Luke's Hall in Harlem on August 25. The August meeting marked the official beginning of the Brotherhood of Sleeping Car Porters (BSCP), with Randolph as general organizer and the *Messenger* as the union's official publication.[5]

When the porters accepted Randolph as their leader, they did not get a man of proven leadership ability. Indeed, one observer noted that Randolph, already thirty-six years old, "seemed a man whose time had passed him by." Randolph was born in Crescent City, Florida, in 1889 and grew up in Jacksonville. Part of an early wave of black migrants to the North, he moved to New York in 1911, determined to become a Shakespearean actor. Randolph spent his earliest years in Harlem as a roving bachelor, moving from address to address and from job to job. He studied economics and history at City College and the Rand School and steeped himself in Marxian socialism. In 1917, he met and married Lucille Green. That same year he joined another young Socialist, Chandler Owen, as editor of the *Messenger* magazine. The *Messenger* did well for a while, but by 1925 its radicalism had faded and the magazine was in deep financial trouble. In a sense, in 1925 Randolph needed a job as much as the porters needed a union leader.[6]

Despite his inexperience in union organizing, Randolph possessed characteristics that made him superbly suited for the campaign that lay before him. Handsome and almost exquisite in bearing, he struck an imposing figure. Gifted with a booming baritone voice which he had cultivated in his attempt to master the arts of oratory and rhetoric, he delivered speeches damning the "claasses" and exhalting the "maasses." He actually hypnotized his audiences. Moreover, he exuded personal incorruptibility and carried himself with an air of such confidence that opponents found it almost impossible to deny the wisdom of his arguments, while supporters were loyal almost to his every word.[7]

Like most charismatic individuals, Randolph showed little interest in routine organizational functions. Daily tasks of making the union work bored him; they could be carried out by lieutenants. For his part, the "Chief," as porters came to call Randolph, functioned as a symbolic figure. He moved in the public realm, stirring up debate on questions of unionism for blacks generally and generating propaganda to publicize his views and the goals of the BSCP. In fact, some of Randolph's associates—particularly Milton P. Webster, who organized the highly sensitive Chicago area—were far more active in signing up porters than the Chief. But it was Randolph who stimulated widespread public support of the union and made the BSCP a movement for racial equality and not just a small union consisting of the few thousand porters who worked for the Pullman Company.[8]

When, with his characteristic enthusiasm, Randolph set out to organize the porters in 1925 and vowed to "bring the company to its knees," he could not foresee the grave difficulties ahead. Pullman had absolutely no intention of recognizing a union of porters. Its management saw no contradiction between allowing conductors, who were white, to organize and bargain with the company and denying black porters the same privilege. The ERP was good enough for porters, they reasoned, and if any porter wanted to quit, plenty of men were waiting to take his place. Pullman also was willing to call on various segments of the black community to help it "protect" well-meaning porters from wild-eyed radicals like Randolph. It warned that all this talk about a union would cause blacks to jeopardize their racial monopoly in the porter industry. To emphasize its ability to make good on such a threat, late in 1925 the company began bringing in Filipinos and assigning them prized runs. Numerous porters quickly got the message and would have nothing to do with BSCP representatives.

Pullman's money and the general distrust of some blacks toward Randolph and organized labor generated extreme hostility toward Randolph and his efforts, particularly in the black press. One critic complained of Randolph's "bootleg superiority complex," while another pointed out that the Chief had failed in everything he ever tried to do. That path of failures, he added, "was said to be bedecked with shady deeds." A constant criticism of Randolph was that he was a Communist. The St. Louis *Argus* claimed that Randolph was using the porters only to raise money with which to run off to Russia. That story appeared in the same edition in which the *Argus* published a full-page advertisement for the Pullman Company. But blacks rarely rode sleeping cars, and whites, who did, did not read the *Argus*. Though not so blatant as to run ads for the company, even the Chicago *Defender*, whose publisher, Robert S. Abbott, was considered among the most militant opponents of oppression against blacks, attacked the new union. Others, including J. Finley Wilson of the Elks, Perry Howard, and, after a brief effort to gain a leadership post in the BSCP, Robert L. Mays, joined the opposition. The Pittsburgh *Courier* stood almost alone among leading black newspapers in supporting the movement in its early days. The union did gain the support of the NAACP and the National Urban League, the leading black advancement organizations at the time.[9]

Opposition to the BSCP did not end with newspaper articles and comments from a few paid propagandists. In keeping with the style of anti-union corporations, Pullman fired porters identified with the union, particularly those considered ringleaders. Lancaster became the first to go when the company fired him in the summer of 1925, ostensibly because he was drunk on the job.

Pullman management made no effort to camouflage its decision when Totten was fired a short time later. In addition to firing some porters, the company intimidated others. Large numbers of porters, mainly loyal members of the company union, spied on other porters and reported alleged union activities to company officials. Porters whom these "stool pigeons" turned in were subjected to "inspections" by company supervisors. In most cases, supervisors found small infractions of the rules, which resulted in reprimands. The clear implication was that the infraction might be removed from the porter's record when he stopped fooling around with the union.

The Pullman Company, and those who operated on its behalf, were not alone in intimidating the porters. Some who worked on behalf of the BSCP did likewise. One pro-Brotherhood group based in Omaha, Nebraska, the Black Klan, threatened to destroy property, and on at least one occasion even threatened murder, if porters in the region did not cease opposition to the BSCP. The Black Klan eventually disappeared into obscurity.[10]

Randolph seemed undaunted in the face of general hostility. He made a whirlwind tour of the country, damning the Pullman Company and establishing BSCP locals in major rail centers. In addition to Webster at Chicago, Benjamin Smith became the union's organizer in Detroit and Pittsburgh, E. J. Bradley took over in St. Louis, and Morris (Dad) Moore and C. L. Dellums worked on the West Coast, particularly in the Oakland area. Randolph even persuaded E. D. Nixon, who later introduced Martin Luther King, Jr., to the civil rights movement, to try to organize porters in Montgomery, Alabama. These men, all of them porters, operated in the field while Totten, Des Verney, and Lancaster helped to run the national office in New York. Webster eventually emerged as Randolph's chief associate, serving the BSCP as first vice president and chairman of the executive board.

From its origin the BSCP had three goals. First, of course, union leaders wanted to gain recognition from the Pullman Company as the official representative of porters and maids so as to improve their wages and working conditions. Second, and of

equal importance, at least to Randolph, the BSCP was the means
by which black workers would break down barriers to equal
membership in organized labor. Thus, Randolph and his colleagues set their sights on an international charter from the AFL.
The union's third goal stemmed from the first two. A union under
black leadership strong enough to gain recognition from the Pullman Company and to wrest a charter from the AFL would serve
as an example to other working-class blacks of the possibilities
for improving their lives.

The BSCP learned quite early the difficulties it would face in
trying to gain recognition from Pullman. Company management
would not even admit that the union existed, publicly proclaim-
ing that it had no conflict with its porters and dismissing Randolph and his colleagues as a bunch of outside agitators. Even
when discussing the porters' affairs among themselves, Pullman
representatives never mentioned the Brotherhood of Sleeping Car
Porters. Instead, they referred to the whole affair as the "Randolph
matter." The company even refused to answer Randolph's letters.

Given these circumstances and the current status of railway
labor law, the union could do little to force the company to negotiate, short of calling a strike. And this the Brotherhood was in no
position to do. But it appeared that the union's legal position was
about to change. In 1926 Congress passed the Watson-Parker Act,
a railway labor law that explicitly recognized the right of workers
to bargain collectively, though it did not outlaw company unions.
In effect, the new law provided for a Mediation Board that would
investigate disputes and certify bargaining agents. The board
could also mediate between corporations and unions and, if necessary, arbitrate tough cases. The problem, from the BSCP's view-
point, was that although arbitration decisions carried the force of
law, the Mediation Board could not force companies or unions to
submit disputes for arbitration.

Nonetheless, Randolph hoped that the new board would work
in the interest of the porters. After the Pullman Company refused
to reply to his request for a conference in September 1926, Randolph informed the Mediation Board that a dispute existed be-

tween the union and the company and requested an investigation. For its part, Pullman informed the board that it had no dispute with its porters. To its best knowledge, not a single porter belonged to the so-called Brotherhood of Sleeping Car Porters. Moreover, Pullman porters already had a union that the company recognized and negotiated with regularly. Any porter who wished could affiliate with the Employee Representation Plan.

In light of the conflicting statements, the board decided to carry out an investigation of its own. An elated Randolph heralded the board's decision as a new day for the porters and black workers generally. The board, he announced, was about to decide the standing of company unions under the Watson-Parker Act. The Brotherhood chief's elation reached unprecedented heights when the board's agent found that the BSCP did in fact represent a substantial proportion of the porters and maids. The full board announced that it would attempt to mediate the dispute between the BSCP and the Pullman Company.

The Pullman Company remained unperturbed. It continued to refuse to recognize the BSCP, still maintaining that the ERP represented its porters. In fact, the company practically ignored the Mediation Board. The board endeavored through spring and summer 1927 to bring the parties together but was unable to do so. In August, the board informed the union and the company that mediation had failed and recommended arbitration. The Brotherhood immediately accepted the offer. The company, true to its previous stance, pointed out that since no dispute existed there was nothing to arbitrate. Pullman's decision left the board no choice. It withdrew from the case and the BSCP suffered a severe defeat.[11]

The BSCP's problems were far from over when the Mediation Board failed to bring about arbitration in 1927. Within a year it experienced two additional failures that almost destroyed the young union. Ironically, at the same time, the leadership's response in this time of trial established a sound foundation on which to base eventual success.

Shortly after the Mediation Board announced its inability to bring about arbitration, the BSCP initiated one of the most novel tactics in trade union annals. The union claimed that the Pullman Company, by informing applicants for porter jobs that they could expect to increase their wages through tips, and then allowing porters to accept tips on company property, violated Interstate Commerce Commission (ICC) rules because the tips amounted to an unannounced increase in the cost of sleeping car services. Accordingly, the Brotherhood asked the ICC to outlaw tipping on Pullman cars. Such a decision, union leaders believed, would require the company to raise porters' wages because the men would be unable to live on the low pay they received. Emphasizing its motto, "Service not Servitude," the union maintained that its members ought to have a decent regular wage and not have to depend on the whims of the traveling public.

The move to outlaw tips was unpopular with many porters, some of whom earned as much as $300 a month from that source. Some even stated that the union's leadership was not concerned with the members but simply wanted publicity. In any event, in a split decision the ICC ruled in spring 1928 that it lacked jurisdiction to outlaw tipping. On its face, tipping did not violate ICC rules.[12]

Accustomed by this time to moving from crisis to crisis, the BSCP immediately announced that it was ready to take the one action that Pullman would understand. It would ask its members to authorize a strike. The BSCP's strike proposal, better termed the strike debacle of 1928, was about as strange as the anti-tipping campaign of the previous spring and revealed a great deal about the divisions within the union's leadership. It also demonstrated a characteristic of Randolph's personality that he would show again and again throughout his illustrious career. Randolph believed in the big bluff. Convinced, as he put it, that "public opinion is the most important weapon in America," he believed that talk of a strike would cause the public to take an interest in the porters' cause and that eventually right would prevail. Thus, although a majority of the porters authorized the union to call a strike in the summer of 1928, Randolph had no intention of going through with it. Unlike some of his colleagues, particularly Webster in Chicago and Dellums in Oakland, the Chief did not believe the union could win a strike. Rather than a strike, Randolph wanted to make enough noise about impending labor strife to force the Mediation Board to recommend to the President that he declare that an emergency existed in the railroad industry. Under provisions of the Watson-Parker Act, the President could then appoint an emergency board with power to investigate the dispute and order arbitration between the company and the union.

The BSCP set its strike date for June 8, 1928. In the weeks leading up to that date, Randolph took some strange actions. In a public statement he assured everyone that a strike vote did not necessarily mean that the porters actually would strike, and he wrote an extremely accommodating letter to J. P. Morgan, a member of Pullman's board of directors. Randolph detailed all the benefits the company would derive from a contented group of porters and made it clear that the union intended to insure that the employees continued their loyalty to the company. Randolph's comments only served to confuse BSCP members and at the same time convinced the Pullman Company and the Mediation Board that his talk about a strike was simply a bluff. Largely because of Randolph's actions, the Mediation Board refused to certify that an emergency existed in the railroad industry. In fact, the board informed James Weldon Johnson of the NAACP that there would be no disruption of rail service, and thus no emergency, even if every Pullman car in the country stood idle.

The Mediation Board's decision left Randolph and the BSCP in a no-win situation. They could go on with the strike and face certain defeat, particularly in light of elaborate steps Pullman had taken to break it. Or they could call off the strike and risk a loss of union membership. Randolph appealed to the AFL for help. In response, William Green advised him that "times were not right" for a strike in the railway industry, and Randolph ordered the porters not to step down. But his explanation that he had called off the strike on Green's advice carried little weight with the porters, and even some union leaders objected to the decision.

The strike debacle of 1928 almost destroyed the BSCP. Porters left the union in droves, a trend that continued as the nation moved into the Great Depression. By 1933 the union had a total membership of 658, more than a third of whom were in a single local in Chicago. Moreover, shortly after the canceled strike of 1928, the *Messenger,* which had been in financial difficulty during the whole period it had served as the union's official organ, ceased publication, and Randolph was almost finished as a labor leader.[13]

The period from 1928 to 1935 was bleak for the BSCP, as it was for the black working class generally. Indeed, in a time when there were few jobs anywhere, few porters wanted to join a union that would jeopardize their fragile job security. They showed more and more loyalty to the Pullman Company, and the BSCP became little more than a cell of dedicated men who were convinced that if only they could keep the doors of the organization open, they would one day be able to revitalize their membership and become the official representative of porters and maids.

The BSCP's need in 1928, if it ever hoped to succeed, was to achieve legitimacy. Since there was no possibility at that point of gaining recognition from the Pullman Company, Randolph and his colleagues turned again to the AFL. The BSCP's application for an international charter in 1928, was not accepted, but early the next year the Executive Council chartered thirteen BSCP locals as federal unions directly affiliated with the AFL.[14] Though fully aware of the Jim Crow nature of the charters, BSCP leaders believed that they had obtained a platform within organized labor from which to push more successfully for improved conditions for black workers.

BSCP officials not only sought legitimacy for their own union but looked on the union as a vehicle for the advancement of all black workers. During the Great Depression the Brotherhood participated in various grass roots activities and workers' actions. The union joined in the numerous protests throughout the country over the plight of the Scottsboro Boys, nine young blacks convicted of rape in Alabama, and was a leader in the successful efforts of organized labor and civil rights organizations to prevent the confirmation of Judge John J. Parker, whom President Herbert Hoover nominated for the Supreme Court in 1930.[15] The BSCP alone tied together Parker's racist and anti-union sentiments. And though they would not go so far as to support Communist activities, Randolph and other BSCP spokesmen encouraged black workers to form workers' councils so as to demand equitable relief funds from the U.S. government, especially after the origin of the New Deal.

Perhaps the union's most important 'work during these hard times was the efforts of its leaders to force the AFL to admit its racism and to take steps to organize workers without regard to race or class. In convention after convention, Randolph and Webster berated the AFL for its refusal to organize unskilled workers, blacks in particular. They emphasized that they had heard all the old rhetoric about egalitarianism and now wanted to see action. And in convention after convention they met a stone wall. Finally, in 1934 Randolph tried another tactic. He encouraged Walter White, executive secretary of the NAACP, to sanction a picket of the AFL convention in San Francisco. White called out the demonstrators, and while pickets marched and chanted outside, Randolph demanded from the floor of the convention that the AFL expel racist unions and that it establish a blue ribbon committee to study racism in AFL affiliates and recommend remedies at the 1935 meeting. Randolph's proposals met strong opposition in the resolutions committee and caused heated debate on the convention floor. In the end, amid considerable rancor, the convention rejected the demand that it expel racist unions and by a narrow margin approved the creation of a committee to study racial discrimination.[16]

Though bound to appoint the committee, AFL president William Green did not intend to have it conduct an exhaustive investigation. Thus, he waited until June 1935 to appoint the Committee of Five on Negro Discrimination and, contrary to the convention's resolution, ordered the committee to report not to the convention but to the Executive Council. Yet despite efforts at subterfuge, hearings before the all-white Committee of Five were quite revealing. Randolph brought an impressive battery of expert witnesses before the group to point out racism in unions and the impact of discrimination on employment prospects for blacks. Charles H. Houston, the outstanding young dean of the Howard University Law School and the NAACP's first full-time staff counsel, represented the Association. Reginald A. Johnson, executive secretary of the Atlanta Urban League and chief lobbyist in Washington for the National Urban League, testified for his organization, and John P. Davis, executive secretary of the Joint Committee on National Recovery, presented extensive technical and statistical data on the problems blacks experienced because of union discrimination.[17]

Houston's testimony was the most important public statement before the committee and demonstrated that the attitude of the leading black advancement organization toward trade unionism had changed dramatically. The extent of commitment to that change would be demonstrated later. As Houston put it, the NAACP had come to realize that "it was necessary to lay a sound economic foundation in order for civil liberties to survive." The NAACP would in the future be keenly interested in the economic status of blacks, particularly their relationship with unions. Yet Houston, like other witnesses, pointed out that the experts assembled there on such short notice could only begin to show the extent of discrimination. Since depression conditions made it impossible for workers to travel en masse to Washington, the AFL should authorize the committee to hold regional hearings to collect additional evidence. The committee reported favorably to Green on this recommendation, but the AFL president determined that "there was no necessity for holding such hearings." He ordered the Committee of Five to submit its final report.[18]

Debate on the report of the Committee of Five on Negro Discrimination came at one of the most interesting and important conventions in the history of the American Federation of Labor. Its leaders not only had to respond to demands of blacks on discrimination but also had to contend with demands from some white union leaders that the AFL abandon its craft orientation and endeavor to organize workers by industry. At that meeting John L. Lewis of the UMW, proponent of industrial unionism, and William "Big Bill" Hutchinson of the carpenters, a defender of the craft concept, allowed their emotions to spill over into a now famous fistfight. After the fight, the convention voted overwhelmingly to continue the timeworn craft organization and effectively expelled those unions interested in organizing the masses of workers. The expelled unions soon came together as the Congress of Industrial Organizations (CIO), which existed as a rival of the AFL until 1955.

It is not surprising then that amid this uproar the report of the Committee of Five did not fare well. In fact, Green did not even present it to the delegates. Rather, he had George M. Harrison, president of the racist Brotherhood of Railway Clerks and a member of the AFL Executive Council, prepare a revision of the committee's report. It was Harrison's emasculated version that the delegates saw. His "Supplemental Report on Negro Labor" did not even mention the Committee of Five and left out all its recommendations. And Green even delayed discussion of this innocuous report until the last day of the convention, when all the delegates were tired and ready to go home.

Randolph, at his eloquent best that day, refused to allow the Executive Council's maneuver to go uncontested. Excoriating the action as a "dignified, diplomatic camouflage," he demanded that Harrison's report be set aside and that the convention endorse the recommendations of the Committee of Five, particularly those calling for expulsion of racist unions and regional hearings to obtain additional evidence of the extent of discrimination. Leaders of racist unions leaped up to defend Harrison, one emphasizing that in his view the labor movement had done more for advancement of blacks than any other institution in America. Rather than expel racist unions, such speakers argued, the AFL should attempt to educate its members on the importance of accepting black workers. Moreover, they pointed out that when an international union refused to admit blacks, the AFL stood ready to organize them into federal locals. The convention closed by re-

jecting Randolph's demand that it implement the recommendations of the Committee of Five, and instead called for education
of the membership.[19]

The convention's actions in 1935, both in rejecting industrial
unionism and in refusing to oppose racist affiliates, embittered
many blacks. Walter White of the NAACP wrote to John L.
Lewis, who had founded the Committee for Industrial Organization on November 9, the day after the AFL convention closed,
that the AFL's action had "destroyed the last vestige of confidence" blacks had in that organization.[20] But that was going too
far. Though Randolph worked openly with Lewis and others of
the CIO, the BSCP received an international charter in the AFL
at the very session in which the convention had rejected everything else Randolph demanded.[21] Randolph kept the BSCP in the
AFL until it merged with the CIO in 1955.

When Randolph took the lead in arguing for acceptance of the
Committee of Five's report in 1935, that was the first convention
at which he could speak from a position of strength. The long
years of darkness for his union had come to an end, and though
the BSCP had not yet negotiated a contract with the Pullman
Company, it was on the verge of doing so. Between 1928 and the
1935 convention, the laws governing labor-management relations
had changed dramatically. In July 1935, shortly before the AFL
meeting, President Franklin D. Roosevelt signed into law the
Wagner-Connery Act, which guaranteed workers the right to
organize. But more important to the BSCP, Congress had passed
the Amended Railway Labor Act of 1934 which guaranteed railroad workers that right. Moreover, that act required corporations
to negotiate with unions that could prove that they represented
the majority of a particular class of workers, and created the National Mediation Board to protect workers' interests. Unlike previous legislation, that law explicitly included the Pullman Company under its definition of railways.[22]

BSCP officials, by maintaining the legitimacy of their union
through the long period of darkness, had performed an amazing
feat of leadership. They now stood ready to profit from the im-

proved public policy. When Pullman's management refused the union's new appeal for recognition, the BSCP appealed to the National Mediation Board. The board ordered an election among porters and maids to determine who represented them. The result was an overwhelming vote of confidence for the union and began a series of events that led to settlement of the dispute between the Brotherhood of Sleeping Car Porters and the Pullman Company. The company accepted the decision of the National Mediation Board that the BSCP represented a majority of the porters and maids, but it did not rush to recognize the union. Indeed, in its first meeting with the BSCP, Pullman's director of negotiations made it clear to Randolph and other union representatives that "we ain't recognizing no union." Pullman maintained that attitude for two more years, eventually bowing under federal pressure to recognize the union but determined to present the BSCP as an inept union unable to negotiate a contract. Then abruptly, on the morning of August 25, 1937, Pullman vice president Champ Carey astonished BSCP representatives and National Mediation Board officials with the laconic statement, "Gentlemen, we are ready to sign."[23]

Thus, on the twelfth anniversary of the founding of the Brotherhood of Sleeping Car Porters, the union finally had won the porters a contract. But even more important than improved working conditions and increased wages, the union's victory was of exceptional symbolic value to black working-class people. Under the dogged and farsighted leadership of its officials, the union had succeeded in bringing the powerful Pullman Company to its knees. It had also forced the AFL to grant a black union an international charter. Moreover, as Randolph and others had continuously emphasized, the BSCP had struck a major blow against company unionism. The union was a black institution that had proved itself capable of succeeding under black leadership in competition with first-rate white institutions. And, at least in the rhetoric of its leaders, it stood ready to work for all black workers regardless of their occupation.

It must be emphasized that the union's undisputed public figure, A. Philip Randolph, personally became as much a symbol of black advancement as the union. Few observers failed to recognize that his rhetoric, determination, and skill in pushing the porters' cause were crucial in making the BSCP more than merely a union of porters. Armed with the Pullman contract in 1937 and president of an international union of the AFL, he appeared a man of courage and strength, capable of and willing to mobilize the masses of black workers in a unified assault against racism in both corporations and organized labor. The union had succeeded because of him, and its very success was the basis of Randolph's later claims to a place among black spokesmen.

5

Black Workers
During Depression and War

The shift from the farm to the factory, therefore, is by far
the most outstanding change that took place in the male
labor force during the war. Between 1940 and 1944, the
number of Negroes employed as skilled craftsmen and fore-
men doubled, as did the number engaged as operatives.
. . . Altogether, the number in both categories rose from
about 500,000 to about 1,000,000.

Monthly Labor Review, 1945

In late October 1929 the Wall Street stock market collapsed, and
Americans generally believed that the Great Crash brought on the
Great Depression of the 1930s. But for rural blacks and many city
dwellers as well, what happened on Wall Street was of no concern at all. Few even knew where Wall Street was; fewer still had
any interest in the stock market. The sad fact is that rural America had not experienced the great prosperity of the 1920s and, as
usual, blacks had been the poorest of the poor. As one young
black man in rural Georgia put it, most blacks did not even know
the Great Depression had come. They had always been poor and
only thought whites were beginning to catch up. But what he
and others did not realize was that the United States had never
before experienced a general destruction of the economy and the
immense human suffering the nation was to endure during the
"Hoover Days" and the first years of the New Deal. Nor could
they visualize that at the end of an era that saw the misery of
depression compounded by the largest war in world history,

black workers in general would have attained the greatest improvements in their employment status than at any time before, with the exception of the aboltion of chattel slavery.

The era of the Great Depression and World War II was a time of increased militancy among workers, both black and white. Among whites, the Depression years saw the origin of the Congress of Industrial Organizations, for example, and the resulting effort to organize workers on an industrywide basis. Black workers, of course, participated in all these activities. But their militancy was expressed in other ways as well. They organized sharecroppers' unions, boycotted white businesses which refused to hire blacks, demonstrated against organized labor, and organized a march on Washington to protest actions of the federal government. By 1945 their activities had produced important results for black workers and for the working-class in general.

In order to understand the changes in the black working class by the end of World War II, we must look at the prevailing conditions in the South during the Great Depression. First, as late as 1945 a majority of blacks still remained in the South, despite the massive migration to northern cities. And if the rural South generally had been economically depressed during the 1920s, the condition for large numbers of black agricultural workers was wretched. Collusion by white landowners and local officials that had produced peonage after the Civil War had become ingrained in local custom. Just as in the antebellum South, black people had no rights in the 1920s—even the right to life—that whites were obliged to respect. In the whole South between 1877 and 1966, only one white person was ever indicted for the murder of a black person.

The case of John S. Williams, a white man who was indicted, convicted, and eventually sentenced to life in prison by a Georgia court, tells much more than a simple case of murder. Just as clearly, it shows the widespread existence of debt peonage in the South, a system of virtual slavery that continued in some parts of the country until as late as 1969.[1] Williams and his sons held numerous black men and women on their Georgia plantation against their will, allegedly in payment of debt, employing systematic violence and psychological intimidation to keep their workers in line. The murders for which Williams went to prison occurred after federal agents visited the plantation to investigate complaints that the Williamses held peons. Though the agents found no blacks willing to testify against the owners, they did note some irregularities, such as chains in some of the rooms and locks on doors by which workers could be secured throughout the night. They warned Williams of the seriousness of the complaint against him, and he promised to make improvements.

Convinced that the federal agents would return, Williams set out to destroy any evidence of workers being held as prisoners. Williams's trial in 1921 revealed that he and one of the black peons systematically killed several men and disposed of their bodies across a wide area of two adjoining counties. The evidence, and the gruesomeness of the deeds, presented in open court by the black accomplice, outraged local white Georgians and, though they would not convict Williams of peonage, they did send him to prison for murder. The black accomplice, Claude Manning, also received a life sentence for his part in the murders and later died on a Georgia chain gang. Williams, who became a prison trusty, was killed trying to prevent a prison break.[2]

Even if situations in which workers lived in conditions approaching slavery, forced to live on plantations because of debt, were unusual, the lives of southern farm workers were bleak at best. Few black farmers owned the land they worked, a situation that was to worsen during the Depression and war years, and whether they worked as sharecroppers or as day laborers, they remained in the same position as their ancestors after the Civil War. The South was still basically a cashless economy, with many black families receiving less than $100 annually in real money. Lack of land and capital, and the systematic oppression of the region, continued to lock blacks in an ever-widening cycle of perpetual poverty from which there seemed little hope of escape.[3]

More than the rapacity of landowners contributed to the deplorable condition of rural blacks. Beginning as early as 1920, successive waves of boll weevils ate up whatever earnings farmers could expect. Then in 1927 the Mississippi River overflowed its banks, unleashing a torrent of disaster throughout the Mississippi Valley. The great flood of 1927, and subsequent efforts to aid the many refugees, revealed the depths of the misery in which rural people lived in that section of the South. Even during this tragedy, white southerners insisted on maintaining the social and economic status quo. Black and white refugees lived in segregated camps. More seriously, the landowners compelled officials of relief organizations, headed by Secretary of Commerce Herbert Hoover, to cooperate with them in keeping black workers in the area, even when they would have no work the next year.[4] When a committee of blacks investigated the conditions of black refugees, they found most of them living in virtual concentration camps under armed white guards. Later studies also revealed that numerous landowners received free seeds from the Red Cross and charged them to their sharecroppers' accounts. Robert R. Moton, president of Tuskegee Institute, who headed the committee of blacks, rightly pointed out that the conditions in the Mississippi Delta brought them not only face to face with the problems of the emergency, but with "one of the greatest labor questions of America, which found itself in the relation between the planter and these tenant farmers." The committee found that the black tenants "lived not only in a state of fear but a state of abject poverty although they work from year to year," and pleaded with Hoover to make recommendations that would remove them from the "hopeless situation that face [sic] them in the future."[5]

Black rural workers did not accept their lot passively. Indeed, in the long tradition of agrarian protest, they struck out against the system that held them in virtual slavery. Black farm workers knew well the price they could expect to pay if they attempted a direct attack on the landowners. Some remembered the ill-fated cotton pickers' strike of the 1890s; still more knew of the massacre of blacks in Elaine, Arkansas, in 1919, when angry white landowners and police officials put down an alleged uprising of local black sharecroppers who had formed a union. Yet, as conditions worsened during the Depression, black farmers in Alabama tried again to form a union. In 1931, aided by a few organizers from the Communist party, blacks in Tallapoosa County founded the Alabama Sharecroppers Union. Despite the help of some Communists, the Alabama Sharecroppers Union could not be called a Communist organization. Its members remained overwhelmingly black, and though some of them might have read copies of the *Southern Workman,* the party's newspaper in the South, few of them understood much about Marxian political economics. Moreover, the union's existence raised fears of racial unrest in the minds of landowners, not fears of communism.[6]

Members of the Sharecroppers Union met in secret enclaves, utilizing the underground network that blacks had perfected during slavery. Most meetings took place in black churches, disguised as religious services. The union's economic gains were slim at best, but its very existence led to new violence in rural Alabama. A shootout between union members and a local deputy sheriff resulted in the death of some sharecroppers at Camp Hill in 1931. Even more violence erupted the next year at Reeltown when union members resisted efforts of law officers and a large party of deputized whites to confiscate the livestock of a union member who allegedly had not paid a debt.[7] In the face of this violence, the union strengthened and continued to grow. Even conservative estimates placed its membership at 3,000 in 1934.[8]

In the larger scheme of southern agriculture, the Alabama Sharecroppers Union was only a minor effort to combat abject poverty. In the election of 1932 the country swept Franklin D. Roosevelt into the White House, and with him a broad range of innovative programs known as the New Deal. One of the first proposals of the new administration aimed at improving conditions in agriculture, particularly in the cotton South. The devastation of that region can be seen in the fact that at 6 cents a pound in 1933, cotton was selling for a third of its price in 1929. Thus, during the fabled Hundred Days, Congress passed the Agricultural Adjustment Act, establishing the Agricultural Adjustment

Administration (AAA) to preside over rehabilitation of the rural economy.

The AAA, at least in the beginning, actually did more harm than good for black farm workers. New Deal planners were concerned with the total problem in agriculture, not with maldistribution of wealth within that society. Accordingly, large landowners benefited most from the new programs. A striking example of government action working against working-class people was the cotton plow-up scheme. New Dealers, believing that they could raise the price of cotton by creating a shortage, persuaded cotton farmers to plow up part of the cotton already planted in 1933. The federal government agreed to pay the farmers from $7 to $20 per acre for the plowed-up cotton. Southern farmers accepted the plan with reluctance. Some, particularly sharecroppers, knew many of them would be displaced, and it is reported that the mules, which had been whipped in the past for stepping on the precious cotton rows, now had to be forced to move. Yet, the scheme worked. By December 1933, cotton was selling at an average of 9.5 cents per pound, compared with about 6 cents per pound the year before.[9]

But as John P. Davis, a black critic of the New Deal, was to ask later, "at what price national recovery?" Southern landowners took the government payments for plowed-up cotton and pocketed the tenants' share. Moreover, despite contracts to the contrary, landowners also evicted thousands of sharecroppers, further worsening their condition. Tenants found themselves reduced to day laborers, forced to accept work at wages from 75 cents to $1 a day, and then only when work was available. Finally, they were denied access to the furnishing system or the rent-free shacks that had previously been available.

Government statistics tell the story of displacement of blacks during the Depression, particularly among sharecroppers. But advocates of white sharecroppers complained that landowners removed whites and replaced them with blacks.[10] The number of black sharecroppers declined by almost a quarter between 1930 and 1940, dropping from 392,897 to 299,118 by the end of the decade. The Amberson Report is accurate in pointing out that white sharecroppers and other tenants suffered from land use changes caused by the Depression and New Deal policies, but data do not support the view that black tenants and croppers replaced whites. Blacks suffered declines in all classes of agricultural workers, while the number of white farm owners actually increased.[11]

Sharecroppers cheated by landowners had little recourse. The New Deal was a democratic experiment, with programs controlled by local committees that knew best the needs of their communities. But the government made no provisions for equitable representation of various classes on these committees, let alone racial balance. Therefore, landowners monopolized the local administration of New Deal programs.[12] When black sharecroppers complained about their treatment, the very people responsible heard their grievances. And discrimination against landless blacks did not stop with local committees. When officials in charge of the Federal Emergency Relief Agency recognized the impropriety of making relief payments through landlords and decided to send funds directly to eligible citizens, whites were paid more than blacks. Government publications even reported the differential. The *Monthly Labor Review* pointed out in 1936 that "Negro families of any specific size received smaller than average relief benefits than did white relief households of the same size. The discrepancy between the average relief benefits received by whites and Negroes was only slightly smaller in the Eastern cotton area when computed on a per-person rather than on a per-household basis."[13] The average rural white family on relief received $15 in February 1935, while the average black family received only $9.[14]

The AAA was only one of several agencies the New Deal used to ease conditions for rural populations. And though the national government looked on all Americans equally, refusing to recognize the special needs of blacks, local administrators did in fact discriminate. The National Youth Administration (NYA), under the direction of Aubrey Williams, a white Mississippian, recog-

nized the needs of black youths and brought Dr. Mary Mc-
Leod Bethune, founder-president of Bethune-Cookman College,
to Washington to serve as director of the NYA's Division of Negro Affairs. Leaders of the Civilian Conservation Corps (CCC)
were not nearly so farsighted. Indeed, officials in Washington allowed field directors wide latitude in running the CCC and even
insisted on maintaining segregation in the agency. The CCC's director of recruitment in Georgia, under mild pressure from Washington to bring more blacks into the organization, reported that
it could not be done because "at this time in the farming period
in the state, it is vitally important that Negroes remain in the
counties for chopping cotton and for planting other produce. The
Negroes in this way are able to obtain work on the farms throughout the state." On another occasion he informed Washington that
white county committees believed that "there are few Negro families who . . . need an income as great as $25 a month in cash."[15]
And in Delaware, where there were too few blacks to form an all-
black CCC unit, and where the state's relief director wanted the
government to force integration of whites and blacks, the CCC
director in Washington informed her that nonexistence of CCC
opportunities for blacks in Delaware was a fact "she would have
to accept." The CCC would not be integrated.[16]

Many considered the AAA's efforts to help southern agricultural
workers, particularly sharecroppers and tenants, inadequate. Several agrarian revolts developed in the South. The most remarkable organization, and one which challenged racial segregation,
developed in the Mississippi Delta. In 1934, on the Arkansas side
of the river near Memphis, Tennessee, young Socialists and sharecroppers organized the Southern Tenant Farmers Union (STFU)
at Tyronza. Norman Thomas, an internationally known Socialist
and a leader of the League for Industrial Democracy (LID), was
the intellectual father of the STFU. From its inception, the sharecroppers' union had interracial leadership; its president was white
and its vice president was black. The white director of the STFU
and its guiding spirit throughout its history, was a sometime tenant farmer, tailor, and small businessman, Harry L. (Mitch)

Mitchell. By the end of the Depression decade, the STFU had established a network of influential supporters throughout the country and had become powerful enough to force the President to appoint a special committee to study the problems of share-croppers. Aside from Norman Thomas, the union's supporters included the indefatigable Washington lobbyist Gardner (Pat) Jackson, an influential New Dealer, and Walter White, secretary of the NAACP. A. Philip Randolph also aided the STFU.

As one would expect, the union existed amid violence and intimidation. And from time to time, the STFU met its oppressors on their own terms. It built an effective underground network, for example, and organized several successful cotton pickers' strikes. After one year, the STFU claimed 10,000 members; by 1936 the figure was 25,000. In 1939, when landowners in Arkansas evicted a large number of black and white sharecroppers, O. H. Whitfield, a black STFU vice president, led 500 of them onto the main highway between Memphis and St. Louis, determined to remain there until the federal government provided relief. But by that time the union, engulfed in national labor union intrigue, had largely fallen apart. Its national leaders were gravely concerned about Communist influence within the STFU. H. L. Mitchell would carry on the struggle to improve working and living conditions for agricultural laborers for decades, but by the outbreak of World War II, for all practical purposes, the day of the STFU had passed. Yet it had left an indelible print on the rural South and symbolized what poor blacks and whites could attain if they could forget race and see their problems as essentially the same.[17]

The Great Depression was hardly a southern rural phenomenon. People in all sections of the country and in both large cities and small towns suffered as well. Hosea Hudson, a steel worker in Birmingham, Alabama, and one of the few black Communists in the country during the 1930s, describes blacks in his town as so destitute that they tore boards from abandoned houses and burned them for firewood. Landlords often allowed tenants to live in the houses rent free just to keep them from being burned.[18]

During this time of desperation, workers even killed other la-

borers to take over their jobs. The grave misfortune, but one that
underscores the pervasive influence of race in the United States,
is that much of the labor-related violence pitted whites against
blacks. In Atlanta, for example, a group of local whites known as
the Black Shirts made strong efforts to have urban blacks ban-
ished to the farms so that whites could have all the jobs in town.
They visited employers who hired blacks, demanding that they
be dismissed and white workers put in their places.[19] Even more
ominous were the actions of white railroad workers. They carried
out a reign of terror, intimidating, beating, and in some cases
murdering black firemen in a conspiracy to force them off the
railroads.[20]

Not all the displacement occurred in the South. At a time when
much of the population was finding it hard to make a living, few
people had time to think about the kind of job they held. Whites
began to drive coal and ice trucks, jobs that had been largely
black for decades, while restaurants and other service facilities
replaced their black crews with whites. Ironically, the Pullman
porters were the only group that remained all-black.

The New Deal attacked urban poverty as vigorously as it had
the terrible rural conditions. Early in 1933 Congress passed the
National Industrial Recovery Act (NIRA), legislation designed
to increase employment by, among other things, shortening the
work week. Nor would workers suffer; minimum wages were set
for most occupations. Moreover, by this omnibus act, the federal
government recognized the right of workers to organize and bargain with employers, and explicitly supported the closed shop
concept.

Congressional debate on the NIRA raised searching questions
about the position of black workers under the New Deal. Particular interest centered on whether the government would allow
them to be paid less than whites for the same work. Leaders of
black organizations and workers themselves vigorously protested
such suggestions, arguing that the government could not officially
support overt discrimination. But proponents of wage differentials
were no less outspoken. Some pointed out that the only reason

blacks found work at all, particularly in the South, was that they accepted lower wages than whites. The message was clear: if the government forced employers to grant equal pay, black workers would be replaced by whites. Yet proponents of unequal pay generally insisted that they were interested not in race but in efficiency. And since blacks were less efficient than whites, they should receive less pay. One company, the Scripto Manufacturing Company of Atlanta, was explicit. It reminded its black workers that:

This company does not base wages on color but entirely on efficiency. Our records show that the efficiency of colored help is only 50 percent of that of white help in similar plants. . . . If the "false friends" of the colored people do not stop their propaganda about paying the same wages to colored and white employees this company will be forced to move the factory to a section where the minimum wage will produce the greatest production. *Stop your "false friends" from talking you out of a job.*[21]

In the end, the government did not accede to the demand that it establish racial differentials for workers, but racist employers and white workers still got what they wanted. The NIRA provided for regional wage rates based on the perceived standard of living in various areas of the country. Also, Congress granted companies the right to classify various types of work, thus completely exempting some blacks from coverage while placing the remainder in the lowest possible classification. Indeed, the legislation did not call for equal pay for equal work, but rather equal pay for equal classification. And in all too many areas, whole fields of work that blacks performed were exempted from minimum wages. The codes did not cover agricultural employees, domestic servants, cooks, and "yard" workers at various southern textile mills.[22]

It must also be kept in mind that inequities established during the early New Deal would affect workers a generation later. Social Security, the federal agency established to provide old age insurance for workers, also exempted from coverage those job classifications in which blacks were heavily employed.[23] And as is often the case, women suffered most. The percentage of black women among covered black workers was far below that of white women among all white workers—16 percent to 30 percent. A 1941 government report laconically stated that "in any analysis of taxable wages it should be emphasized that large numbers of Negroes are in agriculture and domestic service (uncovered employment) and that the *wages in such employment are low*."[24]

As the New Deal wore on, blacks grew increasingly critical of its activities. While whites who opposed equal pay for black workers called the NRA the "Negro Relief Act" and pledged that it would mean "No Roosevelt Again," blacks looked on the legislation as the "Negro Removal Act." "Negroes Rarely Allowed," they claimed, was the motto of NRA agencies. But criticism did not stop with ridicule. Some blacks claimed that administrators of federal work relief agencies, such as the Works Progress Administration (WPA) and the Public Works Administration (PWA), actually lowered the occupational level of black workers because blacks rarely found relief work commensurate in skill with the work they had performed in the private market.[25] And John P. Davis, an especially keen observer of the conditions of black people during the Great Depression, argues that their status actually deteriorated under the New Deal. Davis writes that in October 1933, 2,117,000 Afro-Americans were receiving support from relief agencies; by January 1935 the number reached 4,000,000, or about 30 percent of the black population.[26]

Federal sources on long-term unemployment support Davis's claim and show that as early as the Great Depression young blacks had experienced an alarmingly high unemployment rate, a condition that has remained almost constant except during World War II. The federal unemployment census for November 1937 makes the point. As reported in the *Monthly Labor Review*, "18 percent of all colored youth in the 15–24 age group, and 31 percent of all colored young people in the labor market were wholly unemployed. An additional 2.2 percent of all colored young people—or 3.8 percent of all colored young people in the labor market—were on emergency work, making about 20 percent of all colored young people—or approximately 34 percent of all of them in the labor market—who were entirely jobless or engaged only on emergency work."[27]

As on the farms, black urban workers organized to force improvement of their condition. Such organization took various forms. Some protestors joined groups that allegedly engaged in purposeful bumping of white shoppers and office workers on downtown streets, while some black women participated in a loosely organized "stand a lady up for work" program. This job action, in which black women would agree to do housework on a given day and then refuse to show up, resulted from the low wages domestic workers received and the indecent manner in which they were treated. Conditions were so tight that black women seeking housework in New York would go to a subway station in Harlem and stand along the platform as white housewives who needed a maid for the day came along and casually surveyed them. The conditions closely resembled those of the domestic slave markets of the antebellum South. Still other blacks formed "Don't Buy Where You Can't Work" campaigns, an effort of dubious value since blacks had little money to spend anyhow. Nevertheless, these activities demonstrated the growing militancy of black workers and their determination to refuse to accept employment discrimination as inevitable.

Boycott actions achieved their greatest success in New York City. Under the leadership of the Reverend John H. Johnson of St. Martin's Protestant Episcopal Church, blacks had been negotiating with the major department stores on 125th Street, particularly Blumstein's, to open jobs to them. These negotiations failed, Blumstein's management reminding Johnson that the store already hired blacks as janitors, porters, elevator operators, and other service workers. Various black groups in the city then organized the Citizens' League for Fair Play and instituted a boycott of Blumstein's. The Citizens' League not only picketed the premises but photographed blacks who crossed the picket lines, and embarrassed them by publishing their pictures prominently in the New York *Age,* a black newspaper that supported the boycott. As in most such situations, some blacks opposed the boycott. The *Amsterdam News*, another black newspaper in the city, was notorious in its opposition, claiming that the boycott would only work to the disadvantage of blacks already employed on 125th Street. Though editors of the *Amsterdam News* might have been sincere in opposing the boycott, its supporters noted that the newspaper carried most of Blumstein's advertisements in the black press. Nonetheless, after six weeks, the store finally capitulated and agreed to hire blacks as clerical and professional personnel. Its management did insist, however, that the Citizens' League recommend only light-complexioned Afro-Americans for the jobs.[28]

After its initial success at Blumstein's, the Citizens' League fell apart as some blacks, particularly Ira Kemp and Arthur Reed, began to complain about the large number of "high yaller" women who got the sales jobs. They also insisted that the Citizens' League boycott other Harlem stores. When the group picketed the A. S. Beck Shoe Store, the store sued Reed and Kemp, claiming that they did not represent a labor union but simply one racial group against another. Their actions threatened a race riot. A New York judge upheld Beck's view and outlawed picketing on that basis. But the blacks would eventually win. In 1938 the U.S. Supreme Court upheld the right of blacks to boycott businesses which refused to hire them. As for New York City, the concerted actions of black workers that year led to numerous jobs for blacks in stores and with public utilities, including the telephone and bus companies. Also in 1938, blacks forced New York merchants to accept the first affirmative action plan in the country. In August the New York Uptown Chamber of Commerce agreed with the Greater New York Coordinating Committee for Employment to grant one-third of all retail jobs—executive, clerical, and sales—to blacks. Whites currently employed would not be fired to make room for blacks, but blacks were to receive preferential hiring until they held at least one-third of the jobs.[29]

Despite successes such as those in New York, blacks generally made little progress in employment or promotion to higher skill levels, particularly in industry. Sometimes the frustration spilled over into riots, even in New York, where some success had been achieved. On March 19, 1935, black residents in Harlem went on a night-long rampage, smashing buildings and looting stores, following the spread of rumors that a black youth had been killed by police after being caught stealing a small knife from a local store. By morning three blacks had been killed and numerous others wounded as black New Yorkers showed their resentment of "racial discrimination and poverty in the midst of plenty."[30]

On the national level, black organizations tried to increase pressure on the federal government to take a special interest in the sufferings of black people during the Depression. The two leading groups, the NAACP and the National Urban League, organized workers' councils and tried to instill worker consciousness in blacks. Such activities marked a great change in the traditional policies of both organizations and had come about only because of the Depression. As early as 1933, younger members of the NAACP had insisted that the Association either take an interest in the economic conditions of blacks or disband. About the same time, W. E. B. Du Bois came to a similar conclusion, going so far as to insist that the NAACP's goal of creating an integrated society was now impossible and calling on blacks to create a separate society and attend to their own needs.[31]

More important than such organizational efforts were the activities of a new group formed solely to lobby Congress and the administration on behalf of blacks. Two young Harvard-educated blacks, one with a law degree and the other with a Ph.D. in economics, John P. Davis and Robert C. Weaver, respectively, founded the Joint Committee on National Recovery in the summer of 1933. Many national black organizations, eventually twenty-two in all, affiliated with the Joint Committee. The National Urban League, which viewed the Joint Committee as a competitor for both its field of work and the meager funds available for black advancement groups, refused to participate. The Committee's informal organizational structure and limited resources—an annual budget of just $5,000—seriously restricted its potential achievements. The Committee suffered even more when Weaver resigned to become advisor on Negro affairs to Secretary of the Interior Harold Ickes. Yet the work of the Joint Committee was impressive. It attended more than 100 hearings on NRA codes, examined most government publications and pointed out sections that adversely affected blacks, and led the agitation that convinced the NRA that the government could not sanction different wage and hour standards for blacks and whites.[32]

Despite the Committee's success in limiting the discriminatory impact of federal regulations, many sensed that black workers needed a larger and more powerful organization to change the system permanently. Indeed, the administration's efforts to make structural improvements for the working-class actually worked to the disadvantage of blacks, even though the federal government had ceased being "aggressively racist."[33] The problem, as far as blacks were concerned, was that the government had not become aggressively antiracist. Passage of the Wagner-Connery Labor Relations Act of 1935, hailed by white workers—particularly unionists—as the Magna Carta of American workers, makes the point. During debate on the bill, black spokesmen lobbied hard for an amendment that would deny federal protection to racist unions. They feared that unions, which had continually discriminated against Afro-Americans, would use the new closed-shop clauses to eliminate them from many jobs. But white unionists lobbied just as hard for exclusion of such a clause, and in the end Congress went along with them. Senator Robert Wagner of New York, who privately favored the blacks' position, explained his decision not to support a nondiscrimination clause on the grounds that to do so would have risked losing the whole piece of legislation.[34] Blacks simply needed better organization.

Accordingly, in February 1936 representatives of approximately 200 black groups throughout the country met in Chicago to outline a program and to establish an organization that would more effectively push the economic interests of Afro-Americans. Some progressive white groups, particularly CIO unions, attended the sessions, which resulted in the founding of the National Negro Congress. The Congress elected A. Philip Randolph, president of the Brotherhood of Sleeping Car Porters as its president and chose John P. Davis as executive secretary.

Randolph's eloquent appeals for an end to discrimination in organized labor, the AFL's decision to grant the BSCP an international charter in 1935, publicity surrounding the Brotherhood's official talks with the Pullman Company which commenced that year, and the press coverage that followed this complex individual had catapulted the BSCP president to prominence among black spokesmen. Randolph enjoyed wide name recognition. Although his actual accomplishments in organizing the BSCP touched only a small number of Afro-Americans, he had in fact attained a concrete economic goal while others had contented themselves with theorizing. Moreover, Randolph possessed the ability to make the most routine moral victory appear a broad practical success, and he could turn the narrowest of activities into movements to advance the general black population. The masses of blacks and some leaders, seemingly unaware of the nebulous quality of his achievements, looked on Randolph as the man to lead the struggle to solve their social and economic problems. He was the one person who combined articulate expression of the hopes and desires of blacks with practical experience in trade union matters.

Randolph's presidency of the National Negro Congress was a failure. The organization abandoned the broad base on which it had been founded and endorsed the policies and philosophies of the American Communist party and a few of the more radical white CIO unions. The change came about because though Randolph was president of the Congress, he was not its leader. The real leader was Davis, who, as executive secretary, directed the daily operations. As early as 1935, Davis had shown dissatisfaction with the American capitalist system. A highly sensitive man, Davis had been terribly disturbed by the misery caused by the Great Depression and the seeming inability of the American economy to solve it. Writing in the *Journal of Negro Education,* he cautioned blacks not to limit themselves to any present economic system. Davis pointed out that:

Capitalism is only a few hundred years old; as feudalism is dead so may it die. I believe that the conclusion will be inescapable that there must be an immediate change in emphasis from protection of private property to protection of human beings from misery and poverty.[35]

By 1937 Davis had moved beyond mere musings and accepted the Communist line. By the time the Congress convened for its third session in 1940, Davis and his associates had succeeded in pushing it into the Communist camp. Randolph faced the decision of either resigning as president or being denied reelection.

The National Negro Congress had been extremely active during the intervening years, but its accomplishments were modest. In fact, by the 1940 meeting it was moribund and, except for Randoph, would have little permanent impact on the American scene. But the Congress was important largely because it permitted Randolph the opportunity once again to grab center stage in the black workers' movement. Indeed, far from resigning in disgrace, Randolph mustered all his presence and oratorial powers and quit the Congress with remarkable dignity and aplomb. Ralph J. Bunche, who was present at the session, considered Randolph's resignation speech—in which he warned blacks against simplistic solutions to their problems and the impossibility of depending on whites to lead and finance their organizations—one of the most important statements ever made to black leaders. Randolph argued that white Communists did not understand the conditions of blacks in the United States and cared even less about their future. Violently anti-Communist since the 1920s, when the Communists had tried to take over his union, Randloph warned his listeners—few indeed, because most delegates walked out of the hall during his speech—that "he who pays the fiddler calls the tune." He was right, for in 1940 the National Negro Congress was no longer either national or black, but rather a close-knit group that represented the views of the American Communist party. Randolph walked away from that meeting with the organization in shambles but with his personal reputation intact.[36]

Conditions in the nation had improved significantly during the years of the National Negro Congress as more and more white

Americans found employment in the burgeoning new war industries. Indeed, in 1939–1940 the United States turned increasingly
toward a war economy, and just as blacks had been first fired
when the Depression began, they remained last hired in the turn
toward full employment. In 1940, for example, files presented by
new job applicants showed that the long-term unemployment rate
of blacks ran three times as high as that of whites. Just over 20
percent of blacks had been unemployed four years or more, compared to slightly less than 7 percent for whites.[37] The disproportionately high number of blacks on WPA and other relief job rolls
underscores the unemployment problems of black workers. By
the end of 1939, 14 percent of all WPA workers were black as
whites moved on to permanent jobs.[38] And even in government
service blacks continued to face stiff opposition to job advancement. When less than 10 percent of all federal employees were
custodial workers, 90 percent of all black employees held such
jobs.[39]

Despite the bleakness of the moment, in 1940 blacks stood on
the threshold of the decade that would bring their greatest economic gains, in terms of both real advances and in relation to
whites, since the Civil War. Not only did a few blacks find employment in previously all-white jobs, but by the time the war
ended the combined efforts of blacks and liberal whites, as well
as the changed international realities the war forced on Americans, had laid the foundation for governmental protection of the
rights of blacks to economic equality.

Without question, black advances in American industry during
World War II came largely because of the emergency and the
nation's great need for workers and soldiers. Moreover, they resulted from increasing militancy among blacks. This militancy
was demonstrated both by workers on jobs and by blacks generally, who insisted that for Afro-Americans the war must result in
a "Double V"—a victory against fascism abroad and an equally
certain victory against racism at home. The Fair Employment
Practice Committee and other federal agencies operated with a
clear understanding of the potential for racial unrest, and no one

could overlook the major riots that erupted in several cities in 1943, including New York, Los Angeles, and Detroit. Indeed, the implications of the alleged comment of a black Mississippi share-cropper on the morning after Pearl Harbor—"Boss, I understand them Japanese done declared war on y'all white folks"—was clear to all. Thus, when the National War Labor Board issued an order in 1943 abolishing wage differentials based on race, it took pains to point out that:

whether as vigorous fighting men or for production of food and muni-tions, *America needs the Negro;* the Negro needs the opportunity to work and fight. *The Negro is necessary for winning the war,* and at the same time it is a test of our sincerity in the cause for which we are fighting. More hundreds of millions of colored people are involved in the outcome of this war than the combined populations of the Axis powers. Under Hitler and his Master Race, their movement is back-ward to slavery and despair. In America the colored people have the freedom to struggle for freedom. With the victory of the democracies, the human destiny is toward feedom, hope, equality of opportunity, and the gradual fulfillment for all people of the noblest aspirations of the brothers of men and the sons of God, without regard to color or creed, religion or race, in a world neighborhood of human brother-hood.[40]

Even before Japanese bombs fell on Pearl Harbor and brought the United States formally into World War II, it was clear that the position of black workers would improve. In October 1940, in a case originating in Norfolk, Virginia, the U.S. Supreme Court ruled that states could no longer use race as a basis for paying black and white school teachers different salaries.[41] Even more striking, during 1940 and 1941 black and white leaders of the United Automobile Workers (UAW) worked hard to get black employees at the Ford Motor Company's River Rouge plant to join the union in a strike. Black workers were generally reluc-tant for several reasons. First, given the history of the relation-ship between blacks and organized labor, black automobile work-ers could not depend on the union to protect their interests after the strike ended. Second, in the long tradition of white paternal-ism, Ford had ingratiated itself with both the workers and leaders of the black community. Accordingly, large numbers of black workers believed that they owed their jobs to Ford's benevolence, and numerous voices in the pulpit and press exhorted them to maintain that view. It was, then, an event of major importance when UAW officials, with the help of nationally recognized blacks such as Walter White of the NAACP, convinced blacks to join the strike that led to the unionization of Ford in 1941, a significant victory in organizing the auto industry. Unlike the railroad strike of 1894, in which organized white workers ignored blacks, black participation was crucial to the union's eventual victory.[42]

During World War II, several other CIO unions attempted to organize black workers in basic industries, and when Philip Murray became president of the CIO in 1942, he established a special Committee to Abolish Racial Discrimination. This committee, which included James B. Carey, CIO secretary-treasurer, and Willard S. Townsend, who became the first black member of the CIO executive board in June 1942, conducted a broad educational program among CIO affiliates and even badgered some units to work more vigorously to recruit blacks and to upgrade those already employed. To be sure, the CIO acted partly to win black support in its fight with AFL unions. But in fact, there was no contest. Most AFL unions, as well as the national office, remained staunch supporters of status quo racism. Throughout the war years, A. Philip Randolph and other black leaders implored successive AFL conventions to end union racism. And just as before the war, the AFL showed a decided lack of interest in doing so. Indeed, during the war blacks found that many white unions were as strongly opposed as white employers to the employment and economic improvement of blacks.

Even before the war, blacks had tired of talking about discrimination and had taken steps to force the government to insure the right of blacks to jobs, particularly in the burgeoning war industries. Blacks mounted many protests, the most important of which was the March on Washington Movement led by Randolph and other officials of the Brotherhood of Sleeping Car Porters. In late 1940 and early 1941, Randolph began to talk increasingly about what many others had come to recognize: white workers were coming out of the Depression because of new job opportunities, while blacks remained on unemployment or relief rolls. Even the U.S. Employment Service had noted that blacks were being left out of training programs and new jobs.[43] Randolph proposed that since blacks could improve their position only by showing mass strength, they should band together and march on Washington to demand that the President publicly support an end to racial discrimination in employment.

Randolph announced the creation of the March on Washington Committee and promised that unless President Roosevelt issued an executive order ending racial discrimination in hiring by unions and employers and eliminating segregation in the armed forces, 10,000 blacks would demonstrate in the streets of the national capital. Randolph's movement became even more frightening to white Americans when this formidable personality, following the position he had taken on resigning from the National Negro Congress, demanded that the March on Washington Movement be all black. The time had come, he said, when black people must fight their own battles.

Within weeks black newspapers, preachers, and other community leaders picked up the call for a march on Washington, and as the spring of 1941 wore on, Randolph escalated the number of proposed marchers to 50,000. The March on Washington Movement was becoming the largest mass movement of blacks since the activities of Marcus Garvey's Universal Negro Improvement Association of the 1920s. As summer approached, Randolph began talking about 100,000 marchers coming to Washington, and federal officials began to worry even more. President Roosevelt sent several intermediaries, including his wife Eleanor and New York City Mayor Fiorello La Guardia, to talk Randolph into calling off the march. But their efforts came to no avail. Nothing less than a presidential executive order would stop the march.

After direct conversations between the President and leaders of the march at the White House failed to halt the march, Roosevelt gave in and issued Executive Order 8802, which one historian has called the "greatest single Negro victory since the Civil War."[44] But that evaluation perhaps goes too far, for as with most political actions, the President's decision to issue 8802 was a compromise. Roosevelt, described by many as the consummate politician, had no intention of seeing thousands of blacks parade in protest on the malls of the national capital, particularly when German and Japanese propagandists were trying to exploit any evidence of U.S. racial differences. In the end, he gave up little. Executive Order 8802 does not mention segregation in the armed forces, and the Fair Employment Practice Committee (FEPC) it created was so weak as to have hardly any impact. Indeed, Randolph suffered considerable abuse from some blacks who complained that he had accepted far too little.[45] Yet the important fact is that the March on Washington Movement had forced the federal government to admit publicly that blacks suffered from discrimination in employment and that the government had a responsibility to remedy it. The action forced an end to official racism in one important sector of American life. Of equal importance, Randolph emerged as a man of immense national stature.

Though black workers had forced the establishment of the FEPC, its entire history demonstrated the importance of racism in American society. The majority of the committee members were white because it was thought that they would be more effective in dealing with white employers, labor leaders, and government officials. And except for a brief period when Earl Dickerson served in an acting capacity, the chairman was always white. Moreover, except for Milton P. Webster, vice president of the BSCP, the FEPC had no workers, despite the nominal membership of William Green and Philip Murray, presidents of the AFL and CIO, respectively. Indeed, the FEPC staff, which fortunately had several black members, was more important in the end than the committee itself.

The FEPC faced severe obstacles in trying to erase discrimination against blacks, white women, and religious minority groups. Organized labor gave only lukewarm endorsement to the committee's work. Indeed, in several notable cases, the unions were the

main targets of the FEPC's investigations and directives. Moreover, racist southern congressmen tried at every turn to kill the
committee, while Paul V. McNutt, chairman of the War Manpower Commission, under whose direction Executive Order 8802
placed the FEPC, had no use for it and obstructed its work
whenever he could. The FEPC existed in a virtual straitjacket for
almost two years until in May 1943, President Roosevelt issued
Executive Order 9346, establishing a new President's Committee
on Fair Employment Practice, increasing its budget, and placing
its operations directly under the Executive Office of the President. In addition, the new order explicitly included labor unions
as institutions forbidden to discriminate on the basis of race, sex,
or creed, a stipulation that Randolph had demanded in 1941 but
had been left out of the original order.

By the end of the war, the FEPC had achieved some notable
successes. Aside from its own investigations and directives against
discriminating corporations and unions, the committee's existence
had served to spur militancy among black workers. This new militancy could be clearly seen in the shipbuilding and railroad industries, where the FEPC carried out celebrated hearings. These
hearings on job discrimination on the railroads were particularly
important because collusion between the white firemen's union
and the railroad companies of the Southeast had almost completely removed black firemen from the lines. In February 1941
the National Mediation Board acceded to the Washington Agreement, by which the companies accepted the union's demand that
black workers, described in the document as "nonpromotables,"
be allowed to make up no more than 50 percent of the workers
in any class of employment. With the agreement in hand, the
union had moved by April to replace all black firemen with
whites.

Black firemen organized the Negro Railway Labor Executive
Committee and brought in Charles H. Houston, dean of the law
school at Howard University, to bring their case to court. They
also requested aid from the FEPC. In several days of widely pub-
licized hearings, the committee heard extensive testimony of ra-

cial discrimination in the railroad industry. Union officials maintained that they should not be asked to undo the longstanding
social mores of the states through which the trains ran. In the
end, the FEPC found gross discrimination in the industry generally and particularly in the Washington Agreement. It ordered
the parties to disband the agreement. The union steadfastly refused and threatened the companies with a strike if they complied. Since the FEPC had no coercive powers, black firemen had
little recourse but the courts. Houston filed an unsuccessful suit
on behalf of one of the aggrieved blacks, Bester Williams Steele,
in the U.S. district court in Alabama, and then carried the case
on appeal to the Supreme Court. In December 1944 the Court
ruled that the Washington Agreement violated the constitutional
rights of black workers by arbitrarily discriminating against
them. Accordingly, the agreement was unenforceable.[46]

A similar series of cases that brought together a federal agency,
militant black workers, and the courts to end discrimination in
employment and union affiliation arose in the shipbuilding industry on the West Coast. Shipbuilding was one of the nation's most
important industries during World War II. Near its peak in 1943,
it employed more than 1,722,000 workers and moved from its
normal facilities on the Atlantic Coast as shipyards in California
and Oregon came to rival in importance those of New York and
Newport-News.[47] Unions of shipworkers, particularly the racist
and discriminatory International Brotherhood of Boilermakers,
Iron Ship Builders, and Helpers of America, prospered from this
upsurge in shipbuilding. The union had a white-only clause in its
constitution which it refused to remove. The problem for blacks
was that in April 1941 the Metal Trades Department of the AFL
negotiated the West Coast Agreement with shipbuilding companies, a closed-shop contract that limited employment to union
members and granted unions control over promotions and seniority. Given the boilermakers' history and the fact that the
union had jurisdiction over 65 percent of the job classifications,
blacks could expect to find little work in that industry.[48]

As early as fall 1941, blacks on the West Coast began complaining to the FEPC and the President about discrimination in ship-building. First, they accused the union of using its closed-shop agreement to keep the number of blacks in the yards as low as possible and to deny black workers promotions and access to training programs. Second, and equally odious to many blacks, the union required Afro-Americans to join an auxiliary local of the International Brotherhood of Boilermakers as a prerequisite for gaining employment. Membership in the auxiliary was little more than the right to pay dues. Blacks could not vote for inter-national officers or attend conventions, nor did they have repre-sentation on grievance committees. Their membership dues were simply a tax on their right to work.

By 1942, complaints from the shipyards had moved beyond one or two individual workers and representatives of black ad-vancement organizations such as the NAACP, as militant black workers formed their own groups to press their interests. These included the Shipyard Negro Organization for Victory at Port-land, Oregon, the Shipyard Workers Committee for Equal Par-ticipation in the Unions at Los Angeles, and the Bay Area Coun-cil Against Discrimination in San Francisco-Oakland.[49] These workers' groups were so well organized that an FEPC investiga-tion committee reported to Washington that continued discrimi-nation could cause numerous severe race riots throughout the re-gion. The committee, strengthened by its new charter, agreed to hold formal hearings on shipyard complaints late in 1943. These hearings, in both Portland and Los Angeles, revealed widespread discrimination by both the boilermakers' union and the com-panies. On December 9, 1943, the FEPC directed the union to end its discrimination, in effect ordering it to abolish the white-only clause and to throw out the auxiliary. The committee also directed employers to refuse to discharge blacks on orders from the union until it complied with FEPC directives.[50] The com-panies, though refusing to admit that they discriminated against blacks, generally moved to comply with the FEPC's directives. The union insisted that it would be bound only by the Master Agreement and warned the companies that the FEPC's direc-

tives were simply "an arrogant attempt to destroy collective bargaining agreements" and would serve only to "alienate the good-
will of organized labor and its support of the war effort."[51]

Meanwhile, black shipworkers used the impetus provided by
the FEPC directives to file suit in federal court, seeking injunctions against both the union and the companies. Their litigation
resulted in a decision by the California Supreme Court that in
effect outlawed discriminatory unions with closed-shop agreements because such a union's "asserted rights to choose its own
members does not merely relate to social relations; it affects the
fundamental right to work for a living." In a similar case, a superior court in Providence, Rhode Island, had reached the same
conclusions. Taken together, they marked the end of the system
of discrimination by the boilermakers.[52] When the FEPC ceased
operations in 1946, the boilermakers' union was still trying to
maintain its traditional stance, but the final outcome was obvi-
ous. The shipyard cases demonstrated how the combined efforts
of federal agencies, state and federal courts, and demands of
militant black workers could overturn the impact of racism in the
workplace.[53]

By the end of World War II, major changes had taken place in
the American labor market. Of major importance for the future,
during the war for the first time the increased proportion of
white working women exceeded that of blacks. While the proportion of black women in civilian jobs increased by 40 percent
between 1940 and 1944, that of white women grew by 51 percent.[54] Among black men, the war caused little increase in the labor force, but it did result in wide job diversification. The most
striking change was the great decline in the percentage of black
farm workers. By the end of the war, only 28 percent of black
males worked on farms, a decline of 13 percent since 1940. Indeed, during World War II, as many blacks left the farms for
munitions and other industries as had gone north during the
great migration of World War I. The migration of World War II
was so heavy that by 1947, 1,800,000 blacks—14 percent of all
those born before 1940—lived in a state other than the one in

which they had resided in 1940.[55] Also, 300,000 fewer black males held farm jobs in 1944 than in 1940.[56]

All in all, approximately 1,000,000 black workers were added to the industrial work force during the war, 60 percent of whom were women. About 400,000 of these new female workers were former domestics who left employment in kitchens and scrubbing floors to help win the war. Indeed, "Rosie the Riveter" was as likely to be black as white. There were so many black women in one Campbell Soup Company plant that an assistant personnel manager found it necessary to apologize for their presence. "We never had them before," he told a visitor. And representative of what was to happen to most black workers after the war, he added, "I hope we won't [have them here] again."[57]

The number of blacks employed as skilled craftsmen and semi-skilled operatives doubled between 1940 and 1944. Moreover, the black labor force became considerably more diversified, helping to push up the median income for black workers from 41 percent of the white median in 1939 to 60 percent in 1950. Nonetheless, despite improvement in diversification and numbers, Afro-Americans were still disproportionately engaged in unskilled work. In 1945 just as in 1940, four out of five black men were still unskilled laborers. Moreover, as the Department of Labor pointed out, since most advances for black workers had come in "precisely those occupations, industries and [geographical] areas in which post-war adjustments will be most severe," blacks faced the prospect of losing jobs as the nation returned to a civilian economy.[58]

As the war ended, many blacks thought they faced a bright future. Many had achieved skills for industrial work and believed that the government would continue to guarantee their employment rights. Others were determined to fight if necessary to maintain their improved status. In the excitement of the moment, most blacks did not realize that their fortunes in the American workplace had begun to decline almost as soon as the bombs stopped falling.

6

Black Workers in Postwar America

Negroes have faced a more serious unemployment problem than white workers throughout the postwar period; the jobless rate for Negro workers has remained about twice that of white men and women since the early 1950s. This ratio persists at each level of educational attainment, with the differential even greater among workers with more schooling than among those with a minimal level of education.

Monthly Labor Review, 1968

The decade and a half from the end of the Second World War to the inauguration of President John F. Kennedy in 1961 was a period of immense change in American society. The observation of the historian Richard Hofstadter that the United States is a nation that "grew up in the country and moved to town" more accurately fits this era than any other, for the population growth of both blacks and whites in urban areas far outstripped that of the countryside. In fact, America became so urbanized that the Census Bureau redefined the term "urban" and created a new population category—Standard Metropolitan Statistical Area (SMSA)—in recognition of the fact that millions of Americans now lived in suburbs, those fringe areas around the great cities. Moreover, it was a time of increased mobility and technological change as machines came to do more and more work. Increased mobility and technology obviously affected the lives of citizens, but Americans were affected in other ways as well. As we shall see, black Americans, particularly the working-class, made increasing demands on national and state governments to end official racism and launched the first wave of the modern civil rights movement. And white women, though not yet organized, demanded rights for themselves, particularly the right to work, and entered the labor market by the millions. Such changes would clearly affect the position of blacks in the American economy.

It must be kept in mind that these changes occurred at the onset of unprecedented national prosperity. Indeed, scholars and government officials recognized and extolled the advent of the "affluent society" for many Americans. Fred Vinson, director of War Mobilization and Reconversion, is said to have wondered how Americans would fare "in the pleasant predicament of having to learn to live 50 percent better than they have ever lived before." Americans showed that they adjusted well indeed as they began to spend the billions of dollars they had saved during the war on refrigerators, cars, and other luxuries they had been denied during the wartime shortage. Spending for consumer goods was a major factor in preventing the kind of economic slump that had engulfed the United States after World War I. But all Americans did not fare so well. Those who lived in the "other America" experienced continued and deepening poverty.

Yet, this was also the era of the Cold War. National leaders claimed that Communists had infiltrated the fabric of American society and that the nation was doomed. Some of those, particularly Senator Joseph McCarthy of Wisconsin, used the threat of exposing citizens as Communist sympathizers to deny freedom of speech in the crucible of liberty. In the hysteria of the time, but in a legitimate response to aggression, American soldiers—black and white—rushed off to Korea to stop "Godless Communism," while at home American institutions, including government agencies, universities, and labor unions, worked energetically to purge themselves of supporters of that doctrine. The purges of alleged Communists from labor unions, as we shall see, was a low point of the American trade union movement. They had particularly adverse effect on black workers because the unions usually expelled those black and white leaders who had done most to recruit blacks in the first place.[1]

The immediate postwar period was a time of economic turmoil. Labor leaders were determined to improve their members' wages, which had been held in check by wage and price controls during the war. Prices, which had skyrocketed during the bickering between the Truman administration and Congress over new wage and price legislation, increased union leaders' resolve. They called several strikes, particularly in the steel, mining, and automobile industries, that brought substantial pay increases to their members. But these raises also led to increased inflation, and all workers had to pay higher prices, whether they had jobs or not.

In the immediate aftermath of the war, black workers experienced the layoffs and shorter work weeks that governmental planners and black spokesmen had foreseen. Most blacks who had entered the industrial labor market during World War II had done so by helping to build the vast piles of armaments, ships, and airplanes required to fight the war. But now the nation's return to a peacetime economy required fewer munitions, and black workers, generally the last to enter industry and thus lowest on the seniority rolls, were the first to be fired. Aside from the general decline in the size of the labor force required to do the work most of them performed, black workers also had to compete with the millions of returning white veterans eager to resume their peacetime jobs.

If one looks at the unemployment rate, it does not appear that blacks fared too poorly, since they had always had higher rates of unemployment than whites. And the jobs they held in 1947, for example, show that some real improvement in employment distribution had occurred during the war. But the fact is that in 1945 and 1946, the unemployment rate for blacks increased twice as fast as for whites.[2] And in 1947, the unemployment rate for blacks was 5.4 percent while 3.3 percent of white workers were out of jobs. The differential would continue to increase throughout this period, reaching a 2 : 1 ratio by 1954.[3] But there were apparent signs of hope for black workers. On the surface, one of the more important signs was the significant decline in the proportion of black agricultural workers. It seemed that at last the black

Table 6-1. Unemployment figures, by race and year

Year	White	Black	Black as % of White
1947	3.3	5.4	164
1948	3.2	5.2	163
1949	5.2	8.2	158
1950	4.6	8.5	185
1951	2.8	4.8	171
1952	2.4	4.6	192
1953	2.3	4.1	178
1954	4.5	8.9	198
1955	3.6	7.9	219

Source: Matthew A. Kessler, "Economic Status of Nonwhite Workers, 1955–62," Monthly Labor Review, 86 (July 1963), 782.

labor force was becoming truly industrial. During the 1940s, the proportion of American blacks who lived and worked in the South declined from three-fourths to two-thirds, and the black population became urban for the first time.

Three factors prevented the changing employment structure among blacks from improving their overall work and income status and laid the basis for conditions that would make the black unemployment rate run twice as high as that of whites. First, most black workers at the end of World War II could enter the

Table 6-2. Percentage of blacks employed in agriculture, by sex

Year	Males	Females
1890	60.8	44.0
1900	57.0	44.2
1910	56.1	52.2
1920	46.7	38.9
1930	40.7	27.0
1940	41.5	15.9
1950	23.7	8.9
1960	11.5	3.6

Source: Marion Hayes, "A Century of Change," Monthly Labor Review, 85 (Dec. 1962), 1363.

industrial market only in semi-skilled and unskilled categories, the very sectors that showed a decline in available positions. As late as 1950, for example, more than half of gainfully employed blacks worked as laborers or in domestic service, while only one-fifth of white workers were so occupied.[4] The second factor affecting black workers is that during the decade after the end of the war white workers left rural areas by the millions, adding to the competition for jobs blacks could hope to obtain in urban America. Moreover, during the 1950s the American economy suffered two major recessions, in 1953–1954 and 1957–1958, that influenced both the incomes and employment levels of black workers.[5]

The much ballyhooed great migration of blacks into northern urban areas during World War I palls when compared with the movement of Americans, black and white, into the post–World War II SMSAs. The trend was so strong, particularly among whites, that whereas 30 million Americans lived on farms in 1940, only 10 million, or approximately 5 percent of the national population, would do so by 1970. Seven million people left the land during the 1940s, to be followed by an additional 10 million in the 1950s.[6] The vast majority of white migrants settled in the growing suburbs, whereas the majority of blacks continued to settle in central cities, though more and more in the West as opposed to the North.[7] The migration rate for white workers was much higher than that of blacks. By 1960, approximately 10 percent of black men over age twenty-five had moved from their county of residence in 1955. Of white males of the same age category, 16 percent had moved.[8]

A survey of this migration shows that more highly skilled and better educated workers, those best able to take advantage of increases in operative and professional work, were most likely to migrate. That in part accounts for the higher migration rate among whites than among blacks. Further, racial discrimination made it unlikely that blacks would qualify for such employment despite education or training. The point is emphasized by the situation in the South. Though that region had industrialized con-

siderably during the war and the reconversion period, large numbers of well-educated blacks continued to move out, depriving it
of many of its most talented people. One-third of the college-
educated young men from four southern states—Alabama, Mississippi, Kentucky, and Tennessee—migrated north during the
1950s.[9] Those blacks who remained were greatly affected by the
loss of this leadership pool. Discrimination affected black mobility in other ways as well. Of prime importance was the impact of
discrimination on family income. Black families with relatively
high incomes almost always had more than one worker in the
household. During the 1950s, 80 percent of black families with
incomes between $6,000 and $10,000 and 90 percent of those with
incomes above $10,000 had at least two workers. The comparable
figures for white families in the same categories were 57 percent
and 64 percent, respectively.[10] The fact is that even if the head of
the household could find a better job elsewhere, it would be difficult for the family to move because the new earnings of this
member alone would probably not be high enough to maintain
the family's income level. Black families needed at least two new
jobs if they were to change locations.

The impact of changing conditions in the 1950s on black workers was not immediately evident. The Korean War, along with the
tremendous upsurge in consumer spending, greatly stimulated the
American economy and permitted large numbers of black workers to remain employed. In fact, black workers fared better in the
labor market during the 1950s than at any other time, including
World War II. In 1951, for example, wages and salaries of black
males averaged 64 percent of those of white males, compared
with 54 percent in 1947. Among black males in their early twenties, labor force participation also reached an all-time high; 93
percent of that age group were in the labor force in 1953, compared with an 85.6 percent participation rate in 1948. The unemployment picture also notes the relatively good times blacks enjoyed during the Korean War. Unfortunately, 1953 was the last
year in which black unemployment was low—4.4 percent for
black males and 3.7 percent for black females.[11]

Table 6-3. Rates of migration during 1955–60, of men, by education, race, and age, 1960 (in percents)

	Total, 25 years and over	25–29 years	30–34 years	35–44 years	45–64 years	65 years and over
Total, all men	15.7	31.8	24.5	17.3	10.0	8.4
No school years completed	7.5	13.3	13.5	11.2	7.5	5.9
Elementary: 1 to 4 years	9.1	17.5	16.2	12.8	7.9	6.7
5 to 8 years	10.8	23.2	18.6	13.4	8.4	8.1
High School: 1 to 3 years	14.7	25.6	20.2	14.6	9.9	9.8
4 years	17.5	28.6	21.8	16.3	11.1	10.3
College: 1 to 3 years	22.4	38.2	29.1	23.0	13.5	10.9
4 years or more	31.6	55.4	43.5	30.1	16.0	12.8
Nonwhite men	9.7	19.7	14.3	9.8	6.1	4.8
No school years completed	6.8	14.0	10.9	10.5	6.3	5.2
Elementary: 1 to 4 years	7.2	10.0	12.8	9.4	5.8	4.6
5 to 8 years	8.3	16.7	12.7	8.9	5.6	4.6
High School: 1 to 3 years	11.2	18.4	13.9	9.2	6.1	5.6
4 years	12.5	20.8	13.7	9.8	6.8	4.9
College: 1 to 3 years	15.6	26.5	18.6	12.2	8.1	5.3
4 years or more	20.8	33.2	26.8	19.0	11.1	5.0

Source: Dorothy K. Newman, "The Negro's Journey to the City," Monthly Labor Review, 88 (May 1965), 505.

In retrospect, however, black workers faced a dismal future. Not only did those in northern urban areas face increased competition from growing numbers of whites, but the number of jobs in their areas declined as well. As the white suburbs expanded, the number of plant openings in central cities, which were increasingly becoming black ghettoes, declined. Not only did corporate managers decide to build new plants in the suburbs, where the trained white personnel were moving, but numerous inner-city plants closed down as well, often throwing large numbers of blacks out of work. Plant closings left black workers with three choices. They could look for new jobs; they could pay high commuting costs and go to work in the suburbs; they could join the unemployment lines. In far too many cases, they fell into the last category.

Aside from the movement of plants to the suburbs, automation had a decided impact on black workers in both the North and the South. For example, the largest employment gains for northern black workers during the 1950s came in the semi-skilled occupations, blacks accounting for the entire increase in those categories of employment. Yet, such jobs tend to be in goods-producing and related industries, such as transportation, and are most readily affected by changes in the business cycle. They are also most affected by automation.[12] Thus, by 1962 the proportion of black workers employed in blue-collar jobs fell off to the rate that had prevailed in 1948. The clearest evidence of the impact of automation on southern blacks can be seen in agriculture. By the early 1960s, thousands of mechanical cotton pickers sucked from the bolls the white lint that large numbers of black hands previously had picked. This single technological development contributed significantly to the tremendous decline in the southern farm work force and added to the competition for jobs in cities of the North and South.[13]

The sad fact is that except for the relatively prosperous times of the Korean War period, a large proportion of the black population has lived in a virtual depression since World War II. Although their largest employment gains relative to whites since the Korean War have come in professional and business repair services (70 percent for blacks compared with 35 percent for whites),[14] in every statistical category—unemployment, occupations, earnings—black workers fell further behind whites by 1960 than they had been at the end of World War II. We have already seen that the unemployment differential between black and white workers was 2 to 1. But the impact of that differential is more impressive when we consider that black workers in the twenty-five to forty-four age group suffered even more unemployment than older groups, and at a rate three times that of whites of comparable ages. Those were the age groups of workers most likely to have dependent children. Thus the family as a whole suffered, laying the foundation for poor housing, poor education, and high unemployment for the next generation. Unemployment for black youths was so high that by 1960, more than 20 percent of black males and an even larger percentage of black females became adults without ever having had a job, despite fervent seeking, and with little hope of ever obtaining work. Aside from the economic consequences of joblessness, they bore the heavy psychological burden of being unable to find jobs in a work-oriented society (see Table 6.4).

When we consider that government unemployment figures reflect only those reporting that they are seeking work, it is clear that the problems of black working-class people were even graver than they appear in Table 6.4. Perhaps even more descriptive of the black work force is the large number of blacks who have become casual workers. Considerably more black workers were employed part time for economic reasons than the proportion of blacks in the work force. The trend toward casual employment of blacks—indeed, the maintenance of blacks as a surplus labor supply—developed in the first decades after the Civil War (see Chapter 1). It accelerated during the 1950s. Since the late 1940s, when such data first became available, statistics show that only one-half of the total number of blacks in the labor force worked full time year round. Two-thirds of whites had regular full-time work (see Table 6.5).[15]

Table 6-4. Unemployment by race, sex, and age for selected years since World War II

	White			Black		
	1948	1955	1962	1948	1955	1962
Males						
Over 14	3.1	3.4	4.6	4	8.2	11.0
14–19	8.3	9.6	12.3	7	13.2	20.7
20–24	5.8	6.3	8.0	10	11.2	14.6
25–34	2.4	2.5	3.8	4	8.0	10.5
35–44	1.9	2.4	3.1	4	7.4	8.6
45–54	2.2	2.8	3.5	3	5.8	8.3
55 and over	2.8	3.7	4.1	5	7.5	10.1
Females						
Over 14	3.4	3.9	5.5	5	7.5	11.1
14–19	6.9	8.2	11.5	10	16.2	28.2
20–24	3.6	4.5	7.7	8	11.4	18.2
25–34	3.2	3.8	5.4	6	9.1	11.5
35–44	2.3	3.4	4.5	3	4.9	8.9
45–54	2.5	2.9	3.7	2	4.6	7.1
55 and over	2.6	2.8	3.5	2	4.4	3.6

Source: Matthew A. Kessler, "Economic Status of Nonwhite Workers, 1955–62," Monthly Labor Review, 86 (July 1963), 782.

Table 6-5. Persons employed part time (1–35 hours) in nonagricultural industries, annual averages (in percentages)

Year	Males		Females	
	Nonwhites	Whites	Nonwhites	Whites
1950	14.8	8.3	31.1	21.5
1951	13.6	7.4	37.8	19.9
1953	9.4	7.2	30.0	19.1
1954	20.3	8.6	27.6	21.9
1955	15.3	9.5	35.2	27.7
1956	18.6	11.6	37.4	24.9
1957	18.1	12.0	36.4	25.8
1958	20.5	13.3	37.0	27.0
1959	21.8	14.7	38.6	29.6
1960	20.1	13.7	37.3	29.4
1961	19.0	12.8	35.9	28.1

Source: Alan B. Batchelder, "Decline in Relative Income of Negro Men," Quarterly Journal of Economics, 78 (Nov. 1964), 544.

Aside from the heavy representation of blacks among part-time workers, two other statistical areas highlight the casual nature of their employment. In keeping with the longstanding adage that blacks are last hired and first fired, black workers were much more likely than whites to be laid off when cutbacks occurred. In short, spells of unemployment for economic reasons were likely to be both more frequent and longer-lasting for blacks than for whites. Still first fired, blacks now faced the possibility of never being rehired. Moreover, black male workers generally have a shorter work life than whites. Numerous factors, including longer life expectancies for white men, contribute to this condition. But blacks also experienced a much higher disability rate than whites. In addition, black workers showed a much greater concentration in jobs in which age and physical disability were likely to shorten employment. Clearly, "the shorter length of a black man's working life has significant effect upon the security of his dependents."[16]

An unfortunate but understandable result of these obstacles to employment is that black workers increasingly drop out of the labor force. In 1910, a larger proportion of black than white males were in the labor force. Whites maintained approximately the same rate of participation over the next half century, but the black rate clearly declined.[17] Of black males aged twenty to sixty-four in 1954, an estimated 270,000 were outside the labor force. A decade later, the number in the same age group rose to 405,000.[18]

Interestingly, the decline in labor force participation among black men between 1945 and 1965 has not been followed by that of black women. Indeed, as Table 6.6 shows, except for teenagers, black women in every age category have increasingly entered the labor market. Even more striking is the increase in participation among white women. In fact, it is the growing number of white women workers that has brought so much recent attention to the role of working women—for, as we saw during the Civil War period, black women have always worked. The increasing white female work force has led to the development of day-care centers and other conveniences unheard of just a short while ago and has made it possible for women to have permanent jobs and not ne-

Table 6-6. Civilian labor force participation by age, sex, and race (in percentages)

	White			Nonwhite		
	1948	1955	1962	1948	1955	1962
Both sexes	56.7	57.1	56.1	63.5	61.9	60.0
Males (all ages)	84.2	82.8	78.6	84.8	81.8	76.4
14–19	50.7	45.6	40.8	58.4	48.8	38.4
20–24	84.4	86.5	86.5	85.6	89.7	89.3
25–34	96.0	97.8	97.4	95.3	95.8	95.3
35–44	98.0	98.3	97.9	97.2	96.2	94.6
45–54	95.9	96.7	96.0	94.6	94.2	92.2
55–64	89.6	88.4	86.7	88.4	83.1	81.5
Over 64	46.6	39.5	30.6	44.4	44.4	45.6
Females (all ages)	30.6	33.7	35.6	44.4	44.4	45.6
14–19	32.8	30.5	29.7	30.4	25.3	24.0
20–24	45.1	45.8	47.1	47.1	46.7	48.6
25–34	31.3	32.8	34.1	50.6	51.3	52.0
35–44	35.1	39.9	42.2	53.2	56.0	59.7
45–54	33.3	42.7	48.9	51.1	54.8	60.5
55–64	23.3	31.8	38.0	37.6	40.7	46.1
Over 64	8.6	10.5	9.8	17.3	12.1	12.2

Source: Matthew A. Kessler, "Economic Status of Nonwhite Workers, 1955–62," *Monthly Labor Review,* 86 (July 1963), 786.

glect dependent children. In the two decades after World War II, the increased participation of white women in the labor force exceeded that of black women by two to one. By 1960, 42 percent of all black women over fourteen years of age were in the labor force, compared to 34 percent of white women. The trend among white women was to continue; by 1970 an equal percentage of black and white women—40 percent—worked full time.[19]

Analysis of the occupations and earnings of black and white women helps us to understand the differences in family income between blacks and whites and highlights even more the serious decline in the income of black males. Such analysis also points up the general discrimination against women in American society as well. Despite the large number of black women still employed as domestics, their occupational distribution has improved considerably since World War II, while that of white women has remained relatively unchanged. By 1970, more than four times as many black women held clerical and sales jobs as had been in those occupations in 1950, for example. Moreover, the number of black professional women doubled during the same period, while the proportion of those employed in agriculture declined to less than 1 percent.[20]

In terms of earnings, data show that while the income of black men declined relative to whites in the decades after World War II, the gap between the earnings of black and white women narrowed considerably. And compared to black men, the earnings of black women increased relative to those of whites with increased education. By 1970, black women with college or higher education earned more than white women with the same education (see Table 6.7). But before we make too much of this, it must be emphasized that black educated women earned more than white women as a group, not as individuals. For example, elementary and secondary schools employ 54 percent of all professional black women and 39 percent of all professional white women. Of this group, black women earned an average of $7,311 in 1970, compared to $5,902 for white women. The most important single reason for the differential is that married black women, because of the low earnings of black men, are more likely to remain continuously in the work force than are white women so as to provide essential family income. Accordingly, as a group, black women have longer years of service in relatively well-paying professional jobs.[21]

Though black women, much more than black men, have approached parity with their white counterparts in receiving equal pay for the same work, black women are much more likely to hold lower-paying jobs. In 1960, when one in eight employed women was black, black women made up one-sixth of low wage earners. Black men fared even worse. One quarter of all black men were low wage earners, while only one of twelve nonfarm workers was black.[22] Blacks thus had extremely low annual fam-

Table 6-7. Income of working women over age 25, by race and education

Years of school	1950			1960			1970		
	White	Nonwhite	Percent nonwhite/ white	White	Nonwhite	Percent nonwhite/ white	White	Nonwhite	Percent nonwhite/ white
0–7	$ 710	$ 490	69	$1090	$ 732	67	$1440	$1290	90
8	925	734	80	1180	970	82	1815	1605	88
9–11	1110	807	73	1680	1196	71	2388	2393	100
12	1590	1093	69	2220	1732	78	3380	3491	103
13–15	1680	1247	74	2420	2166	90	3616	4558	126
16 or more	2320	2103	91	3770	3740	99	5995	7744	129

Source: Alan L. Sorkin, "Education, Occupation and Income of Nonwhite Women," The Journal of Negro Education, 41 (Fall 1972), 348.

Table 6-8. Total money income of families by race since World War II

Family income, All classes	1948 White	1948 Nonwhite	1955 White	1955 Nonwhite	1961 White	1961 Nonwhite
Under $3,000	42.6	78.1	25.7	57.3	18.6	47.5
$3,000–$4,999	35.2	16.3	30.3	28.3	19.4	24.4
$5,000–$9,999	19.1	5.3	36.6	13.7	44.7	22.8
$10,000 and up	3.1	.4	6.5	.6	17.1	5.6
Median income	$3,310	$1,768	$4,605	$2,549	$5,981	$3,191

Source: Matthew A. Kessler, "Economic Status of Nonwhite Workers, 1955–62," Monthly Labor Review, 86 (July 1963), 787.

ily incomes and were greatly overrepresented among the working poor. Median family income was higher for whites in 1948 than for blacks in 1961.

Depression conditions for blacks developed despite the best efforts of workers and leaders to maintain the gains of World War II. The fact is that white organized labor was too busy with other matters to give much attention to efforts to find work for displaced blacks. The unions had suffered a decline in public support after the rash of strikes that followed the war and were in no mood to risk what little influence that remained on what many considered the foolish idea of fighting for the rights of blacks. Moreover, organized labor was under pressure from another front as well. Not only did public sentiment turn against unions after the war, but the government did as well. In June 1947, Congress passed the Taft-Hartley Act, which placed numerous restrictions on unions, while several southern states enacted right-to-work laws. The immediate result was to destroy the southern organization drives that both the AFL and the CIO had launched shortly after the end of the war.[23] Feeling the heat of the government, particularly the inquiries of the House Committee on Un-American Activities (HUAC), organized labor also vigorously fought communism in all its manifestations. Ironically, and of grave importance for the future of blacks, the CIO joined the always more conservative AFL in Red baiting and in moving away from its sustained and energetic support of black workers.[24]

The union activities probably did not directly affect the ability of blacks to get jobs, but they did stifle black leadership and dampen hopes. In 1947, for example, the CIO sent Willard S. Townsend, a black member of its Committee Against Racial Discrimination, to North Carolina in an effort to take over a local of the United Tobacco Workers that had, under the leadership of a black woman, Miranda Smith, won a strike against the R. J. Reynolds Tobacco Company. The CIO claimed that the leaders of the local were Communists and sent in Townsend and other black organizers to save the American labor movement. The result was that in a contested election the workers refused to endorse any organization, leaving themselves without a recognized agency to bargain with the huge corporation. The CIO attacked other allegedly Communist-dominated unions as well. At its meeting in 1949, the CIO expelled eleven unions with a combined membership of over one million. The expelled unions included the International Mine, Mill and Smelter Workers; the Food, Tobacco, Agricultural and Allied Workers; and the National Union of Marine Cooks and Stewards,[25] all known to be vigorous in organizing blacks. Surprisingly, the CIO did not expel the United Packing House Workers of America, a union that continued to chide CIO leadership on its Red baiting but remained within the organization.

In addition to their concern with organized labor's efforts to improve their employment opportunities, blacks stepped up their activities in the postwar decades to increase their representation in union leadership. Southern blacks in Birmingham, Alabama, took up arms in an unsuccessful attempt to prevent the Steel Workers Organizing Committee from ousting Hosea Hudson as head of Local 2815 in 1947.[26] Blacks were particularly incensed when CIO Red baiting led to the deportation in 1951 of Ferdinand C. Smith, a long-time militant leader of the National Maritime Union. Black workers wanted more than simply a black person in a leadership position. They wanted strong men who could speak at the highest level about the way union policy kept black workers in the meanest, most back-breaking jobs, requiring them to do the hardest work. Charles Denby, an assembly line worker in the

Detroit automobile plants, has written vividly and passionately about the jobs required of blacks, emphasizing the monotony of assembly lines and pointing out that at the end of a day he was often too tired to shower. Denby and others claimed that UAW leaders did nothing to change their condition or to combat management's incessant speedups.[27]

Ironically, the UAW, which was generally known for its advanced position on racial matters, was a target for militant black unionists, who demanded black representation at the union's national level. As early as 1939, black delegates to UAW conventions had called for the election of blacks to leadership positions. They even demanded that the UAW create a special vice presidency for blacks, and for expansion of the national staff to include more black members. All factions of the white leadership opposed a special vice presidency, Walter Reuther terming it "racism in reverse." UAW officials claimed that the union was a big, democratic organization which elected its leaders on the basis of ability, without regard to race. But in fact, though blacks held various offices in the shops and at the local level, the first black vice president was elected only in 1962.[28]

Black workers were in no mood to wait for white labor leaders to give them the right to participate in the union movement. In 1950 black unionists, of whom UAW members were prominent, met in Chicago to discuss ways of improving the situation of black workers, both inside and outside unions. In a subsequent meeting the next year, they founded the National Negro Labor Council (NNLC). William R. Hood, recording secretary of Local 600, the largest black local in the UAW, became president of the NNLC and led the organization in pressuring organized white labor and company managements alike on behalf of blacks. The NNLC participated in strikes, boycotts, and job training programs, and continually demanded black representation in the high councils of organized labor. The Chicago Negro Labor Council took a leading role in helping to galvanize public support for a strike against the International Harvester Company in 1952, and the national group was heavily involved in a strike of sugar cane workers in Louisiana in the fall of 1953.[29] The members of the NNLC took increased interest in gaining representation in the national union movement after George Meany and Walter Reuther became presidents of the AFL and CIO, respectively, in 1952, and stepped up discussions of merging the two organizations.

The NNLC faced stiff opposition from both white organized labor and the government. Walter Reuther railed against that "Communist-dominated, dual unionist organization," while the government called the NNLC before the Subversive Activities Control Board. HUAC even issued a special pamphlet, "The American Negro in the Communist Party," in which it condemned the NNLC as detrimental to the interests of black workers. When called to defend itself before the subversives board in 1955, the NNLC was a broke organization, unable to raise money for the hearings. One member borrowed money to buy a ticket to Washington and went before the board to announce that the NNLC had ceased its work.[30]

The early 1950s, then, were troubled times for the relationship between blacks and the general organized labor movement as the two groups looked in different directions for allies to help them improve their lives. CIO leaders became increasingly convinced that merger with the AFL was the key to its survival. Accordingly, the CIO deemphasized those issues—one of which was the aggressive organizing of black workers—that had most sharply divided it from the AFL. For their part, black people in general began to emphasize government support to improve their legal status. Good relations between black organizations and the CIO never wholly ceased, but as one scholar has put it, by the time of the AFL-CIO merger in 1955 "there was little save nostalgia to put in the way of the CIO's capitulation" to the more conservative views of the AFL.[31]

Black workers viewed the AFL-CIO merger with alarm. In the first place, 75 percent of the positions on the executive council went to the AFL, as did the presidency of the new organization. And no black unionist could overlook the insult when the AFL-

CIO admitted to membership the Brotherhood of Locomotive Firemen and the Brotherhood of Railroad Trainmen, both of which had constitutional bars against membership for blacks. Blacks were hardly mollified by the election of A. Philip Randolph and Willard S. Townsend to the executive council. Indeed, Randolph was the least content of all, and used his seat on the council to raise embarrassing questions about AFL-CIO actions. Randolph's opposition to the AFL-CIO's countenancing of segregated locals led to heated exchanges with George Meany, as the two men maintained an uneasy truce.

AFL-CIO activities, such as siding against blacks in the courts or before civil rights agencies in cases of alleged union discrimination, increasingly divided black and white unionists. Following the convention of 1959, a group of blacks founded the Negro American Labor Council under Randolph's leadership. Randolph, a man who had dedicated his life to building a coalition between black and white progressives, had been burned so many times by whites that in 1959–1960 he was again talking about creating an all-black organization that would strive to "secure membership of Negro workers in the unions and employment and promotion on the job as well as participation in the executive, administrative and staff areas of the unions."[32] Randolph's insistence that only blacks could lead efforts to accomplish these goals echoed his position on the participation of whites in the March on Washington Movement in 1941.

At this point, Randolph was not alone in attacking the racial policies of organized labor, as the NAACP in particular increasingly attacked discriminating unions. No organization, not even the UAW or the ILGWU, escaped the NAACP's attacks when its officials considered their comments justified.[33] The black press also joined the condemnation of union discrimination. The Pittsburgh *Courier* carried a long denunciation of the Jewish Labor Committee and the ILGWU in late 1959, and though it went further than some black spokesmen wished, it symbolized the deteriorating relationship between blacks and whites in the labor movement.[34] White leaders like Meany and Reuther rushed to condemn both the activities of the NAACP and editorials in the black press, and Charles Zimmerman, a leading Jewish attorney and labor leader, resigned from the NAACP's Legal Defense Fund.[35] There was a tempest in the Negro-labor alliance.

But tempest is not destruction, and on many issues blacks and organized labor could still cooperate. At about the time of the AFL-CIO merger, the U.S. government was on the verge of preparing the way for blacks to launch an all-out assault on official racism. For several years NAACP attorneys, under the leadership of Thurgood Marshall, had been pleading with federal courts to declare segregated schools a violation of the Constitution, which granted equal protection to the rights of all citizens. The cases eventually went to the Supreme Court, which heard extensive argumentation on the negative impact of racial segregation on the life chances of black people. On May 17, 1954, the Court handed down a unanimous decision in the case of *Brown* v. *Board of Education of Topeka, Kansas.* Written by Chief Justice Earl Warren, the decision affirmed that separate but equal educational systems violated the U.S. Constitution. The Court, in a subsequent decision, ordered the states to dismantle their segregated schools with "all deliberate speed."

The Court's decision was narrow, embracing only public education, and anyone who reads the daily newspapers even in the 1980s is aware of how long and hard school districts have deliberated. But in fact the Court's decision in *Brown* had a tremendous psychological impact on blacks and made possible assaults on economic discrimination. Unlike their response to obscure presidential executive orders such as 8802, which was itself of questionable constitutionality, few Americans were likely to ignore a judgment of the Supreme Court. In the eyes of many blacks, the NAACP's appeal to the Supreme Court had been like Joshua fighting the Battle of Jericho, and in the words of the spiritual, "the walls come tumbling down." Little did they know in 1954 and 1955 how many walls there were in the edifice of American racism.

Lawyers are hardly workers, and it is impossible to claim the

Brown decision as a victory of working-class blacks, even though they would profit from it. But the first major community action that followed the Court's decision in *Brown* was clearly a working-class movement. On December 1, 1955, Rosa Parks, a seamstress in a Montgomery, Alabama, department store, sat down on a city bus on her way home from work—in a section reserved for whites under the segregationist laws that had existed in Alabama for decades. To make matters worse, she refused to move when ordered to do so by the driver of the Montgomery City Line bus, one of those men in whom custom, tradition, and a negligent state government had vested virtual police powers. When it came to black passengers, a bus was like a ship on the high seas, and the white driver was the captain with all the powers thereof.

Rosa Parks was not the first black person in Montgomery to refuse to obey segregationist orders on a bus, but the quiet manner in which she confronted the driver, as well as her standing in the community, made her a person around whom blacks of the city could rally and put into action long dormant plans to end discrimination in transportation in that city. The fact that black community leaders had planned to protest segregation on the buses is not to imply that Mrs. Parks's action was prearranged. To say that would distort the truth and, in a sense, detract from the human drama that developed in Montgomery late in 1955 and continued throughout 1956. In fact, Mrs. Parks explained that she had remained in her seat because she was tired. "My foots was tired," she said later, "but my soul is rested."

The simple fact that Mrs. Parks was a seamstress who worked hard all day was not enough to make the Montgomery Bus Boycott, as subsequent events were to be called, a working-class movement. Nor was the demand that the company hire blacks as bus drivers of major importance. But when one considers that 75 percent of the passengers in Montgomery were black men and women who rode the buses to and from work, then the picture becomes clearer. Moreover, within hours after Mrs. Parks's arrest, it was Edgar D. Nixon, a working sleeping car porter and a vice president of the Brotherhood of Sleeping Car Porters, who showed up at the jail to bail her out, and it was Nixon who spent much of the night on the telephone lining up the support of various well-placed blacks to insure that a steering committee would be ready to move into action at dawn the next morning. When Nixon called the vested black leadership, the head of the NAACP, for example, informed him that he would have to write to NAACP headquarters in New York before committing that organization to a boycott of segregated buses in Montgomery. In the tradition of the militant BSCP, and true to the spirit of his idol, A. Philip Randolph, Nixon informed the local NAACP leader that he did not have time to wait for a letter from New York—indeed, a telephone call would take too much time. Black working-class people in Montgomery had waited long enough, and now was the time to act.[36]

Aside from the extreme importance of galvanizing the black community to stand together to signal that they would no longer endure such indignities as those common on city buses (and pay for the privilege of being abused), the Montgomery Bus Boycott is the event that introduced Martin Luther King, Jr., as a national black leader. Soon after the boycott began, its leaders determined that they needed a formal organization to press the demands of the walking people. Accordingly, they formed the Montgomery Improvement Association (MIA). Everyone involved in the discussion leading to the creation of the MIA understood that Nixon, who had the greatest political power among blacks in the city, would choose the leader. Nixon had heard Martin Luther King, Jr., speak shortly before the arrest of Rosa Parks and had told his friend, Rufus Lewis, that King was the man to mobilize Montgomery blacks. Nixon had told Lewis that he was going to "hang King to a star." He was convinced that King had not been in Montgomery long enough either to antagonize a sizeable portion of the black population or to "get a free suit" from the white power structure. Moreover, King was still young. If the boycott backfired, the leader should be someone who could move on with ease.[37]

The choice of King was superb, for this brilliant, articulate man convinced the blacks of Montgomery that theirs was a holy cause that could result only in victory. His use of rhetoric and oratory, and his personal aura of confidence and incorruptibility, instilled in all a sense of pride and renewed wavering spirits. Indeed, the women of the movement came to call him "Little Lord Jesus," the Son of God returned to lead his children into the promised land. But the Montgomery Bus Boycott involved more than leadership. Although the MIA organized a car pool system that city officials claimed worked with military precision, numerous working-class blacks made severe sacrifices for the movement. Many lost their jobs for participating in the boycott, while thousands of others walked long distances to work as the buses rumbled by empty. One elderly woman disdained an offer of a ride in a car, and as she shuffled on, she informed the driver that she was walking for her children and grandchildren so that in the future they could ride in dignity. The Montgomery Bus Boycott touched the spirits of the people.

In addition to enlisting the support of the people themselves, working-class connections were crucial in helping to raise badly needed funds to carry on the boycott. Ed Nixon, a longtime operator in the labor movement, convinced numerous national white unions to provide money for the MIA. His success raises an important question about the motives of white union leaders. For decades, leaders of the major unions had said that they could not hire more black organizers and other union officials because they did not have the funds and because southern rank and file members would object. Even at the time of the Montgomery Bus Boycott, the unions were still refusing to bring blacks into leadership positions. It seems probable that white rank and file members would have objected just as much to having their money donated to a black assault on the sacred racial relations in the South. It is likely that white union leaders themselves had no desire to share leadership and power with blacks and used the alleged racism of white southern members as an excuse.

During the long year that the Montgomery Bus Boycott dragged

on, it became national and international news. And despite the
heroic actions of the people in the streets, the MIA actually won
because of NAACP attorneys who argued successfully before the
Supreme Court that the Montgomery segregation law was unconstitutional. The decision came down on the very day that a
Montgomery judge upheld the city's request for an injunction out-
lawing the boycott. Black workers had banded together in Montgomery in the face of bombings and intimidation, and in so doing
they had created a watershed in the struggle to establish their
rights. And though they did not understand that black workers
needed more than equality to survive, they had identified a man
who seemed able to lead them to freedom. It is common to recall
what Martin Luther King did for Montgomery, but E. D. Nixon
is perhaps right in suggesting that we ought to look at the Montgomery Bus Boycott again and to reflect on what the working-
class people of Montgomery did for King.[38]

Taken together, the Supreme Court decision in *Brown* and the
Montgomery Bus Boycott signaled the arrival of a new age in the
relations between blacks and whites in the United States. After
the *Brown* decision, for the first time in the twentieth century,
blacks and whites opposed to racial discrimination had the law
on their side. The federal government had come down on the side
of establishing an equitable society and it seemed that the people, in Montgomery at least, were willing and ready to push toward its conclusion. As the evidence cited above clearly shows,
blacks generally were still wretched at the end of the 1950s. But
the victory in Montgomery and the national attention that had
come to King and his new organization, the Southern Christian
Leadership Conference (SCLC), imbued many with hope that
the future would be considerably better for black workers and
enabled many to determine that the future must be now, and not
at some far-off time. The 1950s ended with black people, significantly in the South, no longer willing to wait for "pie in the sky,
by and by."

7

Hope and Illusions of Progress

The sanctity of private property takes second place to the sanctity of the human personality. It falls to the Negro to reassert this priority of values, because our ancestors were transformed from human personalities into private property. It falls to us to demand full employment and to put automation at the service of human needs, not at the service of profits.

A. PHILIP RANDOLPH, 1963

Until justice is blind, until education is unaware of race, until opportunity is unconcerned with the color of men's skins, emancipation will be a proclamation but not a fact.

LYNDON B. JOHNSON, 1963

The decade of the 1960s was without doubt one of the most exciting periods in the history of the United States. It was a decade that began with the youngest man ever elected President replacing the oldest man who ever held that job, and it seemed that the new young President would infuse the nation with his own unlimited vigor. It mattered not to most Americans that John F. Kennedy continued—and even stepped up—the Cold War, or that he was almost universally unsuccessful in dealing with Congress. He generated excitement and gave the nation a sense of movement, and the American people loved it. They even applauded his monumental blunders like the ill-fated invasion of Cuba at the Bay of Pigs, and though they shuddered at the prospect of world destruction in an atomic holocaust during the Cuban Missile Crisis of 1962, they admired the President's courage and de-

termination in those trying days and showered him with adula-
tion when the crisis had passed. When an assassin's bullet ended
Kennedy's life just before Thanksgiving in 1963, the nation
wrapped him in martyrdom and vowed to move on toward the
new world he had envisioned.

Black Americans were no less excited about the prospects of
the time and, indeed, they held the key to what would make the
1960s the people's decade. Even before Kennedy became President, young blacks throughout the South had begun what would
become the Civil Rights Movement.[1] They felt that they were at
last on the verge of "facing the rising sun of a new day begun,"
of which the poet and civil rights leader James Weldon Johnson
had prophesied decades before in a poem commonly called the
"Negro National Anthem." Before the decade was over, the Civil
Rights Movement would test the fiber of the American nation as
no other domestic event had done, with the possible exception of
the Civil War, since Thomas Jefferson handed out his draft of the
Declaration of Independence in 1776.

The times were filled with possibilities. Despite growing evidence of distrust between black and white unionists, there seemed
to be a chance that a powerful, forward-looking alliance would
develop between blacks and white organized workers. Numerous
progressive white labor leaders joined with blacks in the Civil
Rights Movement, clasping hands and chiming "We Shall Overcome." But appearances did not wholly represent reality. Be-
neath the placid surface lay the determination of black unionists
to end racism and tokenism in the union movement.

Like so many other periods that opened with hope and expec-
tation for blacks, the 1960s would see those hopes dashed in a
rash of murders, deceit, war, and the benign neglect of the Nixon
White House. As we shall see, by the end of the decade the occupational diversity of blacks remained remarkably unchanged from
what it had been at the end of World War II. To be sure, a few
fortunate blacks, through a combination of luck and talent, had
moved into prestigious positions, some sitting at the highest levels of American government. Observers rhapsodized about how

blacks "made very dramatic gains" in employment between 1959 and 1969, and emphasized that the number of black professionals and technicians doubled during that period from slightly over 250,000 to more than 580,000. They were even more ecstatic in pointing out that the number of black officials and managers had increased by 236 percent. Indeed, 18.8 percent of all black workers held high-status jobs by 1969.[2] But the masses were still over-represented in low-paying jobs and on unemployment rolls, they still occupied wretched housing units, and the income gap between white and black families had widened. The only real change was that for the first time, at least in law, the United States government had become aggressively anti-racist.

The actions of working-class blacks had been directly responsible for the legislation overturning states' rights to practice racial discrimination. Several major organizations and exceptional individuals made outstanding contributions to efforts to rid the nation of racism. But in the end, the sacrifices and sufferings of working-class black people in both rural and urban areas throughout the South, people whose names we will never know, stirred the consciousness of the nation and made it possible for the Civil Rights Movement to succeed. All the proclamations, negotiations, and pleas of black spokesmen would have been in vain had not the masses poured into the streets to demonstrate to white Americans that black people were determined to have equal rights.

The Civil Rights Movement lasted a brief few years; no more than a half decade passed between the sit-in at Woolworth's in Greensboro, North Carolina, in 1960 and the explosion of violence in Watts, California, in 1965. But between those two events, one beginning the Civil Rights Movement and the other emphatically showing that it was over, thousands of blacks (and liberal whites, too) waged an unrelenting nonviolent war against legal discrimination. Determined that "we shall overcome," these people, particularly the young, vowed that "before I'll be a slave, I'll be buried in my grave, and go home to my Lord and be free." Little did they know how prophetic the word grave would be, as far too many black people died in the wave of violence with which white Americans generally greeted this unarmed crusade for freedom. Yet, despite the violence, intimidation, loss of jobs, and threats of starvation, the working people of the South persevered, and with the help of television, which brought the sight of anti-civil rights violence vividly into the living rooms of American families, American public opinion on racial discrimination slowly began to change. Civil rights forces, under the leadership of black unionists in the Negro American Labor Council (NALC), organized a massive march on Washington in the summer of 1963 which attracted more than 300,000 participants and became one of the biggest media events of recent times. Martin Luther King, Jr., mesmerized the assembled thousands at the foot of the Lincoln Memorial, and millions of others who watched television, with his talk about his dream for America. It seemed for a brief period that day that the time was soon to come when Americans would "let freedom ring" for all the nation's citizens from Stone Mountain in Georgia to Mt. St. Helens in Washington State.

Congress seemed no less mesmerized than the common citizenry. Early the next spring, the House of Representatives passed by a wide margin the most far-reaching civil rights bill in the history of the United States. Even more amazing, for the first time in its history the Senate voted cloture to end a filibuster against a civil rights measure and passed the bill as well. This omnibus bill, which wiped out discrimination based on race, sex, or national origin, became law when President Lyndon B. Johnson signed the Civil Rights Act with much fanfare on July 2, 1964. Indeed, it seemed that there was no limit to which the nation would not go in order to create equality for all. Congress hastily followed the Civil Rights Act with the Voting Rights Act of 1965, a measure that authorized the federal government to protect the right of all citizens to vote, even in state elections. The Justice Department now even had power to send federal registrars into states so as to insure that everyone had free and equal access to the ballot. Taken together, these acts brought absolute success to the Civil Rights Movement. After 1965, there was no enforceable law anywhere in the land that discriminated against individuals on the basis of race. Legally, America was a wholly egalitarian society. But what had really changed?

Nothing! That seems to have been the message from California in August 1965 when Watts, a black Los Angeles ghetto, erupted in violence and destruction. The Civil Rights Movement had fulfilled the goals of generations of black leaders—*de jure* discrimination had been wiped out. But the movement had not affected the lives of the people, despite the fact that just two months before Watts, President Johnson had used a commencement address at Howard University, entitled "To Fulfill These Rights," to promise that his administration would make every effort to eliminate the suffering and discrimination of poverty and racism. The sad fact is that by the summer of 1965 polls showed that whites were fed up with efforts to improve conditions for blacks—and Johnson loved the polls—and the President himself was becoming more and more involved in the war in Viet Nam. Time had run out for blacks. Members of the Student Nonviolent Coordinating Committee (SNCC) turned to talk of "Black Power," young blacks in California organized the Black Panther Party, and in city after city in the North, signs emerged that indicated troubled times for the United States on the question of race.

Few people recognized the dangers more clearly than Martin Luther King, who had received the Nobel Prize for Peace because of his efforts to end official racism in America. Even before passage of the Voting Rights Act, he had begun to warn that the real problem in America lay in the inability of large numbers of people to provide adequate food, shelter, and clothing for themselves and their families. Moreover, he recognized that the problem was much more severe in the ghettos of the North than in the South. A man of great insight, King had begun to tell Americans that the nation could not afford both a war in Viet Nam and a domestic "War on Poverty." The violence in Watts broke King's heart, but unlike President Johnson's expression of surprise, the sad and beleaguered civil rights leader understood the conditions that had produced the outbreak he so deeply abhorred. His efforts to improve the conditions of urban workers would continue and would lead to his own violent death at a rundown Memphis motel in 1968.[3]

The clearest evidence that during the 1960s black workers faced a difficult future lay in housing and neighborhood segregation. Ghettos were nothing new in America but, as the National Advisory Commission on Civil Disorders reported after the urban disturbances of 1967, segregation worsened as the twentieth century wore on.[4] When whites continued to move to the suburbs, those areas ceased being only bedroom communities as more and more companies located there at the expense of jobs in the central cities. During the 1960s, 2.6 million whites left the central cities of the fifteen largest metropolitan areas and settled in the suburbs; in the same decade, the black population of the central cities increased by 3.1 million.[5] A survey by the *New York Times* found that during the 1960s the suburbs of the great American cities gained 3,000,000 jobs, an increase of 44 percent, while the central cities suffered a decline of 836,000 jobs.[6]

Segregated housing affected black workers in several ways. Such housing usually existed in the most rundown areas of the central cities, forcing blacks to live in substandard housing for which they were required to pay high rents. High rents and low incomes led to overcrowding and to associated social problems. Nor could blacks in such neighborhoods hope to take advantage of the new jobs opening up in the suburbs and thus move to new homes. Few ghetto blacks owned automobiles and thus could not afford to travel to the jobs. But perhaps more important, their distance from the jobs decreased significantly their information regarding new job openings. Suburban job announcements rarely appeared in ghettos, and blacks had little access to union newsletters and other methods of advertisement. Moreover, blacks suffered the subtle discrimination of suburban employers reluctant to hire blacks for fear of being accused of bringing blacks into white neighborhoods.[7] Sometimes discrimination was more than subtle as blacks faced actual physical violence by seeking work in white neighborhoods. One of the tragedies of efforts to find housing and employment for blacks in the Chicago suburbs was the death by beating of seventeen-year-old Jerome Huey on a Cicero streetcorner in the summer of 1966.[8]

One result of housing segregation and discrimination was the development of what the U.S. Census Bureau officially defined as "poverty neighborhoods" during the 1960s. To be sure, millions of whites lived in such neighborhoods, but an exceptional proportion of the residents were black. Further, of the black population as a whole, the proportion of those living in poverty neighborhoods far exceeded that of the white population. In 1967, 11.6 million people lived in such neighborhoods—approximately 9 percent of the nation's population over sixteen years of age and 16 percent of the total population of the metropolitan areas. But while blacks made up about 10.6 percent of the national population, more than 4.5 million blacks lived in poverty neighborhoods, about 40 percent of the total. The impact of poverty on the black population as a whole is manifest when we consider that half of all urban blacks lived in officially designated poverty neighborhoods during the heyday of the War on Poverty.[9]

Residents of poverty neighborhoods experienced a plethora of economic and social problems that stemmed, for the most part, from the sorry employment conditions under which they lived. Though unemployment was the most severe problem, workers in those neighborhoods also endured short working hours in low-paying, low-status jobs and exhibited weak labor force participation. In fact, 15.3 percent of all unemployed Americans in 1967 lived in poverty neighborhoods compared to only 8.6 percent of the labor force. Among the unemployed, most were men and women in the prime working ages of twenty-four to fifty-five, those most likely to have dependent children. Prime-age men who lived in poverty areas were three times as likely to be unemployed as men of the same ages in other urban neighborhoods.[10] Despite the relative prosperity of the 1960s, unemployment in the poverty areas was higher than it had been for the overall population at any time since the Great Depression of the 1930s.[11]

Besides being unemployed for extended periods, black residents of poverty areas were concentrated in low-status, low-

paying jobs. For example, 57 percent of poverty area people who
had jobs in 1967 worked in semiskilled, unskilled, and service occupations; fewer than one-third had white-collar jobs. Large
numbers of poverty area individuals worked in blue-collar manufacturing, a sector of the economy marked by decreasing employment and sharp reactions to cyclical changes in the years since
World War II.[12]

In significant ways, the concept of poverty neighborhoods makes
sense only in regard to whites, for black urban residents were
likely to be poor regardless of where they lived. During the 1960s,
blacks in nonpoverty areas had an unemployment rate higher
than that of white workers who lived in poverty neighborhoods.
During the relatively good employment situation of the mid-
1960s, 6 percent of poverty area whites were unemployed compared with 7.2 percent of blacks who lived in non-poverty areas.
The impact of joblessness on black families is heightened even
more, however, when we consider that black men were even
more likely to be out of work than black women. Analysts theo-
rize that availability of domestic service jobs helped to mitigate somewhat the unemployment situation of black women.[13]
But such women were likely to have low incomes, increasing the
likelihood that they would become heads of households with dependent children. In 1969, eight out of every ten poor black families had dependent children under eighteen. In that same year, 90
percent of black children in families with incomes of $7,000 or
more lived with both parents. But when incomes fell below
$3,000, only about 25 percent of black children lived with both
parents.[14] It is essential, in order to understand the importance of
poverty in American life, to keep in mind that 40 percent of families with incomes below the poverty mark had fully employed
family heads, and that among blacks five out of six such families
were headed by males.[15] We have heard enough from welfare
critics who argue that the poor are people who are too lazy to
work or black families deserted by the male head.

The seeming hopelessness of the employment situation in the
cities is highlighted by the unconcern of employers for the suffer-

Table 7-1. Unemployed persons by race, sex, and age, 1967

| | Urban poverty neighborhoods | | | | Other urban neighborhoods | | | |
| | White | | Nonwhite | | White | | Nonwhite | |
	Thousands of persons	Unemployment rate	Thousands of persons	Unemployment rate	Thousands of persons	Unemployment rate	Thousands of persons	Unemployment rate
Total	206	5.3	248	8.9	1087	3.2	169	6.1
Men	124	5.0	126	8.0	562	2.6	79	4.9
16–19 years	30	17.2	44	31.4	170	11.6	31	28.5
20–24 years	19	6.5	17	9.1	91	4.3	13	6.7
25 years and over	74	3.7	65	5.2	300	1.7	34	2.6
25–54 years	56	3.7	52	5.3	205	1.4	30	2.7
55 years and over	18	3.8	13	5.1	95	2.5	4	2.5
Women	82	5.7	122	10.1	526	4.3	90	7.6
16–19 years	17	12.3	42	37.2	139	10.8	23	25.0
20–24 years	15	7.0	22	14.5	89	5.0	18	10.1
25 years and over	50	4.6	58	6.2	298	3.3	49	5.4
25–54 years	41	5.1	53	7.0	246	3.5	41	5.4
55 years and over	9	3.2	5	2.8	52	2.5	8	4.9

Source: Paul M. Ryscavage and Hazel M. Willacy, "Employment of Nation's Urban Poor," Monthly Labor Review, 91 (Aug. 1968), 17.

155

ing and squalor around them. Even in the aftermath of the de-
structive urban violence during the late 1960s, surveys of major
employers report that they did not view unemployment as a major problem in urban America. In fact, employers were more concerned about pollution than they were about unemployment, 27
percent of those interviewed calling unemployment "not serious."
The National Advisory Commission on Civil Disorders found that
though employers generally agreed that the private sector of the
economy had a social responsibility to provide jobs for minority
group members, they were "less likely than other occupational
groups to rate unemployment as a serious problem."[16]

As is often the case, blacks turned to the federal government
to take the lead in removing racial discrimination in employment.
As you will recall, President Roosevelt had taken the first timid
step toward governmental intervention in job discrimination when
he issued Executive Order 8802 and created the Fair Employment
Practice Committee (FEPC) in 1941. A number of presidential
orders against discrimination had followed Roosevelt's action,
mainly affecting jobs involving government contracts. Some administrations, particularly Democratic ones, had paid vigorous
lip service to efforts to outlaw discrimination.[17]

Shortly after beginning in 1961, the Kennedy administration,
largely through the Equal Employment Opportunity Commission
(EEOC) and some department heads, moved vigorously against
discrimination. The EEOC made a major breakthrough in May
when Lockheed, the giant aircraft manufacturer, agreed to take
steps to hire and upgrade blacks. Perhaps more important, the
company also promised to use its resources to make blacks aware
of opportunities in the industry generally, particularly those at
Lockheed. Secretary of Labor Arthur Goldberg ordered recruiters
to find blacks for employment in his department, while the U.S.
Post Office, particularly in the South, ordered an end to separate
assignment lines. Moreover, the Postmaster General refused to
allow segregated employees' organizations to use the department's
name. Even the Veterans' Administration (VA) took action. It issued orders to field agents that the VA would no longer honor

contracts or do business with unions that practiced racial discrimination. The President himself forbade segregated employees' organizations to use government facilities. He also recognized that it was not enough simply to require those doing business with the government to include nondiscrimination clauses in their contracts if such clauses could be ignored with impunity. Accordingly, he issued Executive Order 10925 which required contractors to file periodic compliance reports with the EEOC, thus making it easier for the commission to monitor efforts to end discrimination in employment.[18]

But clearly, more than administrative remedy was required before major changes would take place in the job market. In general, all the good work of the administration affected mainly governmental offices or independent agencies doing work for the government, a small proportion of the total work force. In 1961, only about 20 percent of the contracts in the United States had antidiscrimination clauses, and approximately one-third of those had been negotiated by either the UAW or the electrical workers' affiliates of the CIO.[19] Placement agencies, even those at colleges and universities, still received and filled discriminatory job requests, and blacks were hardly noticeable in the numerous apprentice programs throughout the country. In 1962, for example, Office Temporaries, Inc., a large employment agency in New York, used the code "NFU" ("Not For Us") to indicate that applicants were black, while another firm, Lynhall Placement Associates, used the code "POK" to distinguish "people of color," thus skirting the New York State ban on using racial information on applications. As for apprentices, in that same year General Motors had 775 employees in a special training program, of whom only 10 were black, and all clustered in the Chevrolet Gear and Axle Division. The same corporation's "Employees in Training" program covered 11,125 persons in the greater Detroit area, of whom only 60 were black.[20]

Thus, despite the psychological and social value of legislation on equal access to public and private accommodations, Title VII, an explicit ban on discrimination in employment, promotion, and job security, was the most important part of the Civil Rights Act of 1964. It signaled that the legislative branch had finally come to recognize the necessity of protecting the job rights of blacks, and it placed the EEOC on a statutory basis for the first time. Title VII was not as effective as it could have been. For example, Congress denied the EEOC authority to issue cease-and-desist orders on its own when it found evidence of discrimination, thus requiring aggrieved parties to seek remedy through slow and expensive court proceedings. Title VII also included a ban against discrimination on the basis of sex. Congress's linking of race and sex discrimination, as if their history and purpose were the same, further hampered the EEOC's efforts to erase racism from the workplace. The commission's small, overworked staff had to spend an inordinate amount of time and effort on sex discrimination complaints, leaving little time and energy to concentrate on the cancerous racial discrimination.[21]

Despite the inadequacies of Title VII, blacks quickly demonstrated their faith in the federal government's ability to improve their situation, while the EEOC tried to fashion new ground rules to wipe out discrimination. During its first year in operation, the new commission received more than 9,000 complaints of discrimination, 4.5 times as many as drafters of the legislation had anticipated.[22] While the staff struggled with this immense workload, the commissioners themselves engaged in intense debate over the intent of Congress in passing Title VII. Some commissioners insisted that the Constitution required color blindness in the administration of American law. But a growing majority maintained that "society has not discharged its duty when it passes a law which opens the gate to opportunity, while requiring some to carry on their backs the burdens of inherited poverty and prejudice."[23] The EEOC's responsibility, they argued, was not simply to live up to the letter of the law but its spirit as well by "going an extra step to provide sufficient means to enable Negroes to obtain jobs on a basis equal with whites."[24]

As with President Roosevelt's original effort against employment discrimination, federal courts gave firm backing to the administration's interpretation of Congress's intent in passing the legislation. In 1967 in *Ethridge* v. *Rhodes*, for example, a federal court upheld the provision that major contractors must show that they had an integrated work force before they could bid for public contracts. The immediate result was that more and more contractors began turning to black-controlled hiring halls, thus giving blacks a larger share of the jobs and greater involvement in deciding who worked in the building trades industry.[25] The Supreme Court went even further. In *Griggs* v. *Duke Power Company*, handed down in 1971, the Court employed the sociological jurisprudence of the *Brown* decision to attack the root of employment discrimination by both employers and unions. The Court ruled that individuals no longer had to prove that companies discriminated against them. If a company's practices had a discriminatory effect, plaintiffs did not have to show that it had a discriminatory intent.[26] In the same decision, the Supreme Court struck a major blow against artificial credentialism and firmed the ground for affirmative action programs. On the first score, the Court outlawed tests for employment unless they had a direct bearing on job performance. On the second point, it attacked the major obstacle to job advancement for blacks by ruling that union contracts, though apparently neutral, "cannot be maintained if they operate to freeze the status quo of prior discriminatory employment practices."[27] Companies could devise extraordinary plans to promote blacks outside the sainted seniority systems white unions had used for decades to promote whites only.

During the first decade after passage of the antidiscrimination legislation, black women registered more striking gains in employment and job status than black men, continuing a trend that had persisted for most of the post-World War II period. The position of black women continued to improve for several reasons. One is that black women demonstrated a greater commitment to work, and made a greater investment in job skills, than white women. Moreover, both black and white women are generally employed in occupations that do not have steep age-earnings profiles. Accordingly, black women who moved into previously closed

clerical or factory operative work began at incomes not far below
those of white women, whereas black men in new jobs were both
fewer and started at far lower wages compared with white men
already at work. Put another way, black women increased their
incomes relative to those of white women, but both groups of
women fell further behind the income levels of white men. It is
also apparent that black women profited at the expense of black
men when corporations took steps to comply with federal man-
dates to end discrimination. Employers could hire black women
and meet the charges of both race and sex discrimination in one
stroke. And since women generally commanded lower salaries
than men, such steps could be taken without major increases in
labor costs. But despite their seeming improvements, we cannot
escape the fact that black women in the 1960s and 1970s continued to work out of necessity, as they had since the end of the
Civil War. Indeed, black women were the only major sector of
the labor force that responded to a weak job market by increasing their labor force participation. While most workers pull back
during periods of recession, more black women look for work.
They undoubtedly do so because of the impact of recessions on
the employment status of black men.[28]

As in other sectors of American life, blacks were no longer willing to bear the brunt of economic oppression and to treat their
situation as inevitable. Black workers, particularly those in trade
unions, were prepared to employ "Black Power" tactics to force
both unions and employers to accord black people a greater share
of the economy. Moreover, unlike past years, black trade unionists demanded more than simply an end to denial of membership
to blacks by white unions. They demanded a share of the power
to make decisions concerning the well-being of workers and of
the unions. In all these efforts, black workers had the support of
long-established black advancement organizations like the NAACP
and the National Urban League, as well as the help of newer
groups, particularly the SCLC's Operation Bread Basket. In
short, by the mid 1960s blacks had come to realize that they
suffered far less from discrimination by individual whites than

from the fact that whites controlled the major institutions of American life.[29]

It is, of course, inaccurate to say that recognition by blacks of the need for power in unions was something new. As early as the 1920s, A. Philip Randolph had insisted that blacks must have leadership and organizational roles in the organized labor movement if they wished to improve their wages, employment, and working conditions. But his efforts, and those of black automobile workers and others associated through the National Negro Labor Council (see Chapter 6), had been ineffective.

Despite his advancing age, Randolph was determined at the beginning of the 1960s to try again to force the labor movement to live up to its egalitarian principles. He pointed out, as a NAACP report that was published in 1961 confirmed, that in spite of splendid resolutions against racism since the AFL-CIO merger of 1955, "the national labor organization had failed to eliminate the broad pattern of racial discrimination and segregation in many important affiliated unions."[30] At the 1959 AFL-CIO convention, Randolph and Milton P. Webster introduced a resolution calling for the expulsion of unions practicing segregation and discrimination, and demanded that the convention deny the International Longshoremen's Association a charter because it discriminated against black workers. Randolph argued that racism was as detrimental to the U.S. labor movement as communism and asked how the AFL-CIO leadership could continue to sanction racist unions at the very time it was expelling individuals, and at times whole unions, for alleged Communist leanings. The BSCP group lost the vote—but not until after heated debate, during which the firey Webster called George Meany a weak politician. In response, Meany argued that black workers themselves wanted segregated locals and implied that Randolph and his associates were only seeking publicity. It was then that Meany, screaming with anger, demanded to know from Randolph "who in the hell appointed you as guardian of the Negro members in America?"[31]

Randolph lost to the Meany forces at the meeting in 1959, but he left with his dignity intact. More important, Meany's outburst strengthened the resolve of black unionists as they rallied to support the BSCP president. At the NAACP meeting in 1959, Randolph again called for creation of a National Negro Labor Committee, a goal he had cherished since coming into the organized labor movement in the 1920s. Such a committee, Randolph believed, would function like the Jewish Labor Committee and press the special needs and interests of black workers. In May 1960 a meeting of black trade unionists created the Negro American Labor Council (NALC) and elected Randolph president.[32] Randolph remained president until 1966, and though the NALC did not achieve its goal of forcing AFL-CIO unions to cease discrimination against blacks, it did much to improve relations between black labor and civil rights groups. The NALC provided much of the funding and leadership for the March on Washington in 1963. Indeed, a massive march on the nation's capital was another of Randolph's longtime dreams; it was the NALC's most important accomplishment as well.

Despite the harsh words and heated debate between George Meany and Randolph at labor conventions, both Randolph and the NALC represented a segment of the black labor movement that white spokesmen like Meany found acceptable. Though the two sides obviously did not always accept each others' views, they could at least talk. But by the time Randolph left the NALC in 1966, a new breed of black trade unionists had developed, men and women who would demand power in the union and expansion of union activities to fields previously untouched by organized labor.

At first, black workers focused their attention on the most blatant discrimination in unions: separate promotion/seniority systems for blacks and whites and discrimination in hiring hall unions.[33] The EEOC and the federal courts facilitated the efforts of black workers to eliminate these clear examples of discrimination. Hiring hall unions were most effective in the construction industry, which had some of the most powerful unions in the country in the 1960s and 1970s. For example, while organized labor represented 23 percent of the American labor force, referral unions represented 60 percent of the labor force in the building trades.[34] Unions in the construction industry gained their immense power from control of the labor market, largely through apprentice programs and maintenance of the closed shop, which, though outlawed by Taft-Hartley amendments, "continued to thrive in this country on a de facto basis." Such arrangements worked to the disadvantage of blacks because the unions referred workers to employers on a strictly seniority basis. In effect, the system compounded past discrimination because blacks had previously been denied access to jobs and were thus unable to build seniority.[35]

President Lyndon B. Johnson struck a telling blow against hiring hall discrimination in 1965 when he signed Executive Order 11246. This order imposed additional requirements on federal contractors to hire and upgrade blacks and established the Office of Federal Contract Compliance in the Department of Labor to insure that the business sector met its obligations. In 1969, after a broad investigation documented the extent of discrimination within the construction industry, the Labor Department invoked Executive Order 11246 to impose quotas on the building trades unions in Philadelphia that would force them to cease discrimination against blacks and bring more of them immediately into the industry.

General organized labor was adamant in its opposition to the "Philadelphia Plans," as the series of efforts to end discrimination in the U.S. building trades industry in cities throughout the country came to be called. George Meany, in a comment that was as much a strategy suggestion for white unionists as it was a criticism of the programs, charged that the plans would make "no contribution to the overall problem of increasing minority group representation because a contractor can achieve compliance by transferring minority workers already in the area work force to Government projects."[36] Interestingly, though he pointed out what was wrong with the government's program, Meany proposed nothing, short of "education," that would improve the chance for employment of blacks and members of other minority groups.

The Contractors' Association of Eastern Pennsylvania went even further than the president of the AFL-CIO. They sued the government, claiming that it had no power to impose quotas. A district court, in *Contractors of Eastern Pennsylvania* v. *United States* (1970), ruled that the President did have authority to issue Executive Order 11246. Moreover, the court held that regional specificity was constitutional and that goals/quotas did not violate the ban against reverse discrimination that Congress had written into the Civil Rights Act of 1964.[37]

Of the various "hometown plans" that developed following the government's actions in Philadelphia, the St. Louis Plan was among the most imaginative and effective. That plan permitted blacks with some construction experience to become journeymen within two years, while blacks who had not previously worked in the industry could attain journeyman status within two and a half years. The program, endorsed by the major unions in the city, even permitted inexperienced trainees to cross craft lines for six months, after which they were required to choose a specific trade for advanced training. Of major importance, the St. Louis Plan included an aspect that wholly vitiated Meany's opposition. It covered both private and federally assisted construction.[38] Unfortunately, these plans did not prove as effective as many had hoped. As William Gould has pointed out, the plans were generally privately negotiated, and in too many cases they left intact "so many of the basic assumptions behind union practices that discriminate against racial minorities."[39]

Nonetheless, taken together, the *Ethridge* v. *Rhodes* decision, which stimulated increased use of black-controlled hiring halls, development of hometown plans, the Workers' Defense League, and various branches of the Urban League, began to reap dividends for black workers and increased their militancy. Of major significance was the growing number of blacks admitted to apprentice programs. By 1971, the proportion of blacks in the joint plumbers' and pipe fitters' apprentice program had increased from 2.7 percent in 1961 to 5.0 percent, while the proportion in the roofing and trowel trades, already high, increased from 17.2 percent to 17.9 percent for the two years, respectively.[40] In addition, some corporations took the first steps to implement affirmative action hiring and training programs. Federal funds fueled such activities in northern automobile plants, while blacks made a major breakthrough in the South when Litton Industries agreed in 1971 to guarantee heavy hiring, upgrading, and apprenticeship of black workers at its shipyards in Pascagoula, Mississippi.[41]

Despite the development of some cracks in the generally solid wall of union discrimination, many problems remained. Nor were charges of discrimination by blacks idle complaints. The EEOC found "cause" in 70 percent of allegations brought by blacks claiming union discrimination. The EEOC's failure to bring a settlement through peaceful negotiations indicated how strongly the unions resisted change. Efforts to settle grievances against unions through arbitration were hardly more successful than EEOC endeavors. Arbitration usually failed because blacks, lacking control of the unions, had no standing in choosing arbitrators. Moreover, without questioning the integrity of individual arbitrators, it would be to question their intelligence to suggest that they ignored the fact that organized "labor and management—and not rebellious minority employees—[would] decide whether the arbitrator is selected to arbitrate in the future."[42] In 1968, 170 civil rights cases were pending in federal courts against labor unions.[43]

Black workers also insisted that they stood little chance of ending union discrimination through internal labor grievance procedures. Black steelworkers in 1968 appealed to their president and head of the AFL-CIO Industrial Union Department, I. W. Abel, to help them in removing white paternalist Donald Slaiman as director of the huge federation's Civil Rights Department. Slaiman, they argued, did not know black workers and did not represent their interests. Black workers had stopped filing complaints with the Civil Rights Department, they informed Abel, because "experience has taught us that the department is unable to function on our behalf. Most often it represents the discrimination in organized labor rather than black workers who are victims of white racism within the house of labor."[44] As usual, their appeal went unheeded.

During the late 1960s, black workers began organizing militant caucuses within the unions and issued direct challenges to established union leaders. Caucuses of black teachers were particularly active in the unions in New York City and Chicago, and black postal workers functioned through the National Alliance of Postal and Federal Employees and the National Postal Union. The postal workers claimed that the Post Office Department had worked out a "cloakroom deal" with the white craft postal union and argued that the deal was detrimental to the interests of blacks.[45] In 1967 the Congress of Racial Equality (CORE) led in forming the first black caucus in the International Ladies Garment Workers Union (ILGWU). This caucus was in direct conflict with the union's constitution, which forbade caucuses except during a three-month period immediately before the biennial convention. In the same year the ILGWU caucus was formed, federal Judge Constance Baker Motley voided the election of national officers of the National Maritime Union (NMU). Black NMU members argued that the union's constitution, which permitted only individuals who had been members for ten years or more to hold office, discriminated against blacks.[46]

Black workers in the basic industries, particularly automobiles, transportation, and steel, were considerably more militant than other groups. Whereas others turned to the courts for relief, these workers were willing to take on the unions on their own turf. They even established rival unions, while maintaining their regular membership, and called unauthorized strikes when it suited their purposes to do so.

The black members of the United Steel Workers (USW) formed one of the first major black caucuses, the Ad Hoc Committee of Steelworkers, on the eve of the union's convention in 1968. The Ad Hoc Committee made three basic demands of their union: election of a black vice president, more and better jobs for blacks, and better representation of blacks among the union's national and local leaders. Black steelworkers believed their demands would receive a favorable hearing because black votes had been crucial to I. W. Abel's successful ouster of David McDonald as USW president in 1965. But to insure that the union took their demands seriously, the black caucus in East Chicago, Indiana, forced through a resolution at their local meeting, calling on members to withhold per capita taxes from their county and state labor federations as long as those bodies contained discriminatory unions.[47] Withholding money was clearly one way to get the attention of labor leaders.

Those who expected support from Abel were soon disappointed. Even before the convention opened, he assured the Ad Hoc Committee that he would oppose their demands, and he took the floor of the meeting to argue that the request for a special black vice president was reverse discrimination in a union that practiced no discrimination. It was clear that the blacks would lose, but they were straightforward in their warnings to the USW and to Americans in general. One delegate from the floor pleaded with his colleagues not to "miss the tenor of the times. Negro people," he said, "are saying if we can't have our share of America, why have an America?" No one could miss the meaning of those words, coming as they did on the heels of the massive disruptions in American cities the previous summer. Nonetheless, the convention turned down the request for a black vice president. But black steelworkers demonstrated their resolve in the face of this defeat. Workers at the Bethlehem Steel Company at Sparrows Point, Maryland, organized the Shipyard Workers for Job Equality and challenged the regular steelworkers' local on the right to represent blacks. The group also pressured the government to cut off contracts with the company unless blacks got a better share of the jobs, an event that would harm both black and white workers, not to mention Bethlehem Steel. Accordingly, blacks gained some job advancement, but overall, black steelworkers hardly improved their position within the USW.[48]

The year 1968 was a popular one for blacks moving toward leadership posts in their unions. While the steelworkers debated whether that giant union should have a black vice president, black bus drivers in Chicago took on their union over the issue of leadership and employment rights. A major caucus effort came when these workers, comprising 60 percent to 70 percent of the bus drivers, organized as the Concerned Transit Workers (CTW). They demanded better representation of blacks in the leadership of Local 241 of the Amalgamated Transit Union, AFL-CIO. Among their chief grievances was opposition to a constitutional provision that permitted pensioned members of the local to vote in all union affairs. Since the vast majority of the pensioned members were white, their votes helped to maintain all-white leadership even as the union's membership became more and more black. Black bus drivers staged a wildcat strike on July 1 after the local refused to remove the clause that permitted the pensioners to vote. The strike lasted four days before Mayor Richard Daley fashioned a temporary reconciliation between the two factions of employees.

The Daley agreement was only a brief respite in the dispute, for the CTW and leaders of the regular local made no progress in solving their differences. The CTW appealed to the courts and the national union to help solve their grievances. When those appeals failed, the CTW called another strike on August 28, the day before the opening of the Democratic National Convention. Chicago was a city in turmoil. Not only were most of the buses idle, but the city was teeming with thousands of demonstrators there to protest the Viet Nam War. The second CTW strike, a brawling affair, lasted until mid-September, when a court injunction ordered the men back to work. In the end, 42 CTW members lost their jobs, while another 140 were suspended for various periods. But the effort had achieved some success. Despite the CTW's complaint that the actions of Local 241 amounted only to tokenism, the black caucus's activities had forced the union local to find leadership places for blacks.[49]

The most revolutionary black caucus movement developed among black automobile workers, members of one of the nation's largest and most militant industrial unions. The black caucuses had several causes, not least of which were the boom times the automobile industry enjoyed during the 1960s. Employment at the Big Three auto makers (General Motors, Ford, and Chrysler) increased from 693,186 in 1961 to 953,585 in 1966. Employment at

Chrysler alone rose from 75,000 in 1962 to 133,114 in 1966. Employment continued to increase throughout the decade. A large proportion of this greatly increased work force consisted of young men, many under thirty. Blacks were highly represented among these new employees, particularly in Detroit in the aftermath of the riot in the summer of 1967, when UAW officials and other members of the Detroit power structure took extraordinary steps to find jobs for young ghetto youths previously described as the "hard-core unemployed."[50]

The vast majority of the new employees worked at unskilled jobs; practically none of them entered skilled categories. Work in the automobile industry is monotonous and nerve-wracking since workers perform the same task again and again throughout the day. It is particularly monotonous on unskilled and semiskilled assignments. Accordingly, the industry experiences an extremely high turnover rate, and absenteeism among automobile workers is legion. As many as 46,000 new employees moved in and out of the Detroit plants alone during 1968, most of them young unmarried workers.[51]

The black caucus in the automobile industry started from an event that was not a black-white issue. In May 1968, black workers at Dodge Main joined in a wildcat strike to protest the hated speedup, the process by which management, in an effort to produce more units, speeds up the assembly line and requires workers to perform more tasks during a work shift. When the UAW settled the immediate grievance and workers returned to the plant, blacks argued that black workers were disproportionately punished for having taken part in the walkout. They particularly protested the firing of five black men and called on the UAW to institute grievance procedures to get the workers' jobs back. Unable to force the company to rehire these workers, the young blacks organized the Dodge Revolutionary Union Movement (DRUM) to bring pressure on the auto maker and the UAW, which they saw as both ineffective and racist.[52]

Unlike the experienced men in the Ad Hoc Committee, the black caucus in the steelworkers' union, the members of DRUM

were all young men with little seniority in either the workplace
or the union. They demonstrated their differences from older
workers in both their rhetoric and their belief that workers' responsibilities extended beyond the workplace to the community.
The poem "DRUM," which appeared in 1970, sums up their dis-
dain for both their union and the automobile industry:

> Deep in the gloom of the fire-filled pit
> Where the Dodge rolls down the line,
> We challenge the doom while dying in shit
> While strangled by a swine. . . .
> For hours and years with sweated tears
> Trying to break our chain. . . .
> But we broke our backs and died in packs
> To find our manhood slain. . . .
> But now we stand for DRUM's at hand
> To lead our freedom fight,
> And now till then we'll unite like men
> For now we know our might. . . .
> And damn the plantations and the whole Dodge nation. . . .
> For DRUM has dried our tears. . . .
> And now as we die we have a different cry
> For now we hold our spears!
> UAW is scum. . . .
> OUR THING IS DRUM!!![53]

In order to make good on its promise to be militant and revolutionary, DRUM called a wildcat strike in July 1968 which aimed
at forcing Local 3 of the UAW to secure reinstatement of the
seven workers who had been fired in May. Seventy percent of the
black workers at Dodge Main walked out for five days while Local 3 worked to settle the grievance. The strike, which reportedly
cost Chrysler the production loss of 1,900 cars, demonstrated the
close relationship between DRUM and the black community.
Black students from Detroit universities and colleges manned
picket lines on behalf of the workers. Local 3, which negotiated
for the aggrieved workers, eventually accepted a compromise
package from Chrysler management; the company agreed to rehire five of the workers, but two would remain jobless. Though

it was less than the total victory they had demanded, DRUM leaders went along with the deal.[54]

After DRUM's success, several other groups of revolutionary black workers sprang up in automobile plants, among them FRUM at Ford and GRUM at General Motors. Later in 1968 these groups, whose leaders shared a pseudo-Marxist-Leninist view of the world, came together to form the League of Revolutionary Black Workers. In addition to making demands that would improve working conditions for blacks in the plants and make the UAW more responsive to the needs of black members, the League of Revolutionary Black Workers endeavored to organize the black community of Detroit. The League, for example, was instrumental in founding the Detroit branch of the Black Panther Party. Its leaders thought the Oakland Panthers had the wrong ideas about how to organize blacks and wished to take control before young blacks in Detroit could be misled.[55]

In its dealings with the Big Three auto makers and the UAW, the League of Revolutionary Black Workers greatly expanded on the demands DRUM had made. The League called for the immediate firing of Walter Reuther and the hiring of a black worker as president of the UAW, and insisted that the union name blacks to 50 percent of the positions on its staff and the executive board. The League then came to its radical demands, demands so radical as to cause a radical historian to remind us of Eugene V. Debs's comment that "there is a difference between class consciousness and class craziness."[56] The League called for an end to the check-off system for payment of union dues and demanded that the UAW call a general strike to end the war in Viet Nam. The strike should continue until the government ended all taxes on working-class people and imposed additional taxes on industrial profits so as to make up the difference. Monies spent on defense would be reallocated "to meet the pressing needs of the black and poor populations of America." Moreover, the UAW, which the League was at the same time accusing of being too weak to handle the grievances of its members, was called on to force the auto makers to accept a five-hour day and a four-day work week. Nor were workers to suffer from this decline in work time, for the League also demanded a doubling of the wages for all production employees.[57]

Obviously, neither the UAW nor any other union could accomplish what the League of Revolutionary Black Workers demanded. Yet, it is clear that both the UAW and the auto makers paid attention to what the League's leaders said. By 1970 both the union and the companies had brought more blacks into leadership positions than had existed before DRUM came on the scene. UAW leadership also endorsed the "inverse" seniority system by which senior white workers could accept voluntary layoffs with supplemental pay during slow periods so as to enable younger black workers—ineligible for supplemental pay—to remain on the job. Such improvements caused more and more of the black auto workers to place their confidence in UAW leadership, and the influence of the League began to wane.

But conditions over which neither the League nor the automobile companies had control hastened the demise of the League even more. The automobile industry suffered a sharp downturn in sales in 1969–1970 which caused a marked drop in the number of new employees. In fact, the companies were required to lay off some workers already on the job. And the Chrysler Corporation, then already in the slow process of decay that might lead to its demise, even had to pass up about $14 million the federal government had agreed to pay the company to hire and train ghetto workers.[58] As usual, blacks with the least seniority were the first fired, and since there were no new hires, the League lost its membership pool. And, given the tight labor market, workers lucky enough to have jobs were unlikely to risk losing them. Thus the League passed from the scene, but it was hardly forgotten.

Activities among black laborers in the South paralleled the development of militant black workers' groups in northern industrial centers and remind us that large numbers of black people still lived and worked there, despite continual expansion of the northern ghettos. Stirrings among black southern workers also demonstrate how similar the two sections of the country had become. The United States was no longer a country in which blacks in the North demanded to be treated as equal citizens while those in the South cowered in sullen silence in the plantation cotton fields. Indeed, while DRUM mouthed radical rhetoric and talked about mobilizing the black community to help black working-class people, it was in the South that whole cities rallied behind the demands of black workers. It was also in the South that blacks took the most significant steps in forcing recognition of the dignity of all workers, regardless of the types of tasks they performed. Fannie Lou Hamer, who had been one of the moving spirits in founding the Mississippi Freedom Democratic Party during the early 1960s, was in the forefront of attempts to help southern black laborers. In 1965, she founded the Mississippi Freedom Labor Union and called a strike to secure a regular hourly wage and an eight-hour day for sharecroppers in the rich Mississippi Delta. Her effort failed completely as plantation owners evicted the sharecroppers and had their belongings dumped along the highway. But it was only a prelude to events in Memphis, Tennessee, and Charleston, South Carolina, that would capture the attention of the nation and represent the final triumph of the "Negro-Labor Alliance."

The Memphis movement, in the end both tragic and triumphant, centered on the black sanitation workers, who had long-standing grievances against the city. As a whole, Memphis had been left untouched by the Civil Rights Movement. Accordingly, black sanitation workers experienced discrimination beyond that usually associated with their type of work. White workers in the department drove the trucks, while blacks picked up and emptied the garbage cans; white workers had a shower and lounge room where they could eat lunch, while blacks spent their lunchtime, in the words of one worker, "with a sandwich in one hand and a garbage can in the other." Grievances extended to pay and job status as well. Wages were pitiably low, and workers received no pay for time lost because of rain or other conditions beyond their control. Moreover, they had no pension plan. Thus, they had to perform the often backbreaking and always disagreeable work of cleansing the city during their working years with the sure knowl-

edge that their lot would be even more miserable, at least finan-
cially, in their old age.

The sanitation workers had tried unsuccessfully to form a bargaining unit in 1963 and again in 1966, but turned back each
time in the face of stiff opposition from the city, which fired anyone remotely associated with attempts to organize a union. In
1964, the American Association of State, County, and Municipal
Employees hired T. O. Jones, a garbage man whom the city had
fired the year before, to organize the sanitation workers in Memphis. By 1967, Jones had built Local 1733 into a strong union of
1,300 members and was ready to challenge the administration of
Mayor Henry Loeb once more. All that was needed was a specific incident that would galvanize the members and strengthen
their resolve.

The incident that brought the Memphis sanitation workers into
the streets and did much to mobilize the general black community behind them occurred on February 1, 1968. Two black garbage men, who sought shelter from a driving rainstorm in the
back of their truck because they were not permitted to enter the
lounge reserved for whites, crushed to death when lightning
activated the truck's automatic compressor. Grief-stricken, and
angry because of continued incidents of discrimination in pay,
Local 1733 voted on February 12 to go on strike. In so doing,
they made several demands, chiefly recognition of the union as a
bargaining unit for the workers, a wage increase, dues checkoff,
and a written contract.[59]

The ensuing strike, which lasted sixty-five days, soon came to
involve the whole city and attracted national attention as well-
known persons came in to help the "lowly sanitation workers." It
is estimated that blacks in Memphis alone raised $100,000 to help
support the strikers' families, while Walter Reuther of the UAW
made a big splash when his union handed over a check for
$25,000. Supporters of the strikers carried on marches and demon-
strations reminiscent of those of the early 1960s, and ministers,
falling short of calling for a boycott, alarmed city merchants by
preaching sermons calling on blacks to buy "no new clothes for

Easter." Such activities continued in the face of court injunctions, white strikebreakers brought in from Arkansas and rural Tennessee, and the combined forces of Memphis police and Tennessee National Guardsmen, who enforced a curfew over the city.

The strike became a national event, and Memphis attained international notoriety when Martin Luther King, Jr., came to support the strikers' cause. For Memphis was King's last campaign. Court injunctions and schedule conflicts prevented King from ever leading a march in Memphis. But he did have time to give a sermon, perhaps the most memorable of his gifted career. King prophesied in that last talk that the time was soon coming when his dream of an end to racism in America would reach fruition. But he also prophesied something else that was immediately more important. He seemed to foresee his own death. King told the enraptured audience at Mason Temple Church:

Well, I don't know what's going to happen now. But it really doesn't matter to me now. Because I've been to the mountaintop. I won't mind. Like anybody, I would like to live a long life. Longevity has its place. But I'm not concerned about that now. I just want to do God's will. And He's allowed me to look over, and I've seen the promised land.

Working toward an emotional and frenzied finish that unnerved even his closest associates, King continued,

I may not get there with you, but I want you to know tonight that we as a people will get to the promised land. So I'm happy tonight. I'm not worried about anything. I'm not fearing any man. "Mine eyes have seen the Glory of the coming of the Lord."

The next day, April 4, 1968, James Earl Ray shot King from ambush as he stood on the balcony of the Lorraine Motel. King died almost immediately, but he died as he said he wanted to be remembered: "trying to help somebody." His death in the service of the sanitation workers demonstrated to a shattered nation that, as he had said, what was going on in Memphis was "important to every poor working man, black or white, in the South."[60]

As for Memphis, King's assassination undoubtedly speeded a settlement of the strike. On April 16 the members of Local 1733 accepted a package offer from the city that, though it did not include all their demands, at least could be considered a victory. The pay increase was less than they had demanded, and they did not have a written contract. But they had won on the crucial issue of a dues checkoff and recognition of the union as bargaining agent for its members. Moreover, the city had been forced to pledge to cease discrimination against black workers in job status and facilities, and no workers would be disciplined for having taken part in the strike.

Efforts in Charleston, South Carolina, to raise wages and improve working conditions for service personnel in hospitals were as important as the work of Local 1733 in Memphis. The strike, which soon became a citywide demonstration and eventually involved federal cabinet officers and even members of the White House staff, began in March 1969 when Medical College Hospital fired several employees who were trying to organize their co-workers. The strike lasted until July and included all the intimidation, curfews, court injunctions, and boycotts common in such conflicts. The local leadership was made up mainly of black women, including Mary Ann Moultrie, Emma Hardin, and Rosetta Simmons. They gained the support of Coretta King, who had become a national celebrity in the aftermath of her husband's death. Walter Reuther and even George Meany also supported the strikers, as did the leaders of the several black advancement groups. In July, Secretary of Labor George Schultz let it be known that he wanted the strike settled and sent in a federal mediator to help the parties reach an agreement. The hospital workers did not force the hospitals to accept their union as official bargaining agent for its members. But they did gain a package that included a minimum wage, a pay increase for workers already on the job, establishment of a credit union for the employees, and return to service of all who had been fired for participating in the strike. In their view, they had won a major victory.

The 1960s, then, ended with blacks winning some victories in the workplace. But, as the record of employment discussed above shows, there was little reason for optimism. Indeed, Memphis and Charleston were largely symbolic victories, victories that would hardly be recognized, as conditions worsened during the terrible economic downturn of the 1970s.

8

"Who Needs the Negro?"

At the core of the drive to reform our society (whatever other elements might be stressed from time to time) is the pervasive and agonizing question of race. Thus, no matter what other adjectives we may use to characterize the vigorous quest for change, we must also describe it as a black revolution—a basic upheaval about the role of race in this country.

ANDREW BRIMMER, 1969

Even with the recent victories of the alliance between blacks and organized labor at Memphis and Charleston, the 1970s did not promise a bright future for black Americans. Richard Nixon, who became President in 1969, had taken over Lyndon Johnson's war in Viet Nam and had brought to the White House an administration that would do little to solve the pressing problems of black workers. A great misfortune for black workers during the early 1970s is that it fell to a President with limited social vision to implement the recommendations of the National Advisory Commission on Civil Disorders and that that President chose to follow advice that called for "benign neglect" of black people and of the ghettos.

Despite the overwhelming importance of the President's role in setting the national direction, it would misrepresent the history of the decade to hold Nixon wholly responsible for the stagnation that overcame blacks during his administration and continued for years to come. To do so would be to overlook the important changes that occurred in the labor market because of automation and the continued shift from manufacturing to service occupations. These changes caused a shortage of jobs in the employment sector in which blacks were most heavily represented, not to mention a continued decline in the number of jobs in ghettos. Indeed, such shifts, in the view of one scholar, threatened to remove blacks permanently from the labor market and to relegate them even more to a condition of surplus labor, a result prophesied by white workers as early as 1868.[1] Moreover, the nation suffered two major recessions during Nixon's terms that, coupled with a continuing rise in inflation—Nixonomics—caused a turn to the right in general national domestic policy and strengthened the hand of those who called for a "white backlash" against the government's efforts to alleviate the depressing conditions under which blacks lived.

Nor were conditions to improve appreciably during the administrations of Nixon's successors, Gerald R. Ford and Jimmy Carter. As we shall see, despite federal affirmative action and other antidiscrimination procedures, by every statistical measure the socioeconomic status of blacks was as depressed in 1980 as it had been in 1969. Even more striking, black organizations were not in a position to fashion remedies. The success of the Civil Rights Movement that had wiped out *de jure* discrimination had so changed relations between blacks and whites that it was all but impossible to see that overt and blatant discrimination still existed, and black groups had no racist southern sheriffs or union constitutions against which to aim their protests.

Developments of the 1970s, which saw an overall decline in the status of blacks, also sharpened the class lines that had existed in the black community since Reconstruction. As in past periods, some black workers were prepared to take advantage of changes in the labor market and moved into high-paying jobs, while the masses continued to suffer in terms of unemployment, poor housing, and dead-end occupations. Moreover, the proportion of blacks who remained in poverty, even among those who worked regularly, actually increased during the decade. This increase was particularly acute among black families headed by females.

Indeed, one of the anomalies of the time is that the relative poverty of female-headed black families grew more severe even though black women generally fared better during the 1970s than black men.[2]

Not only did conservative Republican administrations desert blacks, but organized white labor abandoned them as well. Indeed, the attitude of the AFL-CIO leadership during the presidential election of 1972 shows conclusively that national labor leaders' claim that they were held back on questions of race because of the opposition of their members is a myth. Organized labor, under George Meany's leadership, joined with the Nixon crowd to "thwart equal opportunity and not advance its cause," and Nixon showed his gratitude when he appointed Peter Brennan, longtime president of the New York Building and Construction Trades Council, AFL-CIO, as Secretary of Labor in 1973.[3] Perhaps even more tragic, rifts that had already begun to develop between black and Jewish groups widened as well, particularly over the issue of affirmative action.

A look at developments in the labor market for black men during the 1970s reveals a mixed picture. Blacks showed a marked upgrading in occupations at the upper employment level, especially in the young, well-educated group. More than twice as many blacks held professional and clerical positions in 1977 as in 1961, while farm and unskilled jobs also declined. But percentage increases in broad occupational categories can be deceiving. Both newspaper boys and stock and bond salespersons are considered sales personnel, for example, but the distinctions between the skills and earnings of the two groups are too clear to warrant discussion. And despite upgrading that had been proportionately astounding, the occupational diversity among blacks in 1980 still did not approach that of whites of a decade earlier. Moreover, when the 1970s ended, it was still too early to see whether occupational changes represented real improvements for black workers because most of the new hired were young employees who still had to face promotional barriers.[4]

If the general occupational structure of blacks improved during the 1970s, the chances of finding jobs for most black workers worsened, providing further evidence of a widening gap between blacks at the top and those at the bottom. Indeed, during the 1970s economists and sociologists began talking about the development of a black underclass.[5] Black unemployment, which had been about twice that of whites since World War II, increased during the 1970s. The recession of 1970–1971 forced fourteen additional blacks onto unemployment rolls for every ten whites. And in 1972, when whites began to recover from the high rate of joblessness that had occurred at the height of the recession, blacks remained without work.[6]

Economically, the 1970s was a terrible decade. Both black and white workers experienced severe increases in unemployment during the recession of 1973–1975, compounding the difficulties of workers who had not recovered from the recession of 1970–1971. The economy started a slow upturn in 1975; by 1978 white workers had come out of the recession, but blacks had not. Though more blacks found jobs, the unemployment rate did not decrease by the end of the decade. Between 1975 and 1977, for example, employment among blacks increased by 700,000 persons; 5,000,000 additional whites found jobs during the same years. But the crucial point is that 1,500,000 blacks remained jobless in the latter year, the same number as in 1975, while the number of unemployed whites declined by 1,000,000. In midsummer 1977, black unemployment stood at its all-time postwar high, with 14.5 percent of the black labor force out of work. In the mid 1970s the black population was enduring a depression, particularly in employment. Indeed, the jobless rate differential actually increased between whites and blacks since the 1973–1975 recession. Beginning at 1.9 : 1, it increased to 2.4 : 1 in 1978, the widest unemployment gap between the races at any time since the government started keeping such statistics.[7] Nor was it likely that the employment picture for blacks would improve soon. Continued racial discrimination, increased participation in the labor force by blacks as they perceived the economy to improve, and their continued high concentration in low-paying and unskilled jobs contributed to the worsening employment condition of blacks in the late 1970s. But these are historical factors. A newer and more controversial cause for increased unemployment among black males, especially, is the phenomenal increase in the number of white female workers. This sector of the work force has shown the largest increase in recent years, rising from 37.7 percent in 1960 to 48.4 percent in 1977.[8]

Not only did black males experience increased unemployment, they also registered a decline in labor force participation, a trend that had been noticed in the 1960s. In 1977, black males over age sixteen showed a labor force participation rate of 71 percent, down sharply from the 83 percent rate of 1960. And such rates did not include those who went uncounted, the "hidden unemployed" whom the government estimated to include as many as 315,000 blacks in 1975.[9]

During the 1970s, black women continued the high labor force participation that had characterized them since the Civil War. Moreover, they continued to make sizeable contributions to family incomes and showed some improvement in occupational status. Educated black women came close to parity with white women of the same age and experience in both income and job diversification. But overall, black females continued to be over-represented in service and lower-level blue-collar positions. In 1977, 37 percent of black women were in service occupations, and though they made up 11 percent of employed women in that year, they held only 7 percent of white-collar jobs.[10] By mid-decade the earnings of black wives averaged approximately one-third the annual income of black husband-wife families. White women in husband-wife families contributed approximately 26 percent of the earnings for the same period, reflecting not so much the superior earnings of black women over whites but the relatively poor earnings of black men.[11]

Generally, incomes of blacks had improved considerably since the end of World War II, reflecting in part the government-enforced decline in discrimination because of the Civil Rights Act of 1964 and various affirmative action plans. Black family income more than doubled from 1947 to 1974. But blacks suffered particularly severe cutbacks during the Nixon recessions of 1970–1971 and 1973–1975. Indeed, black family income was higher in 1969 than it was in 1974. And, in comparison with the earnings of whites, the average family income of blacks in 1977, $9,560, was approximately 57 percent of the $16,740 that whites earned. The income gap had actually widened from the 60 percent of 1974.[12]

Among young families, blacks showed greater promise of reaching income parity with whites during the 1970s than at any other time, and at the end of the decade it seemed that parity among those groups would continue. In husband-wife families in which the husband was thirty-five or less, there was little difference between the incomes of blacks and whites. But even this cheerful development offered little ground for optimism among blacks. Black families reached parity with their white counterparts largely because among blacks both husbands and wives worked more often than did both white spouses. In a sense, a black husband-wife team earned as much as a white male.[13]

Even more discouraging for the future of black working-class people was the alarming rise in the number of female-headed households during the 1970s and the resulting increase in the number of impoverished black families. It is not easy to explain why spouses decided to end their marriages, but it is clear that the depressed wages and occupational status of women meant that an increase in the number of families headed by females would bring about an increasing number of poor black people. Between 1940 and 1975, the proportion of black families headed by women nearly doubled, from 18 percent to 35 percent; by 1978, 39 percent of black families were headed by women. And the proportion of poor black families headed by women had increased as well, from 54 percent of all poor black families in 1969 to an astounding 67 percent in 1974. More than half (51 percent) of the families headed by black women were officially poor in 1977, while 13 percent of those headed by black men fell into that group.[14]

Policymakers and individuals responsible for the future of the

nation can take little solace in the fact that the number and proportion of black people who were officially poor declined from
1959 to 1977; in the former year, there were 9.9 million blacks
(an estimated 55 percent of the black population) in families
with incomes below the poverty level. In 1977, 7.7 million blacks
were still living in great poverty. More important, blacks represented almost a third of the nation's poor at a time when they
made up about 12 percent of the national population.[15]

Massive unemployment and poverty among blacks, particularly
black youth, created an explosive situation as the 1970s ended.
Young blacks, among whom unemployment ran as high as 40 percent, and many of whom reached adulthood never having had a
job and with few skills to expect that the situation ever would
change, felt that they had no stake in America. Many even believed that the forces of the "establishment" intended to lock
them forever into impoverished ghettos and relegate them to a
condition of meaninglessness. Those individuals, as sociologist
Sidney Willhelm observed in 1970, were willing to face death in
order to force the nation to recognize their humanness.[16]

Only the most myopic and thoughtless believed that the several
days of rioting in Miami, Florida, in May 1980 occurred because
of the murder of a black resident by policemen and their subsequent acquittal by a Florida court. The killing was the spark that
set off the riot, as cases of police brutality often do, but the riot
occurred because of long-term economic oppression in the ghetto
of that South Florida city. At the time, blacks there were particularly incensed over the federal government's action in allowing
thousands of Cubans (but not black Haitians) to enter the country and spending millions of dollars "processing" and relocating
them, while at the same time maintaining that there was no
money for rehabilitation of black neighborhoods. In the aftermath
of the Miami riot, national and state leaders showed their abys-
mal ignorance of black communities when they rushed in "national" black spokesmen like Jesse Jackson of People United to
Save Humanity and former UN Ambassador Andrew Young to
quiet the riot and to tell policymakers what to do to prevent a re-

currence. It seemed that no one had paid the slightest attention to the *Report of the National Advisory Commission on Civil Disorders,* which had warned in 1968 that the typical rioter was "extremely hostile to whites, but his hostility is more likely to be a product of social and economic class than of race: he is almost equally hostile toward middle-class Negroes."[17] Despite the hard work of leaders of national organizations, few blacks in the ghettos knew who they were, and the national spokesmen knew nothing about the conditions in the local communities. More important, their presence only made the rioters believe more strongly that no one cared for the ideas of the people in the ghettos. It would be to court disaster if local and national officials believed that Miami was a wholly isolated disruption, for as subsequent developments in Chattanooga, Tennessee, showed, residents pent up in ghettos throughout the country could easily explode into violent counterattack under the increasing weight of economic oppression.

The 1980 Miami riot came at a time when it appeared that the nation had no interest in advancing the cause of unemployed and otherwise neglected black workers. The Humphrey-Hawkins Full Employment Act, which narrowly passed Congress in a weakened form, was likely to have little impact on the employment situation, especially during a national clamor for a balanced budget and a government-inspired recession designed to halt double-digit inflation. Black and other unemployed workers found it difficult to become excited about a policy that constantly deprived them of work and income so that the dollars of those lucky enough to have jobs could have greater spending power. Yet, given the circumstances of the time, the government was in no mood to become an employer of last resort, as the original version of Humphrey-Hawkins had envisioned, and stand as a guarantor against unemployment. Labor unions railed against government inaction, but in a crisis that even saw the near collapse of a major automobile manufacturer, Chrysler Corporation, unions seemed ill prepared to affect national economic policy even for white workers, let alone be of help to blacks.

By 1980, the American people's indifference toward programs

that would help to erase the impact of past discrimination on black workers was manifest. As Patricia Harris, Secretary of Health and Human Services, pointed out, white Americans feel different about blacks than about people who are not black, but "white people are very uncomfortable in acknowledging that."[18] Accordingly, Americans argued that fifteen years of special effort on behalf of blacks, particularly affirmative action programs, had been long enough.

The term "affirmative action" was first used in 1961, when President John Kennedy issued Executive Order 10925. The concept received its most vigorous endorsement four years later, when President Johnson made it clear in his speech at Howard University that equal opportunity, though essential to alleviate the difficulties under which blacks lived, was "not enough, not enough." The President emphasized that black poverty and white poverty were not the same, and that though some of the cures for the two types of poverty might be the same, "there [were] differences—deep, corrosive, obstinate differences—radiating painful roots into the community, and into the family, and [into] the nature of the individual." Black people had had their cultural traditions "twisted and battered by endless years of hatred and hopelessness" in America and in the 1960s had "the heritage of centuries to overcome." It did no good, then, to open the door of opportunity if some people could not walk through it. Johnson told a national television audience and the hundreds assembled on that Washington hill that Friday afternoon that the time had come to "move beyond opportunity to achievement."[19] In September 1965, Johnson issued Executive Order 11246, instructing the Secretary of Labor to insure that contractors hire and upgrade black workers.[20]

Critics of affirmative action argued from the beginning that such programs designed to compensate blacks for past racism were discrimination in reverse. Indeed, they said, such programs, especially when the government mandated specific goals and timetables ("quotas"), strike at the very heart of meritocracy and, in most occupations, threaten to lower standards.[21] But above all, they asked, why should whites be discriminated against for something their ancestors did? These opponents of affirmative action would not admit that past discrimination had burdened black workers so heavily that equal opportunity for everyone was not equality at all. Blacks were being equalized out of existence.

At decade's end, there was no clear consensus as to where the nation would go with affirmative action as the government, particularly the Supreme Court, handed down confusing interpretations. In *Regents of the University of California* v. *Bakke,* the Court ruled that Alan Bakke, a white man who claimed he had been denied admission to the University of California at Davis medical school because sixteen places had been set aside for minorities, should be admitted. But the Court also recognized the principle of race-conscious admission plans. The problem is that the Court did not speak with a clear voice. Four justices clearly supported the affirmative action admission plan, four others clearly opposed special admissions, and one seemed to stand on both sides of the issue. Justice Lewis Powell, whose compromise opinion came out as the Court's decision in *Bakke,* could see the merit in such programs, but he still believed that Bakke had been denied equal protection of the law as an individual.[22] The Supreme Court tried to clarify its position in two cases decided in 1979 and 1980. In *United Steelworkers* v. *Weber,* the Court ruled that a contract between the union and the Kaiser Aluminum and Chemical Corporation which allowed the company to set up two seniority lists—one for whites and one for blacks—from which to choose employees for its new crafts training program did not violate the rights of white workers. The parties could take such overt actions to redress past discrimination against blacks.[23] The Court also decided that Congress did not violate its constitutional authority when it included in the Public Works Employment Act of 1977 a requirement that the Secretary of Commerce set aside 10 percent of federal contracts for minority businesses.[24]

It is important to keep in mind that the cases that have captured the most attention, *Bakke* and *Weber,* deal not with hiring but with training. Employers have long maintained that they would hire blacks if they could find some who are qualified. The clear implication of *Bakke* and *Weber* is that opponents of advancement for blacks want to keep the pool of qualified blacks small so as to maintain the myth of their incapacity, even as the labor market structure of the nation changes.

But the Court's decision in *Bakke* teaches us more. The nation is not prepared to accept the special disability that centuries of racism have placed on black workers. Unlike Justices Harry A. Blackmun and Thurgood Marshall, the full Court was unwilling to agree that the only way to eliminate racial discrimination was to come to grips with the full impact of race on our society. Justice Blackmun observed that "in order to treat some persons equally, we must treat them differently," while Justice Marshall found it quite ironic that "after several hundred years of class-based discrimination against Negroes, the Court is unwilling to hold that a class-based remedy for that discrimination is permissible." When one looks at the decision in *Bakke,* particularly Justice Powell's opinion and his embrace of the Harvard plan with its emphasis on bringing in minority students to create a diverse student body, it is clear that the Court was much more concerned about what blacks could do for institutions than about what institutions could do to improve the chances of blacks in finding employment and earning a living. After fifteen years of affirmative action, the masses of blacks remained in a wretched condition, and it seemed that it would remain so forever.[25]

As the 1970s ended, future prospects for most black workers were about as bleak as they had been when Lincoln signed the Emancipation Proclamation. The nation was fed up with blacks, who were generally perceived to have made amazing progress, and the domestic economy was in a downturn that was predicted to reach the depths of the 1973–1975 recession. With daily newspapers reporting that general unemployment was reaching near record highs and that basic manufacturing in which blacks were heavily employed, such as automobiles and steel, was particularly hard hit, there was little hope for improvement of their employment condition. In the summer of 1980, unemployment of black youth stood at 40 percent. And the evidence of race was still quite clear. It could be seen especially among Viet Nam veterans; unemployment for black veterans was higher than for blacks as a whole, while white veterans had a lower unemployment rate than the population at large.

Yet two changes were under way whose full impact would be felt only in future years. In city after city throughout the country, whites had begun to move back to town, reversing the flight to the suburbs that had begun three decades earlier. This movement, known as "gentrification," was likely to attract jobs to the central cities, but it was also likely to displace large numbers of blacks and other poor persons because the new "gentry" were buying up property and renovating it at such high prices that blacks could not afford to live in the cities they had occupied for so long. In short, the new gentry would reside in exclusive enclaves in the cities, easily segregated from those unable to pay.

In addition to gentrification, census estimates show that blacks had begun an undetermined but unmistakable outmigration from the central cities, and from the North to the South.[26] The land so many had fled now seemed the land of opportunity, though it remains to be seen what job opportunities they will find there. At the beginning of the 1980s, after more than a century of struggle, little had been done to limit the impact of race on employment and income. As W. E. B. Du Bois had prophesied, the problem of the twentieth century has been the color line.[27]

Notes

Chapter 1

1. Mary Frances Berry, *Military Necessity and Civil Rights Policy* (Port Washington, N.Y.: Kennikat Press, 1977), particularly ch. 6.
2. Confiscation was not alien to the actions of the U.S. government, for Congress had confiscated southern property during the Civil War, particularly cotton. And, in fact, abolition was an act of confiscation. Nor was it unreasonable to think of gaining access to federal land. The federal government had granted plots of land to homesteaders for nominal fees and was just beginning a process that would see millions of acres given to railroads in the post-Civil War era.
3. Whitelaw Reid, *After the War: A Tour of the Southern States, 1865–66* (New York: Harper & Row, 1965 [first published in 1866]), 564–65.
4. Quoted in Loren Schweninger, "James Rapier and the Negro Labor Movement, 1869–1872," *The Alabama Review*, 33 (July 1975), 185.
5. Reid, *After the War*, 464–65; W. E. B. Du Bois, *Black Reconstruction in America, 1860–1880* (New York: Atheneum, 1969 [first published in 1935]), 601–4, 611; Vernon L. Wharton, *The Negro in Mississippi, 1865–1890* (Chapel Hill: University of North Carolina Press, 1947), chs. 1–2.
6. Du Bois, *Black Reconstruction*, 167. Nine of the eleven states actually passed such laws, Tennessee and Arkansas being the exceptions.
7. Joseph Reid, "Sharecropping as an Understandable Market Response," *Journal of Economic History*, 33 (Mar. 1973), 107–8; William F. Cohen, "Negro Involuntary Servitude, 1865–1940," *Journal of Southern History*, 42 (Feb. 1976), 47.
8. Harold D. Woodman, "Sequel to Slavery: The New History of the Postbellum South," *Journal of Southern History*, 43 (Nov. 1977), 550.
9. Richard Sutch and Roger Ransom, "Ex-Slaves in the Post-Bellum South: A Study of the Economic Impact of Racism in a Market Environment," *Journal of Economic History*, 33 (Mar. 1973), 134–38; Reid, "Sharecropping," *passim*.
10. Sutch and Ransom, "Ex-Slaves in the Post-Bellum South," 134.

11. Ibid., 137–38.
12. Pete Daniel, *The Shadow of Slavery: Peonage in the South, 1901–1969* (New York: Oxford University Press, 1972), 96–107; N. Gordon Carper, "Slavery Revisited: Peonage in the South," *Phylon*, 38 (Mar. 1976), 90–91; Cohen, "Negro Involuntary Servitude," 35–36.
13. Daniel, *Shadow of Slavery*, ch. 9; Cohen, "Negro Involuntary Servitude," 36–37.

   The mortality rate of convicts forced into industrial employment is an indication of the barbarity of the system. Between 1877 and 1880, for example, South Carolina leased 245 convicts as laborers on the Greenville and Augusta Railroad. Of those, 128 (44.9 percent) died. Moreover, though some whites found themselves relegated to the convict lease system, it was mainly a condition reserved for blacks. Around 1880, the ratio of black to white convicts leased was 13 : 1 in North Carolina, 11 : 1 in Georgia, and 7 : 1 in South Carolina. Both sets of data are from Cohen, "Negro Involuntary Servitude," 56–57.
14. W. E. B. Du Bois, "The Negro Farmer," in U.S. Bureau of the Census, Bulletin No. 8, *Negroes in the United States* (Washington, D.C.: GPO, 1905), 72.
15. Herbert G. Gutman, *The Black Family in Slavery and Freedom, 1750–1925* (New York: Pantheon, 1976), 443–44, 632. See also Appendix A, esp. Tables A-8 thru A-14.
16. Du Bois, *Black Reconstruction*, 637–69; Booker T. Washington, *Up from Slavery* (New York: A. L. Burt, 1901), *passim*.
17. C. Vann Woodward, *Origins of the New South, 1877–1913*, Vol. 9, *A History of the South* (Baton Rouge: Louisiana State University Press, 1951), ch. 2; C. Vann Woodward, *Reunion and Reaction: The Compromise of 1877 and the End of Reconstruction* (Boston: Little, Brown, 1951), is a more extensive discussion of the events surrounding the Compromise of 1877. See also Rayford W. Logan, *The Negro in American Life and Thought: The Nadir, 1877–1901* (New York: Dial Press, 1954), esp. chs. 1–2. The quotation is from Woodward, *Origins of the New South*, 29.
18. Quoted in Woodward, *Origins of the New South*, 221.
19. Ibid., 221–25.
20. Claudia Goldin, *Urban Slavery in the American South, 1820–60* (Chicago: University of Chicago Press, 1976), 129–32, has a good discussion of the impact of slavery on postwar skill distributions; see also John W. Blassingame, "Before the Ghetto: The Making of the Black Community of Savannah, Georgia, 1865–1880," *Journal of Social History*, 6 (Summer 1973), 465–66.
21. Peter Gottlieb, "Migration and Jobs: The New Black Workers in Pittsburgh, 1916–1930," *The Western Pennsylvania Historical Magazine*, 61 (Jan. 1978), 1–15.
22. Jerrell Shofner, "Negro Laborers in the Forest Industry," *Journal of Forest History*, 19 (Oct. 1975), 183.
23. Philip S. Foner, "The IWW and the Black Worker," *Journal of Negro History*, 55 (Jan. 1970), 52.

24. Shofner, "Negro Laborers in the Forest Industry," 183.
25. Walter F. Wilcox, "The Negro Population," in U.S. Bureau of the Census, Bulletin No. 8, *Negroes in the United States,* 60 and Table LXIII. For data on the preponderance of whites in skilled jobs, see Foner, "IWW and the Black Worker," 52.
26. Jerrell Shofner, "The Labor League of Jacksonville," *Florida History Quarterly,* 50 (Jan. 1972), 278–80.
27. Jerrell Shofner, "The Pensacola Workingmen's Association," *Labor History,* 13 (Fall 1972), 555–59.
28. Herbert G. Gutman, "Black Coal Miners in Redeemer Alabama," *Labor History,* 10 (Summer 1969), 519. The miner listed the discrepancies in prices between the company store and stores in town (see table).

Item	Company store price	Town price
Flour per barrel	$ 9.00	$6.00
Meat per 100 pounds	13.00	7.00
Corn meal	2.75	1.75
Sugar, six pounds	1.00	1.00
Coffee, three pounds	1.00	1.00

29. Ibid., *passim;* Woodward, *Origins of the New South,* 213–15, 232–33.
30. Herbert G. Gutman, "Reconstruction in Ohio," *Labor History,* 3 (Fall 1962), *passim.* The quotation is from p. 257.
31. Ibid., 258–59; see also John H. Keiser, "Black Strikebreakers and Racism in Illinois, 1865–1900," *Illinois State Historical Society Journal,* 65 (Autumn 1972), 313–26.
32. U.S. Bureau of Labor, *Sixteenth Annual Report of the Commissioner* (Washington, D.C.: GPO, 1901), 413–65, Table IX. For a discussion of the heavy use of immigrants as strikebreakers and of the myths surrounding that practice, see Richard L. Ehrlich, "Immigrant Strikebreaking Activity: A Sampling of Opinion Expressed in the *National Labor Tribune,* 1878–1885," *Labor History,* 15 (Fall 1974), 529–42.
33. Kenneth W. Porter, "Negro Labor in the Western Cattle Industry, 1866–1900," *Labor History,* 10 (Summer 1972), 346–74.
34. Winthrop D. Jordan, *White Over Black: American Attitudes Toward the Negro, 1550–1812* (Chapel Hill: University of North Carolina Press, 1968), 77–78, 130.
35. Goldin, *Urban Slavery,* 87, 94.
36. Ibid., 87.
37. Claudia Goldin, "Female Labor Force Participation: The Origin of Black and White Differences, 1870 and 1880," *Journal of Economic History,* 37 (June 1977), 101; Carter G. Woodson, "The Negro Washerwoman: A Vanishing Breed," *Journal of Negro History,* 15 (July 1930), 274, n. 12.
38. Goldin, *Urban Slavery,* 97. These figures take on more meaning when it

is kept in mind that census enumerators listed 36.4 percent of black women as "at home" and another 18.8 percent as having no occupation. Gutman, *Black Family*, 628, emphasizes the difficulty one faces in trying to utilize census data on the occupational distribution of black females.

39. Dale Sommers, "Black and White in New Orleans," *Journal of Southern History*, 40 (Feb. 1974), 30–31.

40. Philip S. Foner, *Organized Labor and the Black Worker, 1619–1973* (New York: Praeger, 1974), chs. 2 and 3, is a good discussion of the two unions. Though at no time did the black group speak of itself as such, historians have designated it the Colored National Labor Union. Bettye Thomas, *Journal of Negro History*, 59 (Jan. 1974), provides a novel version of the founding of the black shipbuilding company in Baltimore and asserts, among other things, that Myers has received more credit than he deserves for his part in founding and operating the company.

41. Foner, *Organized Labor and the Black Worker*, 25.

42. Schweninger, "James Rapier and the Negro Labor Movement," 192, 195.

43. Sidney H. Kessler, "The Organization of Negroes in the Knights of Labor," *Journal of Negro History*, 38 (July 1952), 248–76.

44. Melton A. McLaurin, "Racial Policies of the Knights of Labor and the Organization of Southern Black Workers," *Labor History*, 17 (Fall 1976), 569.

45. Ibid., 577–78; Leon Fink, " 'Irrespective of Party, Color or Social Standing': The Knights of Labor and Opposition Politics in Richmond, Virginia," *Labor History*, 19 (Summer 1978), 325–49. The quotation is from Fink, p. 343.

46. William Ivy Hair, *Bourbonism and Agrarian Protest: Louisiana Politics, 1877–1900* (Baton Rouge: Louisiana State University Press, 1970), 176–85; McLaurin, "Racial Policies of the Knights of Labor," 578.

Chapter 2

1. Rayford W. Logan, *The Negro in American Life and Thought: The Nadir, 1877–1901* (New York: Dial Press, 1954), revised and republished under the title *The Betrayal of the Negro, from Rutherford B. Hayes to Woodrow Wilson* (New York: Collier Books, 1965).

2. Ibid., ch. 6.

3. T. Lynn Smith, "Redistribution of the Negro Population, 1910–1960," *Journal of Negro History*, 51 (July 1966), 156–57.

4. U.S. Bureau of the Census, Bulletin No. 129, *Negroes in the United States: 1910* (Washington, D.C.: GPO, 1915), 37; W. E. B. Du Bois, "The Negro Farmer," in U.S. Bureau of the Census, Bulletin No. 8, *Negroes in the United States* (Washington, D.C.: GPO, 1905), 69–98.

5. Du Bois, "The Negro Farmer," 79. See ch. 1, this book, p. 11, for the definition of tenantry.

6. U.S. Bureau of the Census, *Negroes in the United States, 1910*. See esp. Table 2.

7. Ibid., Robert Higgs, "Race, Tenure and Resource Allocation in Southern Agriculture, 1910," *Journal of Economic History*, 33 (Mar. 1973), 159; Gavin Wright, "Comment on Papers by Reid, Ransom and Sutch, and Higgs," ibid., 171–72.

8. Allen W. Jones, "The Role of Tuskegee Institute in the Education of Black Farmers," *Journal of Negro History*, 40 (April 1975), 262–66.

9. Mary Frances Berry, "Reparations for Freedmen, 1890–1916," *Journal of Negro History*, 57 (July 1972), 220–23.

10. William F. Holmes, "The Demise of the Colored Farmers' Alliance," *Journal of Southern History*, 41 (May 1975), 187; Floyd J. Miller, "Black Protest and White Leadership: A Note on the Colored Farmers' Alliance," *Phylon*, 33 (Summer 1972), 170; Martin Dann, "Black Populism: A Study of the Colored Farmers' Alliance Through 1891," *Journal of Ethnic Studies*, 2 (Fall 1974), 62–63; Lawrence Goodwyn, *The Populist Moment: A Short History of the Agrarian Revolt in America* (New York: Oxford University Press, 1978), 118–23. Goodwyn asserts that rather than 1,200,000 members, 250,000 was a more realistic figure for alliance membership (p. 119).

11. Holmes, "Colored Farmers' Alliance," 196–99; Dann, "Black Populism," *passim;* William F. Holmes, "The Arkansas Cotton Pickers' Strike," *Arkansas Historical Quarterly*, 32 (Summer 1973), 107–19; Lawrence C. Goodwyn, *Democratic Promise: The Populist Moment in America* (New York: Oxford University Press, 1976), 292–93.

12. Goodwyn, *Democratic Promise*, 276–306, is a superb discussion of the relationship between black and white Populists. The long quotation is from Lawrence C. Goodwyn, "Populist Dreams and Negro Rights: East Texas as a Case Study," *American Historical Review*, 76 (Dec. 1971), 1452. For quotations from Watson, see C. Vann Woodward, *Origins of the New South, 1877–1913* (Baton Rouge: Louisiana State University Press, 1952), 257.

13. Herbert G. Gutman, *The Black Family in Slavery and Freedom, 1750–1925* (New York: Pantheon, 1976), 631.

14. Carter G. Woodson, "The Negro Washerwoman: A Vanishing Breed," *Journal of Negro History*, 15 (July 1930), 269–77; Howard N. Rabinowitz, *Race Relations in the Urban South, 1865–1890* (New York: Oxford University Press, 1978), 73–76.

15. See, for example, Rabinowitz, *Race Relations in the Urban South*, 71–72; James T. Haley, ed., *Afro-American Encyclopedia or, the Thoughts, Doings and Sayings of the Race* (Nashville: Haley & Florida, 1895), 68; and J. W. Gibson and W. H. Grogman, *Progress of a Race or the Remarkable Advancement of the American Negro* (Atlanta: J. L. Nichols, 1902), 305–8.

16. Arthur M. Ross, "The Negro in the American Economy," in Arthur M. Ross and Herbert Hill, eds., *Employment, Race, and Poverty* (New York: Harcourt, Brace and World, 1967).

17. John W. Blassingame, "Before the Ghetto: The Making of the Black Community of Savannah, Georgia, 1865–1880," *Journal of Social History*, 6 (Summer 1972), 465–66; Claudia Goldin, *Urban Slavery in the*

American South, 1820–60 (Chicago: University of Chicago Press, 1976), 129–32; Richard R. Wright, "The Negro in Unskilled Labor," *Annals of the American Academy of Political and Social Science*, 49 (Sept. 1913), 23. Gutman, *The Black Family*, 627, found that in 1880 all the stationary engineers, bricklayers, and wood sawyers were black in Natchez, Mississippi, and blacks dominated those trades in Richmond, Virginia, and Mobile, Alabama, as well. James Weldon Johnson made much the same point in his autobiography, *Along This Way* (New York, Viking, 1968 [1933]), 31. Referring to the time of his youth in Florida during the 1880s, Johnson wrote, "When I was a child, I did not know that there existed such a thing as a white carpenter or bricklayer or plasterer or tinner. The thought that white men might be able to load and unload the heavy drays of the big ships was too far from my everyday life to enter my mind."

18. Paul Worthman, "Black Workers and Labor Unions in Birmingham, Alabama, 1897–1904," *Labor History*, 10 (Summer 1969), 392; Gutman, *The Black Family*, 627.

19. U.S. Bureau of the Census, Bulletin No. 8, *Negroes in the United States*, 52–64; Gutman, *The Black Family*, 628, emphasizes the age differential that had appeared between black and white skilled workers as early as 1880.

20. U.S. Bureau of the Census, Bulletin No. 8, *Negroes in the United States*, 57–59.

21. Ibid.; Paul Worthman, "A Black Worker and the Bricklayers' and Masons' Union, 1903," *Journal of Negro History*, 54 (Oct. 1969), 398–404.

22. Almont Lindsey, *The Pullman Strike: The Story of a Unique Experiment and of a Great Labor Upheaval* (Chicago: University of Chicago Press, 1942), 94–96; Gerald E. Eggert, *Railroad Labor Disputes: The Beginnings of Federal Strike Policy* (Ann Arbor: University of Michigan Press, 1967), ch. 7. For a discussion of constitutional bans against blacks in the Big Four, see F. E. Wolfe, *Admission to American Trade Unions* (Baltimore: Johns Hopkins University Press, 1912), 119–20, and W. E. B. Du Bois, ed., *The Negro Artisan* (Atlanta, Ga.: Atlanta University Publications, 1902), 167–68.

23. William H. Harris, *Keeping the Faith: A. Philip Randolph, Milton P. Webster, and the Brotherhood of Sleeping Car Porters, 1925–37* (Urbana: University of Illinois Press, 1977), 4; Philip S. Foner, *Organized Labor and the Black Worker, 1619–1973* (New York: Praeger, 1974), 104–5; Eugene V. Debs, *The Negro Worker* (New York: Emancipation Publishing, 1923), 6–7.

24. For an extended discussion of methods unions used to discriminate against blacks, see Wolfe, *Admission to Trade Unions*, ch. 6. In ch. 1 he discusses general trade union admission qualifications. Du Bois, *The Negro Artisan*, 171, emphasizes the power locals exercise over union membership.

25. Kenneth L. Kusmer, *A Ghetto Takes Shape: Black Cleveland, 1870–*

1930 (Urbana: University of Illinois Press, 1976), ch. 4, esp. pp. 69–73; David Katzman, *Before the Ghetto: Black Detroit in the Nineteenth Century* (Urbana: University of Illinois Press, 1973), ch. 4, esp. pp. 125–26; Gilbert Osofsky, *Harlem: The Making of A Ghetto* (New York: Harper Torchbook, 1971), 194–96.

26. *Report of the First Annual Session of the Federation of Organized Trade and Labor Unions of the United States and Canada,* Pittsburgh (Sept. 15–18, 1881), 16. The *Report* is now Vol. 1, *Report of the Proceedings,* American Federation of Labor Conventions. Since the *Report* lists Grandison only by lodge and not by trade, it is impossible to ascertain what type of work he did, though it is safe to conclude from his presence at the meeting that he was a skilled worker.

27. See the discussion of black strikebreakers, ch. 1, *supra.*

28. Herbert G. Gutman, "The Negro and the United Mine Workers of America: The Career and Letters of Richard L. Davis and Something of their Meaning, 1890–1900," in Julius Jacobsen, ed., *The Negro and the American Labor Movement* (Garden City, N.Y.: Doubleday, 1968), 49–127. See particularly p. 111 for membership figures. For a more recent account of Davis's career, consult Stephen Brier, "The Career of Richard L. Davis Reconsidered: Unpublished Correspondence from the *National Labor Tribune,*" *Labor History,* 21 (Summer 1980), 420–29. See also Ira DeA. Reid and Charles S. Johnson, *Negro Membership in American Labor Unions* (New York: Alexander Press, 1930), 68.

29. Foner, *Organized Labor,* 95–96.

30. Ibid., 72–73; Harris, *Keeping the Faith,* 8–10. Important works on Gompers include Bernard Mandel, *Samuel Gompers, a Biography* (Yellow Springs, Ohio: Antioch Press, 1963); Mandel, "Samuel Gompers and the Negro Worker, 1886–1914," *Journal of Negro History,* 40 (Jan. 1955), 34–60; and Arthur Mann, "Gompers and the Irony of Racism," *Antioch Review,* 13 (June 1953), 207. For Gompers's own views, see *American Federationist, passim,* in which he refers to blacks as "niggers," and his ultra-racist diatribe against the Chinese, written in partnership with Herman Gutstadt, *Meat vs. Rice: American Manhood Against Asian Coolieism—Which Shall Survive?* (San Francisco: Asiatic Exclusion League, 1908).

31. Du Bois, *Negro Artisan,* 167–68; Foner, *Organized Labor,* 73.

32. Hugh B. Hammett, "Labor and Race: The Georgia Railroad Strike of 1909," *Labor History,* 16 (Fall 1975), 472.

33. John Michael Matthews, "The Georgia 'Race Strike' of 1909," *Journal of Southern History,* 40 (Nov. 1974), 614–15.

34. Hammett, "Labor and Race," 476.

35. Ibid., 480; Matthews, "The Georgia 'Race Strike,'" 614–15; Foner, *Organized Labor,* 106; Sterling D. Spero and Abram L. Harris, *The Black Worker* (Port Washington, N.Y.: Kennikat Press, 1966 [1931]), 289–95.

36. Charles H. Houston, "Foul Employment Practice on the Rails," *Crisis,* 56 (Oct. 1949), 269.

37. *Report of the President: Brotherhood of Locomotive Firemen and Enginemen* (St. Paul, Minn., 1909), 290–94.

38. See, for example, "Justice for the Negro—How Can He Get It?" n.d.; Elizabeth Gurley Flynn Collection, Wisconsin State Historical Society; R. Laurence Moore, "Flawed Fraternity—American Socialist Response to the Negro, 1901–1912," *The Historian*, 32 (Nov. 1969), 2. A leading Socialist, Victor Berger, the first Socialist to sit in the U.S. Congress, even wrote in 1902 that blacks were socially and politically backward when compared with whites and Orientals. As evidence, he cited what he saw as the large number of rapes that occurred where blacks settled. See Berger, "The Misfortune of the Negro," *Social Democratic Herald*, May 31, 1902.

39. Philip S. Foner, "The IWW and the Black Worker," *Journal of Negro History*, 55 (Jan. 1970), 46–47, 58–59.

40. Ibid., 52.

41. Ibid.; George T. Morgan, Jr., "No Compromise, No Recognition: John Henry Kirby, the Southern Lumber Operators' Association and Unionism in the Piney Woods, 1906–1916," *Labor History*, 10 (Summer 1969), 194.

Chapter 3

1. For the best discussion of the use of immigrant agent taxes and other methods to keep black workers in the South, see William F. Cohen, "Negro Involuntary Servitude, 1865–1940," *Journal of Southern History*, 42 (Feb. 1976), 38–40.

2. Stanley Buder, *Pullman: An Experiment in Industrial Order and Social Planning, 1880–1930* (New York: Oxford University Press, 1967); Neil Betten and Raymond A. Mohl, "The Evolution of Racism in an Industrial City," *Journal of Negro History*, 59 (Jan. 1974), 57–60.

3. Kenneth L. Kusmer, *A Ghetto Takes Shape: Black Cleveland, 1870–1930* (Urbana: University of Illinois Press, 1976); David M. Katzman, *Before the Ghetto: Black Detroit in the Nineteenth Century* (Urbana: University of Illinois Press, 1973); and Gilbert Osofsky, *Harlem: The Making of a Ghetto, Negro New York, 1890–1930* (New York: Harper Torchbooks, 2nd ed., 1971), all stress that occupational and housing discrimination patterns had been established in northern cities long before the onset of the Great Migration.

4. William M. Tuttle, Jr., "Labor Conflict and Racial Violence," *Labor History*, 10 (Summer 1969), 412–18.

5. Elliott Rudwick, *Race Riot at East St. Louis, Illinois, July 2, 1917* (Carbondale, Ill.: Southern Illinois University Press, 1964); William M. Tuttle, Jr., *Race Riot: Chicago in the Red Summer of 1919* (New York: Atheneum, 1970).

6. Tuttle, *Race Riot;* Illinois Commission on Race Relations, *The Negro in Chicago: A Study of Race Relations and of a Race Riot* (Chicago: University of Chicago Press, 1922).

7. Carter G. Woodson, *A Century of Negro Migration* (Washington, D.C.:

Association for the Study of Negro Life and History, 1918); Joseph A. Hill, "Recent Northward Migration of the Negro," *Monthly Labor Review*, 18 (Mar. 1924), 1–14; T. J. Woofter, *Negro Migration*, cited in "Negro Migrations and Migrants," an unsigned article in *Monthly Labor Review*, 14 (Jan. 1922), 42. According to census figures, the net out-migration of blacks from the South represented 8.2 percent of the black population of that region and 2 percent of the total black population.

8. Quotation from "Negro Migration," *Monthly Labor Review*, 16 (June 1923), 33. Government agencies paid considerable attention to the movement of black workers. Numerous stories on the migration appeared in the *MLR* during the 1920s.

9. Abram L. Harris, "Negro Migration to the North," *Current History Magazine*, 20 (Sept. 1924), 923.

10. Woofter, "Negro Migrations and Migrants," 42–43.

11. Quoted in "Negro Migration," *Monthly Labor Review*, 16 (June 1923), 34.

12. Ibid.

13. Hill, "Recent Northward Migration," 11.

14. William H. Harris, *Keeping the Faith: A. Philip Randolph, Milton P. Webster, and the Brotherhood of Sleeping Car Porters, 1925–37* (Urbana: University of Illinois Press, 1977), 1–3; Brailsford R. Brazeal, *The Brotherhood of Sleeping Car Porters* (New York: Harper & Brothers, 1946), 6.

15. Quoted in Chicago *Defender*, Dec. 29, 1928.

16. U.S. Bureau of Immigration, *Annual Reports of the Commissioner-General of Immigration* (Washington, D.C.: GPO, 1913–20).

17. Herbert R. Northrup, *The Negro in the Automotive Industry* (Philadelphia: University of Pennsylvania Press, 1968), 8, writes about both white and black southern migrants to northern cities. In reflecting on the number of blacks who migrated to the North during World War I, one must keep in mind that considerably more whites than blacks quit the South. The difference is that larger white populations in both sections reduced the impact of the white migration. For a contemporary analysis of relative migration of blacks and whites, see "Migration of Negroes to Northern Cities," *Monthly Labor Review*, 12 (Jan. 1921), 201–3.

18. U.S. Department of Commerce, Bureau of the Census, *Negro Population, 1790–1915* (Washington, D.C.: GPO, 1918), 526; U.S. Bureau of the Census, *Negroes in the United States, 1920–1932* (Washington, D.C.: GPO, 1935), 290.

19. Walter A. Fogel, *The Negro in the Meat Industry*, Report No. 12, *Racial Policies of American Industry* (Philadelphia: University of Pennsylvania Press, 1970), 17–18, 25–27.

20. August Meier and Elliott Rudwick, *Black Detroit and the Rise of the UAW* (New York: Oxford University Press, 1979), 3–16; Herbert R. Northrup et al., *Negro Employment in Basic Industry: A Study of Racial Policies in Six Industries* (Philadelphia: University of Pennsylvania Press, 1970), 57.

21. For brief discussions of blacks in the steel mills of Pittsburgh, see

Horace R. Cayton and George S. Mitchell, *Black Workers and the New Unions* (Chapel Hill: University of North Carolina Press, 1939), 7; and Helen A. Tucker, "The Negroes of Pittsburgh," in *Wage Earning Pittsburgh, The Pittsburgh Survey* (New York: Survey Associates, Inc., 1914), 106. U.S. Bureau of the Census, *Thirteenth Census of the United States, Population,* Vol. 4 (Washington, D.C.: GPO, 1914), 590–91, contains statistical data on employment of blacks in steel yards. For percentages of blacks in unskilled jobs, see particularly Blanche J. Paget, "The Plight of the Pennsylvania Negro," *Opportunity,* 16 (Oct. 1936), 310.

22. U.S. Department of Labor, Division of Negro Economics, *Negro Migrations in 1916–1917* (Washington, D.C.: GPO, 1919), 118.

23. U.S. Department of Labor, Division of Negro Economics, *The Negro at Work During the World War and Reconstruction* (Washington, D.C.: GPO, 1921), 59. Figures on the employment of blacks and whites in the shipyards are from Herbert R. Northrup, *Organized Labor and the Negro* (New York: Harper & Brothers, 1944), 210.

24. Division of Negro Economics, *The Negro at Work,* 58–59.

25. Quoted in John O. Finney, Jr., "A Study of Negro Labor During and After World War I" (Ph.D. dissertation: Georgetown University, 1967), 200–201. For a general discussion of blacks in the shipbuilding industry, see Finney, 197–201; Northrup, *Organized Labor and the Negro,* 210–31; and Lester Rubin, *The Negro in the Shipbuilding Industry,* Report No. 17, *Racial Policies of American Industry* (Philadelphia: University of Pennsylvania Press, 1970), 36–41.

26. Hill, "Recent Northward Migration of the Negro," 11–12.

27. "Women in Industry," *Monthly Labor Review,* 29 (Sept. 1929), 54. Italics added.

28. Ibid. See also "Women and Child Labor," ibid., 15 (July 1922), 116–18. Nancy J. Weiss, *The National Urban League, 1910–1940* (New York: Oxford University Press, 1974), 177, 189, and *passim,* discusses the attitudes of whites toward working with blacks.

29. Susan Estabrook Kennedy, *If All We Did Was to Weep At Home: A Story of White Working-Class Women in America* (Bloomington, Ind.: Indiana University Press, 1979), makes all too clear the number of white women who worked and the problems and anxieties they faced.

30. For a discussion of the importance of middle-class status for white working-class women, see ibid., 112–14, and Barbara Klacynska, "Why Women Work," *Labor History,* 17 (Winter 1976), 83. Klacynska also writes about the propensity of black women to remain in the labor force longer than white women. Kennedy points out that often white women "retired" because of a sense of middle-class status long before they acquired the financial status with which to support their new standing; see p. xv. William H. Chafe, *The American Woman: Her Changing Social, Economic and Political Roles, 1920–1970* (New York: Oxford University Press, 1972), 66–88, also discusses women in industry.

31. Mary V. Robinson, "Domestic Workers and Their Employment Rela-

tions," U.S. Department of Labor, *Bulletin of the Women's Bureau*, No. 39 (Washington, D.C.: GPO, 1924), 24, 32–33.

32. Quoted in ibid., 31.

33. Tuttle, *Race Riot;* Rudwick, *Race Riot at East St. Louis;* Illinois Commission on Race Relations, *The Negro in Chicago;* and Oscar Leonard, "The East St. Louis Pogrom," *Survey*, 38 (July 14, 1917), 331–33.

34. Walter F. White, " 'Work or Fight' in the South," *The New Republic*, 18 (Mar. 1, 1919), 144–46; Finney, "Negro Labor," 201–8.

35. Weiss, *National Urban League*, 89–91, 100–101, 123–28; Charles Flint Kellogg, *The NAACP: A History of the National Association for the Advancement of Colored People, 1909–1920* (Baltimore: Johns Hopkins University Press, 1967), I, 34–35; 266–71.

36. Finney, "Negro Labor," chs. III and IV, contains the best discussion of the creation and operation of the Division of Negro Economics. Haynes tells his own story in the Division of Negro Economics, *The Negro at Work*.

37. Finney, "Negro Labor," ch. IV.

38. "Negroes and Organized Labor," *Survey*, 39 (Feb. 9, 1918), 527–28.

39. Quoted in Ira DeA. Reid and Charles S. Johnson, *Negro Membership in American Labor Unions* (New York: Alexander Press, 1930), 27. For other views of the conversations, see Weiss, *National Urban League*, 203–9; Finney, "Negro Labor," 283–93; and NAACP, *Annual Report* (1917–18), 69–70.

40. Reid and Johnson, *Negro Membership*, 27–29.

41. Quoted in Charles H. Wesley, *Negro Labor in the United States* (New York: Vanguard Press, 1927), 278.

42. Amy Jacques-Garvey, ed., *Philosophy and Opinions of Marcus Garvey* (New York: Atheneum, 1969), 69–71. In this section, Garvey makes it clear that he distrusts all whites who speak in favor of equal opportunities for blacks. If required to choose between members of the Ku Klux Klan on the one hand, and whites like Mary White Ovington and J. E. Spingarn of the NAACP on the other, he writes, his choice would be the Klansmen "because of their honesty of purpose" (ibid., 71). The best recent full study of Garvey's career is Tony Martin, *Race First: The Ideological and Organizational Struggles of Marcus Garvey and the Universal Negro Improvement Association* (Westport, Conn.: Greenwood Press, 1976). An earlier book, E. David Cronon, *Black Moses: The Story of Marcus Garvey and the Universal Negro Improvement Association* (Madison: University of Wisconsin Press, 2nd ed., 1969), should also be consulted.

43. Finney, "Negro Labor," 341–51.

44. Chicago *Defender*, June 19, 1926.

45. Finney, "Negro Labor," 349; Reid and Johnson, *Negro Membership*, 118–27; Spero and Harris, *Black Worker*, 116–27.

46. Theodore Kornweibel, Jr., *No Crystal Stair* (Westport, Conn.: Greenwood Press, 1975), ch. 2; Harris, *Keeping the Faith*, 30–31.

47. Harris, *Keeping the Faith*, 31–32.

48. *Messenger,* 7 (Feb. 1925), 89.
49. Wesley, *Negro Labor,* 276–77.
50. William Green, "Our Negro Worker," *Messenger,* 7 (Sept. 1925), 332.
51. Kelly Miller, "The Negro as a Working Man," *American Mercury,* 6 (Nov. 1925), 310–13.
52. A. Philip Randolph, "Economic Radicalism," *Opportunity,* 4 (Feb. 1926), 63; T. Arnold Hill, "The Negro in Industry," *American Federationist,* 42 (Oct. 1925), 915–20; T. Arnold Hill, "The Dilemma of Negro Workers," *Opportunity,* 4 (Feb. 1926), 39–41; see also Weiss, *National Urban League,* 181–91.
53. Harris, *Keeping the Faith,* 23–24.
54. Ibid., 24–25.

Chapter 4

1. William H. Harris, *Keeping the Faith: A. Philip Randolph, Milton P. Webster, and the Brotherhood of Sleeping Car Porters, 1925–37* (Urbana: University of Illinois Press, 1977), is a detailed discussion of the origins and growth of the BSCP through its successful negotiation of a contract with the Pullman Company. The interpretations of this chapter are based on that work. One might also consult Brailsford R. Brazeal, *The Brotherhood of Sleeping Car Porters: Its Origins and Development* (New York: Harper & Brothers, 1946).
2. Harris, *Keeping the Faith,* 15; Charles H. Thompson, "Discrimination in Negro Teachers' Salaries in Maryland," *Journal of Negro Education,* 5 (Oct. 1936), 540.
3. Edward F. Berman, "Brief on Working Conditions of Pullman Porters," n.d., prepared for National Mediation Board hearings in the case of Brotherhood of Sleeping Car Porters and the Pullman Company, 1936–37, copy in Brotherhood of Sleeping Car Porters Papers, The Chicago Historical Society.
4. F. L. Simmons to E. F. Carry, Jan. 15 and Mar. 28, 1924; Carry to Simmons, Apr. 2, 1924; in Pullman Company Papers, Pullman, Inc., Chicago.
5. A. Philip Randolph to Elizabeth G. Flynn, Sept. 21 and Dec. 11, 1925, Garland Fund Papers, The New York Public Library; BSCP "Bylaws," n.d., in National Mediation Board Case File #C-107, *Brotherhood of Sleeping Car Porters v. Pullman Company,* National Archives; *Messenger,* 7 (July 1925), 254–55; (Aug. 1925), 289–90, 306; (Dec. 1925), 403; and ibid., 8 (Jan. 1926), 37.
6. Murray Kempton, *Part of Our Time: Some Ruins and Monuments of the Thirties* (New York: Simon & Schuster, 1955), 244; Harris, *Keeping the Faith,* 34.
7. For a fuller discussion of Randolph's charismatic qualities, see William H. Harris, "A. Philip Randolph as a Charismatic Leader, 1925–41," *Journal of Negro History,* 64 (Fall 1979), 301–15.
8. Harris, *Keeping the Faith,* 217–25.
9. The history of the press coverage of the BSCP during its early years is

in itself an interesting story that brings into play the aims and motives of the various black publishers as well as the effort on the part of the Pullman Company to buy black press opposition to the union. The *Argus* incident, and the longtime support of the company's position by the Chicago *Defender*, show how well Pullman succeeded in that effort. But even more striking was the desertion of the Pittsburgh *Courier* from the BSCP's cause in 1928 amid firm allegations that Pullman officials paid Robert Vann, the *Courier's* publisher, a handsome sum to help stop the union on the eve of its threatened strike. See the Pittsburgh *Courier*, Chicago *Defender*, Chicago *Whip*, and St. Louis *Argus*, all *passim* for 1925–28. Roi Ottley, *The Lonely Warrior: The Life and Times of Robert S. Abbott* (Chicago: Regnery Press, 1955), 259–65, covers the association between the BSCP and the *Defender*, while Andrew Buni, *Robert L. Vann of the Pittsburgh Courier: Politics and Black Journalism* (Pittsburgh: University of Pittsburgh Press, 1974), 162–71, discusses that paper's relationship with the union. Harris, *Keeping the Faith*, 41–49, 129–41, is the fullest account of the various union-press activities.

10. Black Klan to E. R. Estelle, n.d. [1925]; and Black Klan to Estelle, Dec. 17, 1925, both in Pullman Company Papers, Chicago.

11. Various letters and memoranda, *BSCP v. Pullman Company*, National Archives.

12. Interstate Commerce Commission Case #20,007, ICC Files, National Archives.

13. Papers in *BSCP v. Pullman Company*, National Mediation Board Files, National Archives.

14. Several letters, esp. William Green to A. Philip Randolph, May 8, 1929, in Green's Copy Books, No. 400, p. 235; and Green to Randolph, June 18, 1929, ibid., No. 409, p. 534, AFL-CIO Headquarters, Washington, D.C.; Henry T. Hunt to James Weldon Johnson, Apr. 14, 1927, NAACP Papers, C414, Library of Congress; and AFL Convention, *Report of the Proceedings* (Washington, D.C.: AFL, Nov. 1929), 137–38.

15. Walter White, *A Man Called White: The Autobiography of Walter F. White* (Bloomington, Ind.: Indiana University Press, 1970), 106; Richard L. Watson, "The Defeat of Judge Parker: A Study in Pressure Group Politics," *Mississippi Valley Historical Review*, 50 (Sept. 1963), 213–34. The BSCP and other blacks opposed Parker because he had argued during a campaign for the governorship of North Carolina that he opposed the participation of blacks in politics. Organized white labor based its opposition to Parker on the judge's anti-labor stance, particularly his ruling in favor of yellow dog contracts in the Red Jacket case concerning the UMW in West Virginia in 1927. See Irving Bernstein, *A History of the American Worker, 1920–33: The Lean Years* (Boston: Houghton Mifflin, 1960), 406–9.

16. AFL Convention, *Report of the Proceedings* (Oct. 1934), 334.

17. Charles H. Houston, Memorandum to Walter White, NAACP Papers, C414, Library of Congress; *Opportunity*, 13 (Aug. 1935), 247–49.

18. Various letters, Green's Copy Books (Summer 1935).

19. AFL Convention, *Report of the Proceedings* (Oct. 1935), 808–19. For a discussion of the AFL dismissal of CIO unions, see Philip Taft, *The AF of L from the Death of Gompers to the Merger* (New York: Harper, 1959), 140–203.

20. Walter White to John L. Lewis, Nov. 27, 1935, NAACP Papers, C414, Library of Congress.

21. Green to Randolph and Green to M. S. Warfield, both Feb. 15, 1935, Green's Copy Books, No. 484, pp. 75–76, and Green to Warfield, Mar. 21, 1935, ibid., No. 487, p. 877; AFL Convention, *Report of the Proceedings* (Oct. 1934), 709.

22. Amended Railway Labor Act of 1934 (48 Stat. 1185).

23. Interview with A. Philip Randolph, Jan. 19, 1972. The Pullman Company finally agreed to settle the dispute with the BSCP so as to keep the porters, who were again talking about a strike, from involving the company in a threatened general railroad strike. See G. James Fleming, "Pullman Porters Win," *American Federationist*, 44 (Nov. 1937), 332.

Chapter 5

1. Pete Daniel, *The Shadow of Slavery: Peonage in the South, 1901–1969* (Urbana: University of Illinois Press, 1972). The Justice Department got around to making energetic investigations and prosecutions for peonage only in 1940–1941. Those actions came largely because of the government's desire to blunt mounting Japanese and German propaganda on American racism.

2. Ibid., 110–31.

3. Donald Holley, "The Negro in the New Deal Resettlement Program," *Agricultural History*, 45 (July 1971), 180.

4. Daniel, *Shadow of Slavery*, ch. 8, is a superb discussion of the flood and of the widespread evidence of peonage its waters washed into the open.

5. Ibid., 161.

6. Mark D. Naison, "Black Agrarian Radicalism in the Great Depression: The Threads of a Lost Tradition," *Journal of Ethnic Studies* (Summer, 1973), 52–53, discusses the origins of the Alabama Sharecroppers Union.

7. Ibid., 53; Nell Irving Painter, *The Narrative of Hosea Hudson: His Life as a Negro Communist in the South* (Cambridge, Mass.: Harvard University Press, 1979), 83–84, 146–55.

8. H. L. Mitchell, "Report—Sharecroppers Union of Alabama," p. 1, report in the Southern Tenant Farmers Union Papers, microfilm edition, n.d.

9. Raymond Wolters, *Negroes and the Great Depression: The Problem of Economic Recovery* (Westport, Conn.: Greenwood Press, 1970), ch. 1; Donald Holley, "The Negro in the New Deal Resettlement Program," 180.

10. Norman Thomas, *The Plight of the Share-Croppers* (New York: League for Industrial Democracy, 1934), Part II, "Report of the Survey made by Memphis Chapter L.I.D. and the Tyronza Socialist party under the

direction of William R. Amberson," esp. pp. 25–31. The Amberson report contains a strange racial bias in that people associated with him had just organized the Southern Tenant Farmers Union, an organization widely acclaimed for its interracialism.

11. "Nonwhite Farm Operators in the United States, 1940," *Monthly Labor Review*, 53 (Aug. 1941), 400–401. The following table shows the relative changes of black and white farm operators in various classes between 1930 and 1940.

Year	Owners and Managers		Tenants		Croppers	
	Black	*White*	*Black*	*White*	*Black*	*White*
1930	183,000	1,250,000	306,000	709,000	393,000	383,000
1935	186,000	1,404,000	261,000	709,000	393,000	348,000
1940	174,000	1,384,000	209,000	700,000	299,000	242,000

12. Jerald S. Auerbach, "Southern Tenant Farmers: Socialist Critics of the New Deal," *Labor History*, 7 (Winter 1966), 4–5.

13. "Relief Benefits of Rural Negroes," *Monthly Labor Review*, 42 (Jan. 1936), 63.

14. Ibid.

15. Quotations from John A. Salmond, "The Civilian Conservation Corps and the Negro," *Journal of American History*, 52 (June 1965), 78.

16. Ibid., 81–82.

17. H. L. Mitchell, *Mean Things Happening in This Land: The Life and Times of H. L. Mitchell, Cofounder of the Southern Tenant Farmers Union* (Montclair, N.J.: Allanheld, Osmun, 1979), is the most complete published record of the STFU though, as one would expect, it is the story of the union as told by one who obviously has a point to make. Donald H. Grubbs, *Cry from the Cotton—The STFU and the New Deal* (Chapel Hill: University of North Carolina Press, 1971), is a scholarly history of part of the STFU's activities. Naison, "Black Agrarian Radicalism in the Great Depression," esp. pp. 56–62, is also helpful in trying to convey an understanding of the union.

18. Nell Irwin Painter, *The Narrative of Hosea Hudson*, 117–18.

19. Wolters, *Negroes and the Great Depression*, 114–25.

20. Ibid., 116; Hilton Butler, "Murder for the Job," *Nation*, 137 (July 12, 1933), 44; Charles H. Houston, "Foul Employment Practices on the Rails," *The Crisis*, 56 (Oct. 1949), 269.

21. Quoted in Wolters, *Negroes and the Great Depression*, 101. Italics added.

22. Ibid., ch. 6; Robert C. Weaver, "The New Deal and the Negro: A Look at the Facts," *Opportunity*, 13 (July 1935), 202; Jacob Perlman, "Earnings and Hours of Negro Workers in Independent Tobacco Stemmeries in 1933 and 1935," *Monthly Labor Review*, 44 (May 1937),

1153; "Wage Rates and Hours of Labor in the Builders' Trade," ibid., 45 (Aug. 1937), 296.

23. National Youth Administration Conference Statement, Jan. 6–8, 1937, quoted in *Monthly Labor Review*, 44 (Feb. 1937), 347.

24. Charles L. Franklin, "Characteristics of Negroes Under the Old-Age Insurance System," ibid., 53 (Aug. 1941), 402. Italics added.

25. Christopher G. Wye, "The New Deal and the Negro Community," *Journal of American History*, 59 (Dec. 1972), 637.

26. John P. Davis, "A Survey of the Problems of the Negro Under the New Deal," *Journal of Negro Education*, 5 (Jan. 1936), 4.

27. "Negro Youth in the Depression Years," *Monthly Labor Review*, 51 (Aug. 1940), 352.

28. William Muraskin, "The Harlem Boycott of 1934," *Labor History*, 13 (Summer 1972), 362–64.

29. Ibid., 267–68; *Monthly Labor Review*, 47 (Sept. 1938), 557; John Hope Franklin, *From Slavery to Freedom: A History of Negro Americans*, 5th ed. (New York: Knopf, 1980), 398; and *New Negro Alliance v. Sanitary Grocery Co.* (303 US 552 [1938]).

30. Dominic J. Capeci, Jr., *The Harlem Riot of 1943* (Philadelphia: Temple University Press, 1977), 171–73, and *passim;* Franklin, *Slavery to Freedom,* 397; Robert M. Fogelson, *Violence as Protest: A Study of Riots and Ghettos* (Garden City, N.Y.: Doubleday, 1971), 17–22; Allen D. Grimshaw, "A Study in Social Violence: Urban Race Riots in the United States," (Ph.D. dissertation, University of Pennsylvania, 1959), 374–77.

31. B. Joyce Ross, *J. E. Spingarn and the Rise of the NAACP, 1911–1939* (New York: Atheneum, 1972), 169–85; Wolters, *Negroes and the Great Depression,* 219–27, 302–42; Nancy J. Weiss, *The National Urban League, 1910–1940* (New York: Oxford University Press, 1974), 281–87; Guichard Parris and Lester Brooks, *Blacks in the City: A History of the National Urban League* (Boston: Little, Brown, 1971), 227–39.

    Du Bois's impatience with the NAACP's reluctance to take a stronger stand on economic matters during the Great Depression was part of the complicated struggle that led to his resignation from the association in 1934.

32. Ralph J. Bunche, "The Programs, Ideologies, Tactics and Achievements of Negro Betterment and Interracial Organizations," (Research manuscript for the Carnegie-Myrdal Study, Schomberg Collection of New York Public Library), 228–29; Wolters, *Negroes and the Great Depression,* 110–12.

33. Michael S. Holmes, "The Blue Eagle as 'Jim Crow Bird': The NRA and Georgia's Black Workers," *Journal of Negro History*, 57 (July 1972), 276–82.

34. T. Arnold Hill, "Minority Groups and American Labor," National Convention of Social Welfare, *Proceedings of the Convention*, 44 (1937), 402; St. Louis *Argus*, May 24, 1935, and letter, William Green to Walter White, May 2, 1934, in Green's Copy Books, No. 492, p. 557.

Wolters, *Negroes and the Great Depression*, 182–87, discusses in some detail the NAACP and NUL attitudes toward the Wagner Act.

35. Davis, "Problems of the Negro," 12.
36. The material in this section depends heavily upon William H. Harris, "A. Philip Randolph as a Charismatic Leader," *Journal of Negro History*, 64 (Fall 1979), 301–15.
37. "Employment Problems of Negroes in Michigan," *Monthly Labor Review*, 52 (Feb. 1941), 353.
38. "Negroes Under WPA, 1939," ibid., 50 (Mar. 1940), 636.
39. "Employment of Negroes by the Federal Government," ibid., 50 (May 1940), 890.
40. Quoted in "War Labor Board Decision on Wages for Negroes," ibid., 57 (July 1943), 32. Italics added.
41. *School Board of the City of Norfolk* v. *Alston* (61 Sup. Ct. 75). It must be kept in mind, of course, that a decision of the Court did not mean immediate compliance with the decree. Some states, such as South Carolina, for example, set up a system of grades and paid teachers on the basis of their performance on standardized tests, such as the National Teachers' Exam, without regard for teachers' educational background. Other states allowed local communities to pay teachers a supplement in addition to the state salary. White teachers always received larger supplements than blacks.
42. August Meier and Elliott Rudwick, *Black Detroit and the Rise of the UAW* (New York: Oxford University Press, 1979), 82–107, and *passim*; Lloyd H. Bailer, "The Automobile Unions and Negro Labor," *Political Science Quarterly*, 59 (Dec. 1944), 548–70; Philip S. Foner, *Organized Labor and the Black Worker, 1619–1973* (New York: Praeger, 1974), 253–55.
43. "Employment Problems of Negroes," 350–54.
44. Harvard Sitkoff, "Racial Militance and Interracial Violence in the Second World War," *Journal of American History*, 58 (Dec. 1971), 661–81; the quotation is from p. 679. Two other articles in the same journal, Richard M. Dalfiume, "The Forgotten Years of the Negro Revolution," 55 (June 1968), 90–106, and Lee Finkle, "The Conservative Aims of Militant Rhetoric: Black Protest During World War II," 60 (Dec. 1973), 692–713, discuss black militancy during the Second World War. For specific discussions of the origins and development of the FEPC, see Louis C. Kesselman, *The Social Politics of FEPC: A Study in Reform Pressure Movements* (Chapel Hill: University of North Carolina Press, 1948); Louis Ruchames, *Race, Jobs, and Politics: The Story of FEPC* (New York: Columbia University Press, 1953); and Herbert Garfinkel, *When Negroes March: The March on Washington Movement in the Organizational Politics of FEPC* (Glencoe, Ill.: Free Press, 1959). Harris, "A. Philip Randolph as a Charismatic Leader," questions whether the March on Washington Movement was anything more than a bluff.
45. See Garfinkel, *When Negroes March*, esp. pp. 65–71.
46. *Bester Williams Steele* v. *The Louisville and Nashville Company, the*

Brotherhood of Railway Firemen, et al. (65 Sup. Ct. 228). On the same day the Court handed down a similar decision in *Thomas Tunstall* v. *Brotherhood of Locomotive Firemen of Norfolk, Virginia.*

47. Edward M. Gordon, "Employment in the Shipbuilding Industry, 1935–43," *Monthly Labor Review,* 58 (May 1944), 948; "Working Agreement for West Coast Shipbuilding Industry," ibid., 52 (May 1941), 1162; "Labor Requirements for the Shipbuilding Industry," ibid., 52 (Mar. 1941), 573.

48. Master Agreement Between the AFL Metal Trades Department and West Coast Shipyards, 1 April 1941, copy in Fair Employment Practice Committee Headquarters Records, microfilm edition, Roll 13.

49. Numerous memoranda, Fair Employment Practice Committee Headquarters Records, Microfilm edition, Rolls 13 and 15.

50. Fair Employment Practice Committee, "Summary, Findings, and Directives, West Coast Hearings," Dec. 9, 1943, ibid., Roll 14.

51. Charles J. McGowan to Edgar Kaiser, Dec. 14, 1943, ibid.

52. *Joseph James et al.* v. *Marinship Corporation et al.,* California Supreme Court (S. F. No. 17015), 1944; *Hill et al.* v. *International Brotherhood of Boilermakers, Iron Ship Builders and Helpers of America and Local Lodge 308, et al.* (Equity No. 17760), 1944, in Superior Court, Providence County, Rhode Island. For discussions of the significance of the *James* and *Hill* decisions, see Fair Employment Practice Committee, *Final Report* (Washington, D.C.: GPO, 1948), 21; Herbert Hill, *Black Labor and the American Legal System:* Vol. I, *Race, Work, and the Law* (New York: Bureau of National Affairs, 1977), 182n, 205; Foner, *Organized Labor and the Black Worker,* 247–48.

53. For a complete discussion of the shipyard cases, see William H. Harris, "Federal Intervention in Union Discrimination: FEPC and the West Coast Shipyards During World War II," *Labor History,* 21 (Summer 1981), 00–00.

54. Kathryn Blood, U.S. Department of Labor, Women's Bureau, Bulletin No. 205, *Negro Women War Workers* (Washington, D.C.: GPO, 1945), 17–18.

55. U.S. Bureau of Labor Statistics, Bulletin No. 1119, *Negroes in the United States: Their Employment and Economic Status* (Washington, D.C.: GPO, 1952), 5.

56. Seymour L. Wolfbein, "War and Post-War Trends in Employment of Negroes," *Monthly Labor Review,* 60 (Jan. 1945), 1–2.

57. Quotation from William H. Chafe, *The American Woman: Her Changing Social, Economic and Political Roles, 1920–1970* (New York: Oxford University Press, 1972), ch. 6, n. 19.

58. Wolfbein, "War and Post-War Trends in Employment of Negroes," 2.

Chapter 6

1. Eric F. Goldman, *The Crucial Decade—And After: America, 1945–60* (New York: Vintage Books, 1960), is the best general history of the

period. The quotation is from p. 14. John Kenneth Galbraith, *The Affluent Society* (Boston: Houghton Mifflin, 1958), evaluates that aspect of growth in the United States, while Michael Harrington, *The Other America: Poverty in the United States* (New York: Macmillan, 1962), discusses those Americans who have been left out and eloquently calls for a new national policy to alleviate their suffering and eradicate the institutional causes thereof. Sidney M. Willhelm, *Who Needs the Negro?* (Cambridge, Mass.: Schenkman, 1970), deals particularly with the plight of poor and working-class blacks.

2. Mary S. Bedell, "Employment and Income of Negro Workers—1940–52," *Monthly Labor Review*, 76 (June 1953), 596.

3. Matthew A. Kessler, "Economic Status of Nonwhite Workers, 1955–62," *Monthly Labor Review*, 86 (July 1963), 782.

4. Bedell, "Employment and Income of Negro Workers," 598.

5. Ibid., 599. U.S. Bureau of the Census, *Current Population Reports*, Series P-23, no. 80, *The Social and Economic Status of the Black Population in the United States: An Historical View, 1790–1978* (Washington, D.C.: GPO, 1980), x.

6. Walter T. K. Nugent, *Modern America* (Boston: Houghton Mifflin, 1973), 294.

7. U.S. Department of Labor, *Manpower Report of the President* (Washington, D.C.: GPO, 1963), p. 155; Dorothy K. Newman, "The Negro's Journey to the City," *Monthly Labor Review*, 88 (May 1965), 503.

8. *Manpower Report of the President*, p. 155.

9. Newman, "Negro's Journey to the City," 505.

10. *Manpower Report of the President*, p. 156.

11. Arthur M. Ross, "The Negro in the American Economy," in Arthur M. Ross and Herbert Hill, eds., *Employment, Race, and Poverty* (New York: Harcourt Brace and World, 1967), 18.

12. Newman, "Negro's Journey to the City," 503; Kessler, "Economic Status of Nonwhite Workers," 782.

13. Harry C. Dillingham and David F. Sly, "The Mechanical Cotton-Picker, Negro Migration, and the Integration Movement," *Human Organization*, 25 (Winter 1966), 346–47; Willhelm, *Who Needs the Negro?* 140–41.

14. Kessler, "Economic Status of Nonwhite Workers," 781. The percentage is impressive, but given the very small starting base, the total number for blacks is exceedingly small.

15. Ibid., 786.

16. Bedell, "Employment and Income of Negro Workers," 601.

17. Marion Hays, "A Century of Change," *Monthly Labor Review*, 85 (Dec. 1962), 1362.

18. *U.S. Manpower Report*, cited in Ross, "The Negro in the American Economy," 21.

19. "The Changing Status of Negro Women Workers," *Monthly Labor Review*, 87 (June 1964), 671; U.S. Department of Commerce, Bureau of the Census, Series P-60, no. 80, *Income in 1970 of Families and Persons in the United States* (Washington, D.C.: GPO, 1971), 127–28.

20. Alan L. Sorkin, "Education, Occupation and Income of Nonwhite Women," *The Journal of Negro Education*, 41 (Fall 1972), 344.
21. Ibid., 348; Alan B. Batchelder, "Decline in the Relative Income of Negro Men," *Quarterly Journal of Economics*, 78 (Nov. 1964), 532.
22. Laurie D. Cummings, "The Employed Poor: Their Characteristics and Occupations," *Monthly Labor Review*, 88 (July 1965), 830.
23. For an extended discussion of events in the South, see F. Ray Marshall, *Labor in the South* (Cambridge, Mass.: Harvard University Press, 1967).
24. Philip S. Foner, *Organized Labor and the Black Worker, 1619–1973* (New York: Praeger, 1974), ch. 19.
25. *Proceedings, CIO 11th Constitutional Convention* (Cleveland, Ohio: CIO, 1949). See also Sumner M. Rosen, "The CIO Era, 1935–55," ch. V in Julius Jacobsen, ed., *The Negro and the American Labor Movement* (Garden City, N.Y.: Anchor, 1968), 200.
26. Foner, *Organized Labor*, 285; Nell Irvin Painter, *The Narrative of Hosea Hudson: His Life as a Negro Communist in the South* (Cambridge, Mass.: Harvard University Press, 1979), 352–55.
27. Charles Denby, *Indignant Heart: A Black Worker's Journal* (Boston: South End Press, 1978).
28. August Meier and Elliott Rudwick, *Black Detroit and the Rise of the UAW* (New York: Oxford University Press, 1979), 210–22; Foner, *Organized Labor*, 288–90; Denby, *Indignant Heart*, is particularly critical of Reuther's position on upgrading black members in the union's structure. Denby's portrait of Reuther is in striking contrast to contemporary accounts of the UAW president in the black press as an untiring supporter of efforts to end racial discrimination in the union movement.
29. Foner, *Organized Labor*, 293–311, is a good brief discussion of the NNLC. For a discussion of the cane strike, in which both the AFL and the CIO come across as having done little to aid the agricultural workers, see H. L. Mitchell, *Mean Things Happening in This Land: The Life and Times of H. L. Mitchell, Cofounder of the Southern Tenant Farmers Union* (Montclair, N.J.: Allenheld, Osmun, 1979), 284–89.
30. U.S. Congress, House Committee on Un-American Activities, *The American Negro in the Communist Party* (Washington, D.C.: GPO, 1954), 11–12; *Report of the Proceedings, 14th Constitutional Convention, United Automobile, Aircraft, and Farm Equipment Workers, CIO* (Indianapolis: Cornelius Printing Co., 1953).
31. Rosen, "The CIO Era," 193–94.
32. Quoted in F. Ray Marshall, "Unions and the Negro Community," *Industrial and Labor Relations Review*, 17 (Jan. 1964), 190.
33. Ibid., 192.
34. *Pittsburgh Courier*, Dec. 12 and 19, 1959; and Jan. 2, 1960.
35. Marshall, "Unions and the Negro Community," 195–99.
36. Television interview, William H. Harris with Edgar D. Nixon, Bloomington, Ind., January 1980 (Bloomington: Indiana University Radio and Television Archives).
37. Ibid.

38. Ibid. The story of the Montgomery Boycott is superbly told in David
    L. Lewis, *King: A Critical Biography* (New York: Praeger, 1970), ch. 3.
    King remembers the boycott in his book, *Stride Toward Freedom: The
    Montgomery Story* (New York: Harper, 1958).

Chapter 7

1. I purposely capitalize Civil Rights Movement in this discussion because
   I am referring to a specific period in American history which I wish to
   distinguish from the perpetual efforts black people have made to attain
   equality since the first boatload of Africans docked at Jamestown, Virginia, in 1619.
2. Jack E. Nelson, "The Changing Economic Position of the Urban Black
   Workers, 1940–1970," *Review of Black Political Economy*, 4 (Winter
   1974), 40; Joe L. Russell, "Changing Patterns of Employment of Nonwhite Workers," *Monthly Labor Review*, 89 (May 1966), 503; Claire
   C. Hodge, "The Negro Job Situation," *Monthly Labor Review*, 92 (Jan.
   1969), 20–21. Note that 37.8 percent of white workers, more than twice
   that of blacks, had such high-paying jobs.
3. David L. Lewis, *King: A Critical Biography* (New York: Praeger, 1970),
   passim. See also David Brody, *Workers in Industrial America: Essays on
   the 20th Century Struggle* (New York: Oxford University Press, 1980),
   143–44. Brennan was president of the New York council from 1957 to
   1973 and served at the labor department from 1973 to 1975.
4. *Report of the National Advisory Commission on Civil Disorders* (New
   York: New York Times Ed., 1968), *passim*; John F. Kain, "Housing Segregation, Negro Employment, and Metropolitan Decentralization," *Quarterly Journal of Economics*, 82 (May 1968), 177.
5. Nelson, "Changing Economic Position of Urban Black Workers," 36.
6. Cited in Edmonia W. Davidson, "Education and the Black Cities: A
   Demographic Background," *Journal of Negro Education*, 42 (Summer
   1973), 238.
7. Kain, "Housing Segregation," 180; "Employers in Riot Cities Speak
   Out," *Monthly Labor Review*, 91 (Dec. 1968), 43.
8. Lewis, *King*, 321.
9. Paul M. Ryscavage and Hazel M. Willacy, "Employment of the Nation's
   Urban Poor," *Monthly Labor Review*, 91 (Aug. 1968), 15; James R.
   Wetzel and Susan S. Holland, "Poverty Areas of Our Major Cities,"
   Monthly Labor Review, 89 (Oct. 1966), 1106, place the total number
   of poverty area residents at 12.1 million people fourteen years old
   and over, 42 percent of whom were black.
10. Ryscavage and Willacy, "Employment of the Nation's Urban Poor," 15.
11. Wetzel and Holland, "Poverty Areas of Our Major Cities," 1106.
12. Ryscavage and Willacy, "Employment of the Nation's Urban Poor," 17.
13. Wetzel and Holland, "Poverty Areas of Our Major Cities," 1105–6.
14. Laurie D. Cummings, "The Employed Poor: Their Characteristics and
    Occupations," *Monthly Labor Review*, 88 (July 1965), 828.

15. Ibid. Cummings's statistics show that in 1963, a good year economically, 8.5 million people worked full time and earned less than $3,000. Two million of these individuals were primary breadwinners. In the mid-1960s, one-fifth of all American families were classified as poor.

16. "Employers in Riot Cities," 42, 45.

17. In addition to Executive Order 8802, other executive orders affecting black workers included: President Roosevelt's EO 9346 in 1943; President Truman's EO 10308 in 1951, which established the President's Committee on Government Contract Compliance; President Eisenhower's EOs 10479 in 1953 and 10557 in 1954, both of which expanded the responsibilities of governmental contractors, but which languished while Vice President Richard M. Nixon chaired the Committee on Government Contract Compliance. Civil rights activities were not in vogue during the Eisenhower administration, the President himself affirming that "you can't legislate morals" when asked his view on the need for federal legislation against racism.

18. "Report of the President's Committee on Equal Employment Opportunity," *Monthly Labor Review*, 85 (June 1962), 652–53; "Plan for Equal Job Opportunity at Lockheed Aircraft Corp.," ibid., 84 (July 1961), 748–49.

19. "Antidiscrimination Provisions in Major Contracts, 1961," *Monthly Labor Review*, 85 (June 1962), 643.

20. Herman D. Bloch, "Discrimination Against the Negro in Employment in New York," *American Journal of Economics and Sociology*, 24 (Oct. 1965), 361–82.

21. For a brief discussion of the impact of sex cases on the workload of the EEOC staff, see Albert J. Rosenthal, "Employment Discrimination and the Law," *Annals of the Academy of Political and Social Science*, 407 (May 1973), 93. In addition to Rosenthal, the discussion above is based in part on William B. Gould, "Black Workers Within the House of Labor," ibid., 78–90, and Richard Freeman, "Changes in the Labor Market for Black Americans, 1948–72," *Brookings Papers on Economic Activity*, 1 (1973), 67–131.

22. "Significant Decisions in Labor Cases," *Monthly Labor Review*, 90 (Oct. 1967), 54–55.

23. Georgena Potts, "Conference on Equal Employment Opportunity," *Monthly Labor Review*, 88 (Nov. 1965), 1321.

24. Ibid.

25. Herbert Hill, "Black Protest and the Struggle for Union Democracy," *Issues in Industrial Society*, 1 (Jan. 1969), 23.

26. *Griggs* v. *Duke Power Company*, 401 US 424 (1971).

27. Ibid. For further discussion of the importance of *Griggs*, see Rosenthal, "Employment Discrimination and the Law," 94–95, and Herbert Hill, *Black Labor and the American Legal System*, Vol. I, *Race, Work, and the Law* (Washington, D.C.: Bureau of National Affairs, 1977), 61–62. Hill, ibid., 84–88, also discusses other cases on this subject.

28. Freeman, "Changes in the Labor Market for Black Americans," 77–115; Alan L. Sorkin, "Education, Occupation and Income of Nonwhite

Women," *The Journal of Negro Education,* 41 (Fall 1972), 350; Stuart H. Garfinkle, "Occupations of Women and Black Workers, 1962–74," *Monthly Labor Review,* 98 (Nov. 1975), 25; Harvey R. Hamel, "Educational Attainment of Workers," *Monthly Labor Review,* 91 (Feb. 1968), 30; U.S. Bureau of the Census, *Current Population Reports,* Series P-23, No. 80, *The Social and Economic Status of the Black Population in the United States: An Historical View, 1970–1978* (Washington, D.C.: GPO, 1980), 62 and Table 53.

29. See Harold M. Baron, "Black Powerlessness in Chicago," *Trans-Action* 6 (Nov. 1968), 27.

30. Quote from Herbert Hill, "Racism Within Organized Labor: A Report of Five Years of the AFL-CIO," NAACP Labor Department (1960), reprinted in *Journal of Negro Education,* 30 (Spring 1961), 109–18.

31. Quoted in F. Ray Marshall, "Unions and the Negro Community," *Industrial and Labor Relations Review,* 17 (Jan. 1964), 190.

32. Ibid., 192.

33. By 1969, the EEOC had come to define "referral" or hiring hall unions as those that:

    1. Operate a hiring hall or hiring office; or
    2. Have arrangements under which an employer or employers are required to consider for hire persons referred by the unions or their agents; or
    3. Have at least 10 percent of their members employed by employers who customarily look to the unions, or agents of the unions, for employees for hire on a casual day-to-day or temporary basis, for a specific period of time, or for the duration of a specific job.

    Quoted in Herbert Hammerman, "Minority Workers in Construction Referral Unions," *Monthly Labor Review,* 95 (May 1972), 17.

34. Gould, "Black Workers Within the House of Labor," 86; Herbert Hammerman, "Minorities in Construction Referral Unions—Revisited," *Monthly Labor Review,* 96 (May 1973), 44–45.

35. Gould, "Black Workers Within the House of Labor," 86; Alfred Blumrosen, Robert A. Wilson, and Jay S. Siegel, "Reports to the ABA Meetings," *Monthly Labor Review,* 87 (Oct. 1964), 1179.

36. Quoted in "Labor Month in Review," *Monthly Labor Review,* 93 (Feb. 1970), 2.

37. See ibid. and "Significant Decisions in Labor Cases," ibid. (June 1970), 72.

38. Ibid., 93 (Feb. 1970), 2.

39. Gould, "Black Workers Within the House of Labor," 87.

40. Hammerman, "Minorities in Construction Referral Unions—Revisited," 44–45.

41. Pat Watters, "Workers, White and Black, in Mississippi," *Dissent,* 19 (Winter 1972), 75.

42. William B. Gould, "Black Power in the Unions: The Impact Upon Collective Bargaining Relationships," *Yale Law Journal,* 79 (Nov. 1969), 53.

43. Hill, "Black Protest and the Struggle for Union Democracy," 22.

44. Quoted in ibid., 20.

45. Thomas R. Brooks, "Black Upsurge in the Unions," *Dissent*, 17 (Mar.–Apr. 1970), 231; Ewart Guinier, "Impact of Unionization of Blacks on Unionization of Municipal Employees," *Academy of Political Science, Proceedings*, 30 (2) (1970), 180.

46. Hill, "Black Protest and the Struggle for Union Democracy," 27.

47. Philip S. Foner, *Organized Labor and the Black Worker, 1619–1973* (New York: Praeger, 1974), 405–6.

48. Ibid., 407–8.

49. Ibid., 402–4; Brooks, "Black Upsurge in the Unions," 131.

50. Thomas R. Brooks, "Workers Black and White: DRUMbeats in Detroit," *Dissent*, 17 (Jan.–Feb. 1970), 18.

51. Ibid.

52. James A. Geschwender, "The League of Revolutionary Black Workers: Problems Confronting Black Marxist-Leninist Organizations," *Journal of Ethnic Studies*, 2 (Fall 1974), 3. Foner, *Organized Labor and the Black Worker*, 410–19, discusses DRUM and related activities within the UAW. See also Brooks, "Black Upsurge in the Unions." Two white women also lost their jobs for taking part in the Dodge Main walkout in May 1968.

53. Quoted in Foner, *Organized Labor and the Black Worker*, 410.

54. Geschwender, "Revolutionary Black Workers," 6.

55. Ibid., 9.

56. Quoted in Foner, *Organized Labor and the Black Worker*, 418.

57. Brooks, "DRUMbeats in Detroit," 23; Foner, *Organized Labor and the Black Worker*, 418.

58. *Wall Street Journal*, Feb. 16 and Mar. 3, 1970.

59. *Memphis Commercial Appeal*, Feb. 20, 1968; Lewis, *King*, 378; Foner, *Organized Labor and the Black Worker*, 379–80.

60. Quoted in the *New York Times*, Apr. 17, 1968.

Chapter 8

1. Sidney M. Willhelm, *Who Needs the Negro?* (Cambridge, Mass.: Schenkman, 1970), 135–50, 161–73; Letter in *Workingmen's Advocate*, Apr. 25, 1868, reprinted in Philip S. Foner and Ronald L. Lewis, eds., *The Black Worker: A Documentary History from Colonial Times to the Present*, Vol. I, *The Black Worker to 1869* (Philadelphia: Temple University Press, 1978), 332–33.

2. C. Vann Woodward, *Origins of the New South, 1877–1913*, Vol. IX, *A History of the South* (Baton Rouge: Louisiana State University Press, 1951), 218, points out the development of a distinct class stratification among blacks as early as the 1880s.

3. William B. Gould, "Black Workers Inside the House of Labor," *Annals of the American Academy of Political and Social Science*, 407 (May 1973), 78–79.

4. U.S. Bureau of the Census, *Current Population Reports*, Series P-23, no. 80, *The Social and Economic Status of the Black Population in the*

United States: An Historical View, 1790–1978 (Washington, D.C.: GPO, 1980), 188; David L. Featherman and Robert M. Hauser, "Changes in the Socioeconomic Stratification of the Races, 1962–73," *American Journal of Sociology,* 82 (Nov. 1976), 621; Julianne M. Malveaux, "Shifts in the Development and Occupational Status of Black Americans in a Period of Affirmative Action," in *Bakke, Weber, and Affirmative Action, Working Papers, The Rockefeller Foundation* (New York: Rockefeller Foundation, 1979), 148.

5. William J. Wilson, *The Declining Significance of Race: Blacks and Changing American Institutions* (Chicago: University of Chicago Press, 1978).

6. Curtis L. Gilroy, "Black and White Unemployment: The Dynamics of the Differential," *Monthly Labor Review,* 97 (Feb. 1974), 39; U.S. Bureau of the Census, *Current Population Reports,* Series P-23, no. 46, *The Social and Economic Status of the Black Population in the United States, 1972* (Washington, D.C.: GPO, 1973), 23.

7. *Social and Economic Status of the Black Population in the United States: An Historical View,* 188; Ann McDougall Young, "Work Experience of the Population, 1976," *Monthly Labor Review,* 100 (Nov. 1977), 43; "Labor Month in Review," ibid. (Oct. 1977), 2.

8. U.S. Departments of Labor and of Health, Education and Welfare, *Employment and Training Report of the President* (Washington, D.C.: GPO, 1978), 27; *Social and Economic Status of the Black Population: An Historical View,* 211, esp. Table 157; Malveaux, "Shifts in the Employment and Occupational Status of Black Americans," 147.

9. U.S. Bureau of the Census, *Current Population Reports,* Series P-23, no. 54, *Social and Economic Status of the Black Population, 1974* (Washington, D.C.: GPO, 1975), 2; Malveaux, "Shifts in the Employment and Occupational Status of Black Americans," Table 2; Young, "Work Experience of the Population," 43–44; and Robert G. Mogull, "The Pattern of Labor Discrimination," *Negro History Bulletin,* 35 (Mar. 1972), 54–55.

10. *Social and Economic Status of the Black Population: An Historical View,* 187 and Table 164; Young, "Work Experience of the Population," 45.

11. Beverly L. Johnson and Howard Hayghe, "Labor Force Participation of Married Women, March 1976," *Monthly Labor Review,* 100 (June 1977), 33. Comparative earnings of black and white husbands in such families were $7,800 and $11,600, respectively.

12. *Social and Economic Status of the Black Population: An Historical View,* 25–26, 187.

13. Ibid., 185–86.

14. Ibid., 29, 187, and Tables 37 and 148. "The poverty threshold for a non-farm family of four was $5,815 in 1976, $5,500 in 1975, and $5,038 in 1974." Ibid., 202.

15. Ibid., 29, 187.

16. Willhelm, *Who Needs the Negro?* 243–44.

17. *Report of the National Advisory Commission on Civil Disorders* (New York: New York Times Ed., 1968), 129.

18. Quoted in Louisville *Courier-Journal,* July 13, 1980, Sec. G, p. 15. The Department of Health and Human Services came into operation in 1980 when Congress created a new Department of Education as part of President Carter's governmental reorganization. The Department of Education took over the duties previously carried out by the education section of the old Department of HEW, as well as some responsibilities that had been scattered among various other departments.

19. Lyndon B. Johnson, "To Fulfill These Rights," Howard University Commencement Address, June 4, 1965.

20. 30 Fed. Reg. 12319 (Sept. 24, 1965). See also 32 Fed. Reg. 14303 and 34 Fed. Reg. 12985 for amendments to EO 11246.

21. Nathan Glazer, *Affirmative Discrimination* (New York: Basic Books, 1975), is the most sophisticated expression of the views of anti-affirmative action scholars. See also his article, "Why *Bakke* Won't End Reverse Discrimination," *Commentary,* 66 (Sept. 1978), 36–41. Among organizations, the Anti-Defamation League of B'nai B'rith was a leader in opposing affirmative action programs.

22. *Regents of the University of California* v. *Bakke,* 438 U.S. 265.

23. *United Steelworkers of America* v. *Weber et al.,* 432 U.S. 193 (1979).

24. *Fullilove* v. *Klutznick,* 78–1007, U.S. Sup. Ct., July 2, 1980; 42 USC S6705 (f)(2).

25. The various papers in the Rockefeller Foundation Working Papers, *Bakke, Weber, and Affirmative Action,* are quite helpful in formulating an understanding of the Court's decisions in these cases and the probable impact of affirmative action on American workers. C. Eric Lincoln, "In the Wake of *Bakke,*" ibid., 214–37, is especially good in making clear the distinction between the tortured existence of blacks in this country over the centuries and the lives of others who now claim to be members of minority groups. Lincoln also prophesies that in the long run, the greatest advantages of affirmative action will not be gained by blacks but by white women, "against whom such open [anti-affirmative action] attacks are presently less socially acceptable and much more likely to involve feelings of guilt and ambivalence" (p. 233).

26. *Economic and Social Status of the Black Population: An Historical View,* 168 and Table 121.

27. W. E. B. Du Bois, *The Souls of Black Folk* (New York: 1903), The Forethought. *The Souls of Black Folk* is now most readily available in John Hope Franklin, ed., *Three Negro Classics* (New York: Avon Books, 1965). In the memorable passage which is paraphrased here, Du Bois wrote, "Herein lie buried many things which if read with patience may show the strange meaning of being black here at the dawning of the Twentieth Century. This meaning is not without interest to you, Gentle Reader; for the problem of the Twentieth Century is the color line."

Appendix

Fig. A-1. Median income of families by selected characteristics and region: 1974 (revised) and 1977 (adjusted in 1977 dollars).

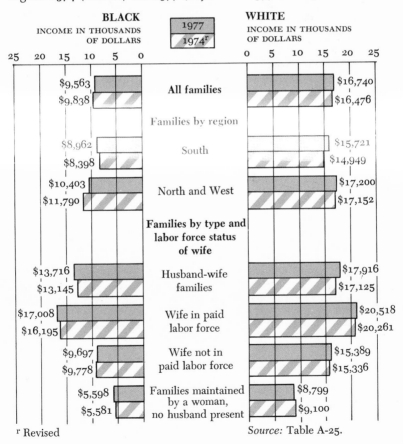

Table A-1. Median income of family head by work experience: 1967, 1969, and 1974 (Adjusted for price changes in 1974 dollars)

Race of head and year	All families[1]	Total	Head worked At full-time job		At part-time job	
			Total	50–52 weeks	Total	50–52 weeks
Black						
1967	$7,201	$8,228	$ 8,760	$ 9,349	$4,122	$4,982
1969	8,074	9,231	9,852	10,635	4,026	4,481
1974	7,808	9,813	10,723	12,136	4,655	5,500
White						
1967	$12,162	$13,104	$13,414	$14,023	$6,911	$7,536
1969	13,175	14,276	14,652	15,336	7,016	7,743
1974	13,356	14,717	15,200	16,467	8,117	8,899
Ratio: black to white						
1967	0.59	0.63	0.65	0.67	0.60	0.66
1969	0.61	0.65	0.67	0.69	0.57	0.58
1974	0.58	0.67	0.71	0.74	0.57	0.62

1. Includes heads who did not work, not shown separately.
Note: Data on income by work experience of family head first became available by race from the Current Population Survey for 1967.
Source: U.S. Department of Commerce, Bureau of the Census.

Table A-2. Median income of husband-wife families with husband under 35 years old, by earning status of husband and wife and region: 1959, 1969, and 1974 (Adjusted for price changes in 1974 dollars)

Area and year	Husband only earner			Husband and wife both earners		
	Black	White	Ratio: black to white	Black	White	Ratio: black to white
United States						
1959	$5,118	$ 8,854	0.58	$ 6,506	$10,174	0.64
1969	7,795	11,851	0.66	11,336	13,359	0.85
1974	8,096	12,031	0.67	12,783	13,639	0.94
South						
1959	$3,910	$ 7,506	0.52	$ 5,178	$ 9,171	0.56
1969	6,809	10,669	0.64	8,977	12,419	0.72
1974	6,548	10,779	0.61	10,850	12,875	0.84
North and West						
1959	$6,904	$ 9,250	0.75	$ 9,002	$10,569	0.85
1969	8,748	12,297	0.71	13,634	13,818	0.99
1974	9,559	12,490	0.77	14,955	13,030	1.07

Source: U.S. Department of Commerce, Bureau of the Census.

Table A-3. Poverty status of persons, families, and unrelated individuals, by selected characteristics: 1977 (Numbers in thousands. In current dollars. Persons, families, and unrelated individuals as of the following year)

Selected characteristic	Black	White
POVERTY STATUS OF PERSONS		
Total, all persons	24,710	185,254
Below poverty level	7,726	16,416
Percent below poverty level	31.3	8.9
Poverty Rate by Type of Residence		
United States	31.3	8.9
Metropolitan areas	28.6	7.6
In central cities	31.2	10.7
Outside central cities	21.3	5.9
Nonmetropolitan areas	39.1	11.2
POVERTY STATUS OF FAMILIES		
Total, all families	5,806	50,530
Below poverty level	1,637	3,540
Percent below poverty level	28.2	7.0
Male head[1]	3,529	44,701
Below poverty level	475	2,140
Percent below poverty level	13.5	4.8
Female head, no husband present	2,277	5,828
Below poverty level	1,162	1,400
Percent below poverty level	51.0	24.0
POVERTY STATUS OF UNRELATED INDIVIDUALS		
Total, all unrelated individuals	2,860	19,869
Number below poverty level	1,059	4,051
Percent below poverty level	37.0	20.4

1. Includes heads with wife present or without wife present.
Note: The poverty threshold for a nonfarm family of four was $6,191 in 1977. Families and unrelated individuals are classified as being above or below the poverty threshold, using the poverty index adopted by a Federal Interagency Committee in 1969. This index centers around the U.S. Department of Agriculture's Economy Food Plan and reflects the differing consumption requirements of families based on their size and composition, sex and age of the family head, and farm-nonfarm residence. The low-income cutoffs for farm families have been set at 85 percent of the nonfarm levels. These cutoffs are updated every year to reflect the changes in the Consumer Price Index. The poverty data exclude inmates of institutions, members of Armed Forces living in barracks, and unrelated individuals under 14 years of age. For a more detailed explanation, see *Current Population Reports*, Series P-60, No. 115.
Source: U.S. Department of Commerce, Bureau of the Census.

Table A-4. Labor force status of persons: 1975 to 1978 (Numbers in thousands. Seasonally adjusted quarterly averages)

Labor force status and year	Black and other races				White			
	1st quarter	2nd quarter	3rd quarter	4th quarter	1st quarter	2nd quarter	3rd quarter	4th quarter
1975								
In civilian labor force	10,390	10,456	10,608	10,658	81,490	82,023	82,365	82,444
Percent of population	59.3	59.2	59.3	59.2	61.4	61.6	61.6	61.4
Employed	8,993	8,974	9,115	9,187	75,368	75,334	75,903	76,154
Unemployed	1,397	1,482	1,493	1,471	6,122	6,690	6,462	6,290
Not in labor force	7,136	7,196	7,268	7,359	51,227	51,196	51,399	51,857
1976								
In civilian labor force	10,773	10,854	10,904	11,047	82,983	83,613	84,281	84,629
Percent of population	59.4	59.4	59.3	59.7	61.5	61.8	62.1	62.1
Employed	9,353	9,452	9,478	9,570	77,206	77,923	78,305	78,635
Unemployed	1,421	1,402	1,427	1,477	5,777	5,690	5,976	5,994
Not in labor force	7,375	7,419	7,497	7,470	51,839	51,690	51,542	51,697
1977								
In civilian labor force	11,109	11,195	11,320	11,570	85,113	85,927	86,222	87,099
Percent of population	59.6	59.7	59.9	60.8	62.2	62.6	62.5	62.9
Employed	9,681	9,764	9,784	10,026	79,403	80,492	80,998	82,062
Unemployed	1,428	1,432	1,536	1,544	5,710	5,435	5,225	5,037
Not in labor force	7,525	7,566	7,574	7,465	51,699	51,406	51,648	51,265
1978								
In civilian labor force	11,794	11,910	(NA)	(NA)	87,439	88,259	(NA)	(NA)
Percent of population	61.5	61.8	(NA)	(NA)	63.0	63.3	(NA)	(NA)
Employed	10,344	10,479	(NA)	(NA)	82,742	83,749	(NA)	(NA)
Unemployed	1,450	1,431	(NA)	(NA)	4,697	4,510	(NA)	(NA)
Not in labor force	7,370	7,372	(NA)	(NA)	51,400	51,064	(NA)	(NA)

NA, Not available.
Source: U.S. Department of Labor, Bureau of Labor Statistics.

Table A-5. Unemployment rates, by sex and age: 1975 to 1978
(Annual averages. Seasonally adjusted quarterly averages)

| | | Selected ages | | |
Year and race	Total, 16 years and over	Both sexes, 16 to 19 years	Men, 20 years and over	Women, 20 years and over
Black and other races				
1975, annual average	13.9	36.9	11.7	11.5
1st quarter	13.4	38.6	10.8	11.1
2nd quarter	14.2	36.7	12.0	11.8
3rd quarter	14.1	36.1	12.1	11.7
4th quarter	13.8	35.9	12.0	11.3
1976, annual average	13.1	37.1	10.6	11.3
1st quarter	13.2	35.5	10.8	11.3
2nd quarter	12.9	39.0	10.2	10.9
3rd quarter	13.1	37.3	10.3	11.5
4th quarter	13.4	36.5	11.1	11.4
1977, annual average	13.1	38.3	10.0	11.7
1st quarter	12.9	37.5	9.9	11.7
2nd quarter	12.8	38.2	9.4	11.9
3rd quarter	13.6	39.2	10.8	11.4
4th quarter	13.3	38.3	10.1	11.8
1978:				
1st quarter	12.3	38.6	9.0	10.8
2nd quarter	12.0	36.9	8.5	10.9
Black				
1975, annual average	14.7	39.4	12.4	12.1
1976, annual average	13.8	39.3	11.2	11.6
1977, annual average	13.9	41.1	10.5	12.2
White				
1975, annual average	7.8	17.9	6.2	7.5
1st quarter	7.5	17.4	5.8	7.5
2nd quarter	8.2	18.3	6.5	8.0
3rd quarter	7.8	18.3	6.4	7.3
4th quarter	7.6	17.6	6.1	7.3
1976, annual average	7.0	16.9	5.4	6.8
1st quarter	7.0	17.3	5.3	6.8
2nd quarter	6.8	16.5	5.2	6.6
3rd quarter	7.1	16.7	5.5	7.0
4th quarter	7.1	17.1	5.5	6.9

Table A-5. (*Continued*)

Year and race	Total, 16 years and over	Selected ages		
		Both sexes 16 to 19 years	Men, 20 years and over	Women, 20 years and over
1977, annual average	6.2	15.4	4.6	6.2
1st quarter	6.7	16.6	5.1	6.4
2nd quarter	6.3	15.9	4.7	6.2
3rd quarter	6.1	14.9	4.4	6.2
4th quarter	5.8	14.1	4.2	6.0
1978:				
1st quarter	5.4	14.4	3.9	5.1
2nd quarter	5.1	13.3	3.5	5.3
Ratio: black to white				
1975, annual average	1.9	2.2	2.0	1.6
1976, annual average	2.0	2.3	2.1	1.7
1977, annual average	2.2	2.7	2.3	2.0

Note: The unemployment rate is the proportion of the civilian labor force that is unemployed.
Source: U.S. Department of Labor, Bureau of Labor Statistics.

Table A-6. Civilian labor force status of women, by marital status: 1976 and 1977 (Numbers in thousands. Annual averages)

Marital status, year, and race	Civilian noninstitutional population	Civilian labor force			Unemployed	
		Number	Percent of population	Employed	Number	Percent of civilian labor force
1976						
Black and other races						
Total	10,056	5,044	50.2	4,356	688	13.6
Married, husband present	4,176	2,291	54.9	2,070	221	9.6
Married, husband absent	1,123	580	51.6	489	91	15.7
Widowed or divorced	1,991	806	40.5	734	72	8.9
Single	2,766	1,367	49.4	1,063	304	22.2
White						
Total	71,147	33,371	46.9	30,739	2,632	7.9
Married, husband present	44,039	19,558	44.4	18,221	1,337	6.8
Married, husband absent	1,750	1,019	58.2	895	124	12.2
Widowed or divorced	12,510	4,634	37.0	4,310	324	7.0
Single	12,849	8,159	63.5	7,312	848	10.4

1977					
Black and other races					
Total	10,346	5,265	50.9	4,528	737	14.0
Married, husband present	4,223	2,361	55.9	2,142	219	9.3
Married, husband absent	1,099	578	52.6	494	84	14.5
Widowed or divorced	2,099	864	41.2	789	75	8.7
Single	2,925	1,462	50.0	1,103	359	24.5
White					
Total	72,118	34,685	48.1	32,156	2,530	7.3
Married, husband present	44,155	20,077	45.5	18,833	1,244	6.2
Married, husband absent	1,765	1,018	57.7	907	111	10.9
Widowed or divorced	12,830	4,929	38.4	4,620	309	6.3
Single	13,368	8,661	64.8	7,796	866	10.0

Source: U.S. Department of Labor, Bureau of Labor Statistics.

Table A-7. Unemployment rates, by industry and sex: 1977
(Annual averages)

Major industry group	Men Black	Men White	Women Black	Women White
Total	13.1	5.5	14.8	7.3
Experienced wage and salary workers	11.5	5.4	12.6	6.7
Private and government nonagricultural wage and salary workers	11.6	5.3	12.5	7.1
Mining	(B)	3.0	(B)	6.8
Construction	18.6	11.3	(B)	8.9
Manufacturing	9.7	4.8	15.6	8.9
Durable goods	8.7	4.9	12.9	8.5
Primary metal industries	10.2	4.8	(B)	6.4
Fabricated metal products	13.6	5.7	(B)	7.6
Machinery	5.9	3.8	(B)	6.7
Electrical equipment	(B)	3.7	14.3	8.8
Motor vehicles and equipment	5.6	3.3	(B)	5.0
All other transportation equipment	8.8	5.4	(B)	13.6
Other durable goods industries	9.4	6.8	15.5	9.4
Nondurable goods	11.4	4.6	17.6	9.4
Food and kindred products	11.6	6.4	19.7	15.3
Textile mill products	8.6	6.3	(B)	6.9
Apparel and other finished textile products	(B)	6.7	15.6	9.9
Other nondurable goods industries	11.3	3.3	19.6	7.5
Transportation, communications, and other public utilities	7.2	4.2	6.7	4.6
Railroads and railway express	(B)	3.3	(B)	3.1
Other transportation	9.0	6.2	(B)	4.9
Communication and other public utilities	6.1	2.2	3.7	4.6
Wholesale and retail trade	15.9	6.1	21.6	8.6
Finance, insurance, and real estate	10.7	2.6	9.0	4.1
Service industries	11.5	4.6	11.7	6.1
Professional services	9.5	2.8	9.0	4.2
Other service industries	12.0	5.1	13.8	7.2
Government wage and salary workers	7.1	2.4	9.4	5.2
Agricultural wage and salary workers	11.1	9.7	(B)	13.6

B, base less than 75,000.
Source: U.S. Department of Labor, Bureau of Labor Statistics.

Guide to Further Reading

I consulted a wide range of published and unpublished material in the preparation of this book. This guide is not an exhaustive account of all those sources. It is intended mainly to provide readers with a handy reference to readily available information on the topics I discuss in the book. Accordingly, I have not included archival materials or unpublished studies, such as dissertations and master's theses, that are available on the subject, and scholars in the field will notice the omission of various general studies of blacks and of organized labor. Since I intend this brief outline of the literature to serve as a guide to readers, I have arranged the materials alphabetically by books and articles in general divisions corresponding to the chapters in the book.

Chapter 1

BOOKS

Du Bois, W. E. B. *Black Reconstruction in America, 1860–1880.* New York: Atheneum, 1969 [first published in 1935].

Gutman, Herbert G. *The Black Family in Slavery and Freedom, 1750–1925.* New York: Pantheon, 1977.

ARTICLES

Blassingame, John. "Before the Ghetto: The Making of the Black Community in Savannah, Georgia, 1865–80." *Journal of Social History,* 6 (Summer 1973), 463–88.

Bloch, Herman. "The National Labor Union and Black Workers." *Journal of Ethnic Studies,* 1 (Spring 1973), 13–21.

Gutman, Herbert G. "Work, Culture, and Society in Industrializing America, 1815–1919." *American Historical Review,* 78 (June 1973), 731–88.

Porter, Kenneth. "Negro Labor in the Western Cattle Industry, 1866–1900." *Labor History,* 10 (Summer 1969), 346–74.

Reid, Joseph. "Sharecropping as an Understandable Market Response: The Post-Bellum South." *Journal of Economic History*, 43 (March 1973), 106–30.

Schweninger, Loren. "James Rapier and the Negro Labor Movement, 1869–72." *Alabama Review*, 28 (July 1975), 185–201.

Shofner, Jerrell H. "The Labor League of Jacksonville: A Negro Union and White Strikebreakers." *Florida History Quarterly*, 50 (Jan. 1972), 178–82.

————. "The Pensacola Workingmen's Association: A Militant Negro Labor Union During Reconstruction Florida." *Labor History*, 13 (Fall 1972), 554–59.

————. "Militant Negro Laborers in Reconstruction Florida." *Journal of Southern History*, 39 (Aug. 1973), 397–408.

————. "Negro Laborers and the Forest Industry in Reconstruction Florida." *Journal of Forest History*, 19 (Oct. 1975), 180–91.

Somers, Dale. "Black and White in New Orleans: A Study of Urban Race Relations, 1865–1900." *Journal of Southern History*, 40 (Feb. 1974), 19–42.

Sutch, Richard, and Roger Ransom. "The Ex-Slave in the Post-Bellum South: A Study of the Economic Impact of Racism in a Market Environment." *Journal of Economic History*, 33 (March 1973), 131–48.

Chapter 2

BOOKS

Durham, Philip, and Everett Jones. *The Negro Cowboys*. New York: Dodd, Mead, 1965.

Woodward, C. Vann. *Origins of the New South, 1877–1913*. Vol. IX, *A History of the South*. Baton Rouge: Louisiana State University Press, 1951.

ARTICLES

Bailey, Kenneth R. "A Judicious Mixture: Negroes and Immigrants in West Virginia Mines, 1880–1917." *West Virginia History*, 34 (Jan. 1973), 141–61.

Berry, Mary F. "Reparations for Freedmen, 1890–1916: Fraudulent Practices or Justice Deferred?" *Journal of Negro History*, 57 (July 1972), 219–30.

Bloch, Herman D. "Labor and the Negro, 1866–1910." *Journal of Negro History*, 50 (July 1965), 163–84.

Brier, Stephen. "The Career of Richard L. Davis Reconsidered: Unpublished Correspondence in the *National Labor Tribune*." *Labor History*, 21 (Summer 1980), 420–29.

Brown, Minnie. "Black Women in American Agriculture." *Agricultural History*, 50 (Jan. 1976), 202–12.

Brown, William, and Morgan Reynolds. "Debt Peonage Re-Examined." *Journal of Economic History*, 33 (Dec. 1973), 862–71.

Carper, Gordon. "Slavery Revisited: Peonage in the South." *Phylon*, 37 (Mar. 1976), 85–99.

Cohen, William. "Negro Involuntary Servitude in the South, 1865–1940: A Preliminary Analysis." *Journal of Southern History*, 42 (Mar. 1976), 31–60.

Daniel, Pete. "The Metamorphosis of Slavery, 1865–1900." *Journal of American History*, 66 (June 1979), 88–99.

Dann, Martin. "Black Populism: A Study of the Colored Farmers' Alliance through 1891." *Journal of Ethnic Studies*, 2 (Fall 1974), 58–71.

Du Bois, W. E. B. "The Negroes in the Black Belt: Some Social Sketches." U.S. Department of Labor, *Bulletin* No. 22. Washington, D.C.: Government Printing Office, 1899.

———. "The Negro Farmer." U.S. Census Bureau, Bulletin No. 8, *Negroes in the United States*. Washington, D.C.: Government Printing Office, 1904.

Goldin, Claudia. "Female Labor Force Participation: The Origin of the Black and White Differences, 1870 and 1880." *Journal of Economic History*, 37 (June 1977), 87–108.

Goodwyn, Lawrence. "Populist Dreams and Negro Rights: East Texas as a Case Study." *American Historical Review*, 76 (Dec. 1971), 1435–56.

Gutman, Herbert G. "Reconstruction in Ohio: Negroes in the Hocking Valley Coal Mines in 1873 and 1874." *Labor History*, 3 (Fall 1962), 243–64.

———. "Documents on Negro Seamen During the Reconstruction Period." *Labor History*, 7 (Fall 1966), 307–12.

———. "Black Coal Miners and the Greenback Labor Party in Redeemer Alabama, 1878–79." *Labor History*, 10 (Summer 1969), 506–35.

Hammett, Hugh. "Labor and Race: The Georgia Railroad Strike of 1909." *Labor History*, 16 (Fall 1975), 470–84.

Holmes, William. "The Arkansas Cotton Pickers' Strike of 1891 and the Demise of the Colored Farmers' Alliance." *Arkansas Historical Quarterly*, 32 (Summer 1973), 107–19.

———. "The Demise of the Colored Farmers' Alliance." *Journal of Southern History*, 41 (May 1975), 187–200.

Jones, Allen. "The Role of Tuskegee Institute in the Education of Black Farmers." *Journal of Negro History*, 60 (Apr. 1975), 252–67.

Keiser, John H. "Black Strikebreakers and Racism in Illinois, 1865–1900." *Illinois State Historical Society Journal*, 65 (Autumn 1972), 313–26.

Matthews, John Michael. "The Georgia 'Race Strike' of 1909." *Journal of Southern History*, 40 (Nov. 1974), 613–30.

Miller, Floyd J. "Black Protest and White Leadership: A Note on the Colored Farmers' Alliance." *Phylon*, 33 (Summer 1972), 169–74.

Miller, Kelly. "Professional and Skilled Occupations." *Annals of the American Academy of Political and Social Science*, 49 (Sept. 1913), 10–18.

McLaurin, Melton. "The Racial Policies of the Knights of Labor and the Organization of Southern Black Workers." *Labor History*, 17 (Fall 1976), 568–85.

Morgan, George T., Jr. "No Compromise—No Recognition: John Henry Kirby, the Southern Lumber Operators' Association and Unionism in the Piney Woods." *Labor History*, 10 (Spring 1969), 193–204.

Ransom, Roger L., and Richard Sutch. "Debt Peonage in the Cotton South after the Civil War." *Journal of Economic History*, 33 (Sept. 1972), 641–69.

Rogers, William Warren. "Negro Knights of Labor in Arkansas: A Case Study of the 'Miscellaneous' Strike." *Labor History*, 10 (Summer 1969), 498–504.

Saunders, Robert. "Southern Populists and the Negro, 1893–95." *Journal of Negro History*, 54 (July 1969), 240–61.

Washington, Booker T. "The Negro's Part in Southern Development." *Annals of the American Academy of Political and Social Science*, 35 (Jan. 1910), 124–33.

Wilhoit, Francis M. "An Interpretation of Populism's Impact on the Georgia Negro." *Journal of Negro History*, 52 (Apr. 1967), 116–27.

Woodson, Carter G. "The Negro Washerwoman: A Vanishing Figure." *Journal of Negro History*, 15 (July 1930), 274–77.

Worthman, Paul. "A Black Worker and the Bricklayers' and Masons' Union, 1903." *Journal of Negro History*, 54 (Oct. 1969), 398–404.

———. "Black Workers and Labor Unions in Birmingham, Alabama, 1897–1904." *Labor History*, 10 (Summer 1969), 375–407.

Worthman, Paul, and James Green. "Black Workers in the New South, 1865–1915," in Nathan Huggins, Martin Kilson, and Daniel Fox, eds., *Key Issues in the Afro-American Experience*, Vol. I. New York: Harcourt Brace, 1971, pp. 47–69.

Chapter 3

BOOKS

Cayton, Horace R., and George S. Mitchell. *Black Workers and the New Unions*. Chapel Hill: University of North Carolina Press, 1939.

Dillard, James H. *Negro Migration in 1916–17*. Washington, D.C.: Government Printing Office (U.S. Department of Labor, Division of Negro Economics), 1919.

Greene, Lorenzo J., and Carter G. Woodson. *The Negro Wage Earner*. Washington, D.C.: Association for the Study of Negro Life and History, 1930.

Osofsky, Gilbert. *Harlem: The Making of a Ghetto: New York, 1890–1930*. New York: Harper & Row, 1966.

Spear, Allan. *Black Chicago: The Making of a Ghetto, 1890–1920*. Chicago: University of Chicago Press, 1967.

Wesley, Charles H. *Negro Labor in the United States*. New York: Vanguard Press, 1927.

Wolfe, F. E. *Admission to American Trade Unions*. Baltimore: Johns Hopkins University Press, 1912.

ARTICLES

Bodnar, John. "The Impact of the 'New Immigration' on the Black Worker: Steelton, Pennsylvania, 1880–1920." *Labor History*, 17 (Spring 1976), 214–29.

Bodnar, John, Michael Weber, and Roger Simon. "Migration, Kinship, and Urban Adjustment: Blacks and Poles in Pittsburgh, 1900–1930." *Journal of American History*, 66 (Dec. 1979), 548–65.

Fickle, James. "Management Looks at the 'Labor Problem': The Southern Pine Industry During World War I and the Postwar Era." *Journal of Southern History*, 40 (Feb. 1974), 61–76.

Foner, Philip. "The IWW and the Black Worker." *Journal of Negro History*, 55 (Jan. 1970), 45–64.

Gottlieb, Peter. "Migration and Jobs: The New Black Workers in Pittsburgh, 1916–1930." *Western Pennsylvania Historical Magazine*, 61 (Jan. 1978), 1–15.

Harris, Abram L. "Negro Migration to the North." *Current History*, 20 (Sept. 1924), 921–25.

Hawkins, Homer. "Trends in Black Migration from 1863 to 1960." *Phylon*, 24 (June 1973), 140–52.

Hayes, Marion. "A Century of Change: Negroes in the U.S. Economy, 1860–1960." *Monthly Labor Review*, 85 (Dec. 1962), 1359–65.

Haynes, George Edmund. "Effect of War Conditions on Negro Labor." *Proceedings of the Academy of Political Science*, 8 (Feb. 1919), 165–78.

Higgs, Robert. "The Boll Weevil, The Cotton Economy, and Black Migration, 1910–1930." *Agricultural History*, 50 (Apr. 1976), 335–50.

Hill, Joseph A. "Recent Northward Migration of the Negro." *Monthly Labor Review*, 18 (Mar. 1924), 1–14.

Klaczynska, Barbara. "Why Women Work: A Comparison of Various Groups—Philadelphia, 1910–1930." *Labor History*, 17 (Winter 1976), 73–87.

Leonard, Oscar, and Forrester B. Washington. "Welcoming Southern Negroes: East St. Louis and Detroit—A Contrast." *Survey*, 38 (July 14, 1917), 331–35.

Robinson, Mary V. "Domestic Workers and Their Employment Relations." *Bulletin of the Women's Bureau* [U.S. Department of Labor], 39 (1934).

Smith, T. Lynn. "The Redistribution of the Negro Population of the United States, 1910–60." *Journal of Negro History*, 51 (July 1966), 155–73.

Tuttle, William. "Labor Conflict and Racial Violence: The Black Worker in Chicago, 1894–1919." *Labor History*, 10 (Summer 1969), 408–32.

———. "Contested Neighborhoods and Racial Violence: Prelude to the Chicago Race Riot of 1919." *Journal of Negro History*, 55 (Oct. 1970), 266–88.

Woofter, T. J., Jr. "The Negro on Strike." *Journal of Social Forces*, 2 (Nov. 1923), 84–88.

Wright, R. R., Jr. "The Negro in Unskilled Labor." *Annals of the American Academy of Political and Social Science,* 49 (Sept. 1913), 19–27.

Chapter 4

BOOKS

Brazeal, Brailsford R. *The Brotherhood of Sleeping Car Porters: Its Origins and Development.* New York: Harper & Brothers, 1946.

Harris, William H. *Keeping the Faith: A. Philip Randolph, Milton P. Webster, and the Brotherhood of Sleeping Car Porters, 1925–37.* Urbana: University of Illinois Press, 1977.

Ottley, Roi. *The Lonely Warrior: The Life and Times of Robert S. Abbott.* Chicago: Regnery Press, 1955.

Reid, Ira DeA. *Negro Membership in American Labor Unions.* New York: Negro Universities Press, 1969 [first published in 1930].

Spero, Sterling D., and Abram L. Harris. *The Black Worker: The Negro and the Labor Movement.* New York: Columbia University Press, 1931.

ARTICLES

Harris, William H. "A. Philip Randolph as a Charismatic Leader, 1925–1941." *Journal of Negro History,* 64 (Fall 1979), 301–15.

Kornweibel, Theodore. "An Economic Profile of Black Life in the Twenties." *Journal of Black Studies,* 6 (June 1976), 307–20.

Mergen, Bernard. "The Pullman Porter: From George to Brotherhood." *South Atlantic Quarterly,* 73 (Spring 1974), 224–35.

Watson, Richard L. "The Defeat of Judge Parker: A Study in Pressure Group Politics." *Mississippi Valley Historical Review,* 50 (Sept. 1963), 213–34.

Chapter 5

BOOKS

Dollard, John. *Caste and Class in a Southern Town.* New Haven: Yale University Press, 1937.

Foner, Philip S. *Organized Labor and the Black Worker, 1619–1973.* New York: Praeger, 1974.

Franklin, Charles L. *The Negro Labor Unionist in New York: Problems and Conditions among Negroes in Manhattan, with Special Reference to the NRA and Post-NRA Situations.* New York: Columbia University Press, 1936.

Grubbs, Donald H. *Cry from the Cotton: The Southern Tenant Farmers' Union and the New Deal.* Baton Rouge: Louisiana State University Press, 1971.

Hope, John, II. *Equality of Opportunity: A Union Approach to Fair Employment.* Washington, D.C.: Public Affairs Press, 1956.

Jacobson, Julius, ed. *The Negro and the American Labor Movement*. Garden City, N.Y.: Anchor Books, 1968.

Johnson, Charles S. *Shadow of the Plantation*. Chicago: University of Chicago Press, 1934.

Johnson, Charles S., Edwin R. Embree, and Will W. Alexander. *The Collapse of Cotton Tenancy*. Chapel Hill: University of North Carolina Press, 1935.

Meier, August, and Elliott Rudwick, *Black Detroit and the Rise of the UAW*. New York: Oxford University Press, 1979.

Mitchell, H. L. *Mean Things Happening in This Land: The Life and Times of H. L. Mitchell: Cofounder of the Southern Tenant Farmers Union*. Montclair, N.J.: Allanheld, Osmun, 1979.

Weaver, Robert C. *The Urban Negro Worker in the United States, 1925–36*. Washington, D.C.: Government Printing Office, 1937.

———. *Negro Labor: A National Problem*. New York: Harcourt, Brace, 1946.

Wolters, Raymond. *Negroes and the Great Depression: The Problem of Economic Recovery*. Westport, Conn.: Greenwood, 1970.

Woofter, Thomas J. *Landlord and Tenant on the Cotton Plantation*. New York: Negro Universities Press, 1969 [first published in 1936].

ARTICLES

Auerbach, Jerome. "Southern Tenant Farmers: Socialist Critics of the New Deal." *Labor History*, 7 (Winter 1966), 3–18.

Bailer, Lloyd H. "The Automobile Unions and Negro Labor." *Political Science Quarterly*, 59 (Dec. 1944), 548–77.

Bloch, Herman D. "Discrimination Against the Negro in Employment in New York, 1920–63." *American Journal of Economics and Sociology*, 24 (Oct. 1965), 361–82.

Bond, J. Max. "The Training Program of the Tennessee Valley Authority for Negroes." *Journal of Negro Education*, 7 (July 1938), 383–89.

Davis, John P. "What Price National Recovery." *Crisis*, 40 (Dec. 1933), 271–72.

———. "A Survey of the Problems of the Negro Under the New Deal." *Journal of Negro Education*, 5 (Jan. 1936), 3–12.

Eatherly, Billy J. "The Occupational Progress of Mississippi Negroes: 1940–60." *Mississippi Quarterly*, 21 (Winter 1967–68), 49–62.

Frazier, Edward K. "Earnings of Negroes in the Iron and Steel Industry." *Monthly Labor Review*, 44 (Mar. 1937), 564–79.

Harris, William H. "Federal Intervention into Union Discrimination: FEPC and the West Coast Shipyards During World War II." *Labor History*, 22 (Summer 1981), 325–47.

Hill, Herbert. "In the Age of Gompers and After—Racial Practices of Organized Labor." *New Politics*, 4 (1965), 26–46.

Holcomb, Ernest. "Wage Laborers and Sharecroppers in Cotton Production." *Monthly Labor Review*, 51 (Nov. 1940), 1151–1155.

Holley, Donald. "The Negro in the New Deal Resettlement Program." *Agricultural History*, 45 (July 1971), 179–200.

Holmes, Michael S. "The Blue Eagle as 'Jim Crow Bird': The NRA and Georgia's Black Workers." *Journal of Negro History*, 57 (July 1972), 276–83.

———. "The New Deal and Georgia's Black Youth." *Journal of Southern History*, 38 (Aug. 1972), 443–60.

Houston, Charles H. "Foul Employment Practice on the Rails." *Crisis*, 56 (Oct. 1949), 269.

Johnson, Charles W. "The Army, the Negro and the Civilian Conservation Corps: 1932–42." *Military Affairs*, 36 (Oct. 1972), 82–88.

———. "The Changing Economic Status of the Negro." *The Annals of the American Academy of Political and Social Science*, 140 (Nov. 1928), 128–37.

Landes, William. "The Economics of Fair Employment Laws." *Journal of Political Economy*, 76 (July/Aug. 1968), 507–52.

Liggett, Malcom H. "The Efficacy of State Fair Employment Practice Commissions." *Industrial and Labor Relations Review*, 22 (July 1969), 559–67.

Muraskin, William. "The Harlem Boycott of 1934: Black Nationalism and the Rise of Labor Consciousness." *Labor History*, 13 (Summer 1972), 361–73.

Naison, Mark D. "Black Agrarian Radicalism in the Great Depression: The Threads of a Lost Tradition." *Journal of Ethnic Studies*, 1 (Summer 1973), 47–65.

Olson, James. "Organized Black Leadership and Industrial Unionism: The Racial Response, 1936–45." *Labor History*, 10 (Summer 1969), 475–86.

Perlman, Jacob. "Earnings and Hours of Negro Workers in Independent Tobacco Stemmeries in 1933 and 1935." *Monthly Labor Review*, 44 (May 1937), 1153–72.

Reed, Merl. "The FEPC, the Black Worker, and Southern Shipyards." *South Atlantic Quarterly*, 74 (Autumn 1975), 446–67.

Salmond, John. "The Civilian Conservation Corps and the Negro." *Journal of American History*, 52 (June 1965), 75–88.

Waggaman, Mary T. "Wartime Opportunities for Women Household Workers in Washington, D.C." *Monthly Labor Review*, 60 (Mar. 1945), 575–84.

Wolfbein, Seymour L. "War and Postwar Trends in Employment of Negroes." *Monthly Labor Review*, 60 (Jan. 1945), 1–5.

———. "Postwar Trends in Negro Employment." *Monthly Labor Review*, 65 (Dec. 1947), 663–65.

Chapter 6

BOOKS

Becker, Gary S. *The Economics of Discrimination*. Chicago: University of Chicago Press, 1957.

Hiestand, Dale L. *Economic Growth and Employment Opportunities for Minorities.* New York: Columbia University Press, 1964.

Leggett, John C. *Class, Race and Labor: Working Class Consciousness in Detroit.* New York: Oxford University Press, 1968.

Lewis, David L. *King: A Critical Biography.* New York: Praeger, 1970.

Tabb, William K. *The Political Economy of the Black Ghetto.* New York: Norton, 1970.

Wächtel, Dawn Day. *The Negro and Discrimination in Employment.* Ann Arbor: University of Michigan–Wayne State University Press, 1965.

ARTICLES

Bedell, Mary S. "Employment and Income of Negro Workers, 1940–52." *Monthly Labor Review,* 76 (June 1953), 596–601.

Farley, Reynolds. "The Urbanization of Negroes in the United States." *Journal of Social History,* 1 (Spring 1968), 241–58.

Hare, Nathan. "Recent Trends in the Occupational Mobility of Negroes, 1930–1960: An Intracohort Analysis." *Social Forces,* 44 (Dec. 1965), 166–73.

Kessler, Matthew A. "Economic Status of Nonwhite Workers, 1955–62." *Monthly Labor Review,* 86 (July 1963), 780–88.

Lunden, Leon. "Antidiscrimination Provisions in Major Contracts, 1961." *Monthly Labor Review,* 85 (June 1962), 643–51.

Manor, Stella P. "Geographic Changes in U.S. Employment from 1950–1960." *Monthly Labor Review,* 86 (Jan. 1963), 1–10.

Ryack, Elton. "Discrimination and the Occupational Progress of Negroes." *Review of Economics and Statistics,* 43 (May 1961), 209–14.

Chapter 7

BOOKS

Geschwender, James A. *Class, Race, and Worker Insurgency: The League of Revolutionary Black Workers.* Cambridge: Cambridge University Press, 1977.

Willhelm, Sidney. *Who Needs the Negro?* Cambridge, Mass.: Schenkman, 1970.

ARTICLES

Anderson, Bernard E. "Employment of Negroes in the Federal Government." *Monthly Labor Review,* 88 (Oct. 1965), 1222–1227.

Baron, Harold M. "Black Powerlessness in Chicago." *Trans-Action,* 6 (Nev. 1968), 27–33.

Batchelder, Alan B. "Decline in the Relative Income of Negro Men." *Quarterly Journal of Economics,* 78 (Nov. 1964), 525–48.

Blau, Peter M. "The Flow of Occupational Supply and Recruitment." *American Sociological Review,* 30 (Aug. 1965), 479–90.

Bonacich, Edna. "Advanced Capitalism and Black/White Race Relations in the United States: A Split Labor Market Interpretation." *American Sociological Review,* 41 (Feb. 1976), 34–51.

Bracket, Joseph A. "Employment of Negroes by Government Contractors." *Monthly Labor Review,* 87 (July 1964), 789–93.

Brimmer, Andrew. "The Black Revolution and the Economic Future of Negroes in the United States." *American Scholar,* 38 (Autumn 1969), 629–43.

Broom, Leonard, and Norval D. Glenn. "When Will America's Negroes Catch Up?" *New Society* (Mar. 25, 1965), 6–8.

Cummings, Laurie D. "The Employed Poor: Their Characteristics and Occupations." *Monthly Labor Review,* 88 (July 1965), 828–35.

Doeringer, Peter B. "Promotion Systems and Equal Employment Opportunity." *Proceedings of the Nineteenth Annual Winter Meeting,* Industrial Relations Research Association (1966), 278–89.

Duncan, Otis Dudley. "Discrimination Against Negroes." *The Annals of the American Academy of Political and Social Science,* 371 (May 1967), 86–103.

———. "Patterns of Occupational Mobility Among Negro Men." *Demography,* 5 (May 1968), 11–22.

Featherman, David L., and Robert M. Hauser. "Changes in the Socioeconomic Stratification of the Races, 1962–73." *American Journal of Sociology,* 82 (Nov. 1976), 621–51.

Freeman, Richard. "Changes in the Labor Market for Black Americans, 1948–72." *Brookings Papers on Economic Activity* (1973), 67–131.

Garfinkle, Stuart H. "Occupations of Women and Black Workers, 1962–74." *Monthly Labor Review,* 98 (Nov. 1975), 25–35.

Geschwender, James A. "The League of Revolutionary Black Workers: Problems Confronting Black Marxist-Leninist Organizations." *Journal of Ethnic Studies,* 2 (Fall 1974), 1–23.

Gillman, Harry. "The White/Nonwhite Unemployment Differential." In Mark Perlman, ed., *Human Resources in the Urban Economy.* Washington, D.C.: Resources for the Future, Inc., 1963.

———. "Economic Discrimination and Unemployment." *American Historical Review,* 71 (Dec. 1965), 1077–1096.

Gould, William B. "Black Power in the Unions: The Impact Upon Collective Bargaining Relationships." *Yale Law Journal,* 79 (Nov. 1969), 46.

———. "Black Workers Inside the House of Labor." *The Annals of the American Academy of Political and Social Science,* 407 (May 1973), 78–90.

Henle, Peter. "Some Reflections on Organized Labor and the New Militants." *Monthly Labor Review,* 92 (July 1969), 20–25.

Hill, Herbert. "Black Protest and the Struggle for Union Democracy." *Issues in Industrial Society,* 1 (Jan. 1969), 19–29.

Hodge, Claire C. "Negro Job Situation: Has It Improved?" *Monthly Labor Review,* 92 (Jan. 1969), 20–28.

Kain, John. "Housing Segregation, Negro Employment, and Metropolitan Decentralization." *Quarterly Journal of Economics,* 82 (May 1968), 175–97.

Kidder, Alice Handsaker. "Racial Differences in Job Search and Wages." *Monthly Labor Review,* 91 (July 1968), 24–26.

Marshall, Ray. "Unions and the Negro Community." *Industrial and Labor Relations Review*, 17 (1963–64), 179–202.

McKersie, Robert B. "The Maturation of the Two Movements." *Monthly Labor Review*, 90 (July 1967), 36–38.

Mogull, Robert G. "The Pattern of Labor Discrimination." *Negro History Bulletin*, 35 (Mar. 1972), 54–59.

———. "Discrimination in the Labor Market." *Journal of Black Studies*, 3 (Dec. 1972), 237–49.

Nelson, Jack E. "The Changing Economic Position of Black Urban Workers/ 1940–1970." *Review of Black Political Economy*, 4 (Winter 1974), 35–48.

Northrup, Herbert R. "In-Plant Movement of Negroes in the Aerospace Industry." *Monthly Labor Review*, 91 (Feb. 1968), 22–25.

Russell, Joe L. "Changing Patterns of Employment of Nonwhite Workers." *Monthly Labor Review*, 89 (May 1966), 503–09.

Ryscavage, Paul M. "Employment Developments in Urban Poverty Neighborhoods." *Monthly Labor Review*, 92 (June 1969), 51–56.

Ryscavage, Paul M., and Hazel M. Willacy. "Employment of the Nation's Urban Poor." *Monthly Labor Review*, 91 (Aug. 1968), 15–21.

Sexton, Brendan. "Unions and the Black Power Brokers." *Dissent*, 18 (Feb. 1971), 41–49.

Siegel, Paul M. "On the Cost of Being a Negro." *Sociological Inquiry*, 35 (Winter 1965), 41–57.

Streifford, David. "Racial Economic Dualism in St. Louis." *Review of Black Political Economy*, 4 (Spring 1974), 63–82.

Tobin, James. "On Improving the Economic Status of the Negro." *Daedalus*, 94 (Fall 1965), 878–98.

Via, Emory F. "Discrimination, Integration and Job Equality." *Monthly Labor Review*, 91 (Mar. 1968), 82–89.

Waldman, Elizabeth. "Marital and Family Status of Workers." *Monthly Labor Review*, 91 (Apr. 1968), 14–22.

Watters, Pat. "Workers, White and Black in Mississippi." *Dissent*, 19 (Winter 1972), 70–77.

Wetzel, James R., and Susan S. Holland. "Poverty Areas of Our Major Cities." *Monthly Labor Review*, 89 (Oct. 1966), 1105–1110.

Willacy, Hazel M. "Men in Poverty Neighborhoods: A Status Report." *Monthly Labor Review*, 92 (Feb. 1969), 23–27.

Willacy, Hazel M., and Harvey J. Hilaski. "Working Women in Urban Poverty Neighborhoods." *Monthly Labor Review*, 93 (June 1970), 35–38.

Chapter 8

BOOKS

Rockefeller Foundation. *Bakke, Weber, and Affirmative Action: Working Papers*. New York: The Rockefeller Foundation, 1979.

Wilson, William J. *The Declining Significance of Race: Blacks and Changing American Institutions*. Chicago: University of Chicago Press, 1978.

ARTICLES

Ashenfelter, Orley. "Racial Discrimination and Trade Unionism." *Journal of Political Economy*, 80 (May/June 1972), 435–64.

"The Black Plight: Race or Class? A Debate Between Kenneth B. Clark and Carl Gershman." *New York Times Magazine* (Oct. 5, 1980), 22.

Brooks, Thomas R. "DRUMbeats in Detroit." *Dissent*, 17 (Jan.–Feb. 1970), 16–24.

————. "Black Upsurge in the Unions." *Dissent*, 17 (Mar.–Apr. 1970), 124–34.

Clark, Kenneth B. "The Role of Race." *New York Times Magazine* (Oct. 5, 1980), 25.

Cooper, Sophia, and Denis Johnston. "Labor Force Participation, by Color, 1970–80." *Monthly Labor Review*, 89 (Sept. 1966), 965–72.

Gellner, Christopher G. "Enlarging the Concept of a Labor Reserve." *Monthly Labor Review*, 98 (Apr. 1975), 20–27.

Gershman, Carl. "A Matter of Class." *New York Times Magazine* (Oct. 5, 1980), 24.

Gilroy, Curtis L. "Black and White Unemployment: The Dynamics of the Differential." *Monthly Labor Review*, 97 (Feb. 1974), 38–47.

————. "Investment in Human Capital and Black–White Unemployment." *Monthly Labor Review*, 98 (July 1975), 13–21.

Hall, Robert E., and Richard A. Casten. "The Relative Occupational Success of Blacks and Whites." *Brookings Papers on Economic Activity*, 3 (Washington: The Brookings Institution, 1973), 781–97.

Hammerman, Herbert. "Minority Workers in Construction Referral Unions." *Monthly Labor Review*, 95 (May 1972), 17–26.

————. "Minorities in Construction Referral Unions—Revisited." *Monthly Labor Review*, 96 (May 1973), 43–46.

Hammerman, Herbert, and Marvin Pogoff. "Unions and Title VII of the Civil Rights Act of 1964." *Monthly Labor Review*, 99 (April 1976), 34–37.

Leigh, Duane E., and V. Lane Rawlins. "On the Stability of Relative Black–White Unemployment." *Monthly Labor Review*, 96 (May 1973), 30–32.

Nelson, Charmeyne. "Myths About Black Women Workers in Modern America." *Black Scholar*, 6 (Mar. 1975), 11–15.

Rabin, Yale. "Highways as a Barrier to Equal Access." *Annals of the American Academy of Political and Social Science*, 407 (May 1973), 63–77.

Rosenthal, Albert J. "Employment Discrimination and the Law." *Annals of the American Academy of Political and Social Science*, 407 (May 1973), 91–101.

Sorkin, Alan. "Education, Occupation, and Income of Nonwhite Women." *Journal of Negro Education*, 41 (Fall 1972), 343–51.

Vroman, Wayne. "Labor Market Changes for Black Men Since 1964." *Monthly Labor Review*, 98 (Apr. 1975), 42–44.

Young, Anne McDougall. "Work Experience of the Population, 1976." *Monthly Labor Review*, 100 (Nov. 1977), 43–47.

Selected Government Publications

U.S. Department of Commerce, Bureau of the Census, *Current Population Reports,* Series P-23, No. 39, *Differences Between Incomes of White and Negro Families by Work Experience of Wife and Region: 1970, 1969 and 1959.* Washington, D.C.: GPO, 1971.

————. *Current Population Reports,* Series P-20, No. 30, *Population, Characteristics, Population Profile of the United States, 1976.* Washington, D.C.: GPO, 1977.

————. *Current Population Reports,* Series P-23, No. 46, *The Social and Economic Status of the Black Population in the United States, 1972.* Washington, D.C.: GPO, 1973.

————. *Current Population Reports,* Series P-23, No. 46, *The Social and Economic Status of the Black Population in the United States: An Historical View, 1790–1978.* Washington, D.C.: GPO, 1980.

————. *Census of Partial Employment, Unemployment, and Occupations, 1937.* Washington, D.C.: GPO, 1938.

————. *Negro Population of the United States, 1790–1915.* Washington, D.C.: GPO, 1918.

————. *Negroes in the United States,* Bulletin No. 8. Washington, D.C.: GPO, 1904.

————. *Negroes in the United States: 1910,* Bulletin No. 129. Washington, D.C.: GPO, 1915.

————. *Negroes in the United States, 1920–1932.* Washington, D.C.: GPO, 1935.

————. *Occupations of the Population of the United States.* Special Report. Washington, D.C.: GPO, 1896.

————. *Population: Characteristics of the Nonwhite Population by Race: 16th Census, 1940.* Washington, D.C.: GPO, 1943.

————. *Population, 16th Census: 1940,* Vol. III, *The Labor Force: Occupation, Employment and Income.* Washington, D.C.: GPO, 1943.

————. *Plantation Farming in the United States.* Washington, D.C.: GPO, 1916.

U.S. Bureau of Labor Statistics, Bulletin 1699, *Black Americans, a Chartbook.* Washington, D.C.: GPO, 1971.

————. *Employment in Perspective: The Negro Employment Situation,* Report No. 391. Washington, D.C.: GPO, 1971.

————. *The Negro in the West . . . Some Facts Relating to Social and Economic Conditions.* Washington, D.C.: GPO, 1966.

————. Bulletin No. 1511, *The Negroes in the United States: Their Economic and Social Situation.* Washington, D.C.: GPO, 1966.

————. Bulletin No. 1119, *The Negroes in the United States: Their Employment and Economic Status.* Washington, D.C.: GPO, 1952.

U.S. Department of Labor, Bulletin No. 10, Vol. 2, *Conditions of Negroes in Various Cities.* Washington, D.C.: GPO, 1897.

————. *Negro Migration in 1916–1917.* Washington, D.C.: GPO, 1919.

————. U.S. Womens Bureau, No. 205, *Negro Women War Workers.*
Washington, D.C.: GPO, 1945.

U.S. Department of the Interior. *The Urban Negro Worker in the United
States, 1925–1936.* Washington, D.C.: GPO, 1937.

U.S. Civil Service Commission. *Study of Minority Group Employment in
the Federal Government, 1966.* Washington, D.C.: GPO, 1967.

Index

241